PRACTICAL SYSTEMS THINKING

Alan Waring

THOMSON

Australia • Canada • Mexico • Singapore • Spain • United Kingdom • United States

THOMSON
™

Practical Systems Thinking

Copyright © 1996 Alan Waring

The Thomson logo is a registered trademark used herein under licence.

For more information, contact Thomson Learning, High Holborn House, 50-51 Bedford Row, London WC1R 4LR or visit us on the World Wide Web at:
http://www.thomsonlearning.co.uk

British Library Cataloguing-in-Publication Data
A catalogue record for this book is available from the British Library

ISBN-13: 978-1-86152-614-4
ISBN-10: 1-86152-614-8

First edition published 1996 by Chapman and Hall
First edition reprinted 1996 and 2000 by International Thomson Business Press
Reprinted 2001 by International Thomson Publishing
Reprinted 2002, 2003, 2005 and 2006 by Thomson Learning

Typeset by Acorn Bookwork, Salisbury, Wiltshire
Printed in the UK by TJI Digital, Padstow Cornwall

Contents

Acknowledgements

I should like to thank the following:

Bob Clark, Head of the Technology Staff Tutor Group and Chair of the T401 Technology Project Course Team at the Open University, both for reviewing the major revisions of this new text and for his contributions to my original book in 1989 on which this new text is based. Also, members of the Open University Systems Group for their comments and support in the development of both books.

Dr Daune West of the University of Paisley for critically reviewing the academic content of the new text and making helpful suggestions for improvement.

Professor Brian Toft of Sedgwick UK, Mr Paul Ransley of London Underground, Dr Ian Glendon of Aston Business School, and Mr Robert Lowe of 3i PLC for reviewing various parts of the draft.

Any remaining errors are entirely the author's responsibility.

Ingmar Folkmans and his colleagues at ITBP for their professionalism throughout the book's preparation.

Last but not least, my wife Mehri for her support over the many months it took to write the book.

INTRODUCTION

THE AIMS AND STYLE OF THIS BOOK

This book is a substantially adapted and revised version of the author's previous book *Systems Methods for Managers: a Practical Guide* published in 1989. The purpose of this new book is to provide students in a wide range of disciplines with a text on applied systems thinking which concentrates on practice and technique. The book should be used as a reference guide to general technique and to three specific systems methodologies which are widely used – HARD SYSTEMS, SOFT SYSTEMS AND SYSTEMS FAILURES. Other systems methodologies are described briefly in Chapter 13; References and Further Reading include definitive and comprehensive texts.

NB In order to emphasize the view that terms such as 'system', 'hard system', 'soft system' and 'system failure' relate to metaphorical and perceptual constructs, throughout the book these terms are printed in SMALL CAPITALS – SYSTEM, HARD SYSTEM, SOFT SYSTEM, SYSTEM FAILURE.

The book is written in open learning style with activities, exercises and suggested answers. The writing style is direct and at a commonsense level and seeks to avoid academic language which may be appropriate to some other books. The text is supported by numerous illustrations, in keeping with the emphasis on diagramming techniques in systems work. Worked case studies are included which bring together concepts and techniques introduced in the main text.

WHO SHOULD READ THIS BOOK?

The book is aimed at a wide readership having a common need, namely seeking to learn methodologies and techniques which could help them resolve work-related problems more effectively i.e. seeking more than a 'quick fix' in their approach to administrative, managerial, technical or social problems. Readers will therefore include second- and third-year undergraduates in a wide range of disciplines.

Examples and case studies have been chosen because they demonstrate principles common to the readership as a whole. Thus, a case study examining market problems in the brewing industry (as in Chapter 7) could quite easily evoke powerful insights into management information systems and decision-making in which a particular reader might be interested. Management students could learn much about monitoring and control systems from a study of why a serious and costly accident occurred on a construction site (as in Chapter 11).

PRACTICAL BENEFITS FOR YOU

This book aims to bring the reader close to what systems thinking can achieve in practice. If you come to regard this book as a do-it-yourself guide to using systems ideas for practical benefit, the author will feel that he has done his job.

Newcomers to systems thinking will soon discover that the beauty of systems ideas lies not just in their usefulness in dealing with 'problems' but also in their lack of professional boundaries. Systems methodologies and the methods and techniques they incorporate are generic tools which can be applied to any discipline and should not be seen as secret knowledge to be jealously guarded by particular professional groups. Systems practice requires *a particular way of thinking*, not particular academic or professional credentials.

Whatever your discipline, you should be able to gain some practical benefit from the book by being able to understand problems more clearly, analyse situations more incisively, and devise solutions and action plans which are more defensible than would otherwise be the case.

AN APPROACH TO SYSTEMS

The author describes three complementary systems methodologies – HARD SYSTEMS, SOFT SYSTEMS, and SYSTEMS FAILURES. These three methodologies have a lot in common, as suggested in Fig. A, yet have distinct features which make each of them ideally suited to particular kinds of perceived problem. It is a mistake to adopt only one approach in some form or other. The three methodologies are best used in a complementary way. To use only one methodology all the time encourages 'tunnel vision' and often produces ineffective results.

It should be appreciated that this book is not an academic treatise and does not claim to present original systems ideas and techniques. The author readily acknowledges the Open University Systems Group, Professor Peter Checkland at Lancaster University and others for inspiring the approach adopted. The book, however, does present in a single text new examples and original case studies of how to use systems ideas and techniques. Further, the author does not claim to present the latest views or research position of the systems movement as a whole or of any particular interest group.

Although a broad swathe of systems ideas and techniques is covered, the book has omitted a number of areas. For example, in the operational research area queuing models are not addressed. Planning models such as Gantt charts and critical path analysis are also left out. Such omissions were a matter of judgement and the author hopes that readers will not be disappointed by them.

ORGANIZATION OF THE BOOK

The book is in two parts. Part 1 (Chapters 1 to 5) provides an introduction to using systems ideas and to three systems methodologies, and Part 2 (Chapters 6 to 12) revisits these in more detail. Chapter 13 outlines other systems methodologies and current developments. A glossary of terms and a list of references are included at the end of the book.

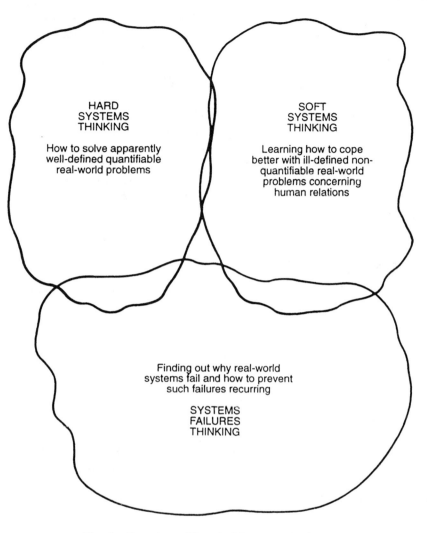

Fig. A. Overview of Practical Systems Thinking

PREVIEW OF PART 1

In taking an initial look at systems ideas, familiar topics from work life are chosen to show how a systems approach to thinking and action can improve the effectiveness of tackling problems or uncertainties about how to proceed. The book is concerned with 'real-world' problems and not with problems contrived for laboratory examination. The three methodologies – HARD, SOFT and FAILURES – are introduced in outline.

Systems thinking extends the scope and boundaries of what needs to be considered for tackling or avoiding perceived problems effectively. Part of the art of systems thinking is making the familiar look strange – being able to look at a perhaps boringly familiar situation in a completely new and stimulating light. For example, imagine you are a farm manager. To a 'non-systems' thinker, a farm is a farm – pleasant, green, smelly, scruffy or whatever. It is where seeds are planted, grow, mature and die. It is where livestock are reared to produce meat, eggs, milk etc. Not a particularly stimulating description. A systems thinker, however, might look at the same farm and describe it like this: 'a habitat system for vegetation and animals (including humans) which is partly controlled by human intervention and from which mutual benefit may be derived'. However pompous this sounds, it does suggest that farms do not just 'happen' and that humans are not the only beneficiaries. Try looking at the farm from the point of view of a farm rat or a greenfly. A systems view of a farm may be a more fruitful start to planning how to develop it, how to cope with plant pests, what to do when you get bored with the same old crops, or how to proceed when a flood of cheap, foreign produce threatens your market position. A systems view may enable you to cope more effectively with labour disputes or to take action to prevent crop failures.

PREVIEW OF PART 2

Part 2 takes a closer look at using systems ideas and three specific methodologies which have been found to be useful in tackling the complexities of situations and changes. For example, suppose you were given the task of reorganizing the work of an office, or a department or even a whole factory. Where would you start? What would you do at 9.00am on the first day? Panic, perhaps? Do your best while relying on experience, intuition and good luck? Muddle through, telling yourself that it will all work itself out in the end? You may well try to be systematic (a good thing) but that may not be enough. Just consider the many examples of disasters which arise in spite of systematic effort. A hard systems approach to such a task would be much more than simply using systematically organized effort.

Consider another example. Morale in a department has been steadily declining; people mutter in corners; lethargy and lack of enthusiasm abound; productivity is falling. There is, however, no obvious reason for staff dissatisfaction. Pep talks have not improved things. So, what is wrong? Do you reorganize the staff, perhaps? Liven up the decor? Introduce incentive schemes? Shooting in the dark like this is unlikely to improve things. A soft systems approach, however, may be able to identify the underlying reasons for conflict or unease so that remedies may be worked out. A first step in resolving conflicts of interest is to identify the issues and get the interested parties to agree that these actually *are* the issues.

In some situations a FAILURE may have occurred. We are all confronted daily with numerous examples, whether in our personal lives, at work, or 'out there'. At the extreme, failures may be described as disasters, for example accidents such as the Kings Cross fire, Bhopal, Seveso, Flixborough, Chernobyl, Piper Alpha, Zeebrugge etc. But small-scale failures may be just as devastating for individuals. A small company going bust can cause great hardship to those who depend on the firm for their livelihood. When things have gone wrong it is easy to point the finger of blame at 'obvious' causes. However, obvious causes may not be (and rarely are) the underlying causes at all. Preventing similar failures requires understanding of *how* and *why* the FAILURE occurred. Analysing system failures helps to gain that understanding.

In a particular situation it is often beneficial to use more than one systems methodology. Chapter 12 outlines how to switch and combine the three methodologies described in this book as things develop.

EXERCISES AND ACTIVITIES

All chapters in Part 1 and Chapters 6, 8 and 10 in Part 2 contain exercises. Suggested answers are given at the end of each chapter. Some chapters also contain activities. The purpose of exercises and activities is to get you to do relevant things. An interactive approach is likely to help you learn more effectively than if you simply read through the book.

REALISTIC EXPECTATIONS

Before starting on Part 1, a word of caution. This introduction may have given you the impression that systems methodologies are a kind of philosophers' stone or magic wand to wave at difficult problems or complex situations. Systems thinking is indeed powerful and useful but like anything else it has its limitations. A good craftsperson selects his or her tools according to the particular task. The system methodologies described, especially in Part 2, should not be regarded as 'recipes' for success.

Whatever the results of a systems study, there is no guarantee that in every case other people will agree with its findings or suggestions. Even if they express agreement, there may be hidden value-systems at work which operate to ensure that changes are not implemented. What a systems approach can do is provide rational tools for analysing perceived problem situations and presenting explicit evaluations that lead to logically defensible decisions.

SOME PERSPECTIVES

THE ISSUES, DEBATES AND ASSUMPTIONS WHICH AFFECT SYSTEMS THINKING AND PRACTICE

This section seeks to alert the reader to some important issues, debates and assumptions which affect systems thinking and practice and which therefore must be borne in mind in order to get the best out of using the book. Systems thinking is a way of looking at the real world for the purposes of understanding and/or improvement. It would be tempting to accept without question that systems methodologies represent an uncontroversial toolkit, rather like a set of spanners available to tackle nuts-and-bolts. However, such an attitude needs to be resisted. Systems thinking and practice carry with them a whole set of assumptions which can affect the outcome. Indeed, although all systems thinking implicitly entails concepts such as control, communication, interconnectivity and so on, there are different ideas and sets of assumptions which underpin different systems methodologies. The student needs to be aware of biases and tensions not only within the academic community but also within the characteristic thinking of social actors in problem settings which are being considered from a systems perspective and within the student's own view of the world and how it works.

As the warning of page 1 notes, in this book the terms SYSTEM, HARD SYSTEM, SOFT SYSTEM and SYSTEMS FAILURE are printed in small capitals to emphasize the view that they are essentially metaphorical and perceptual.

TERMINOLOGY AND MEANINGS

Wherever possible, pedantic distinctions have been avoided where they are likely to be unimportant to the reader and the practical aims of the book. For example, in the non-academic world, terms such as 'method', 'methodology', 'approach', 'technique' and 'analysis' are often used in a loose, interchangeable way. In systems thinking, however, they need to be used more precisely because, although related, they are not equivalent. Since meaning and action are dialectically linked (Denzin 1978; Johnson 1987) – see the later section on participant observation –, different meanings attached to particular terms are likely to result in correspondingly different actions and outcomes. Uncontrolled use of terms in systems work may result either in a naïve formulaic approach with attendant risks of unwarranted faith in the products of that work, or in communication failures with colleagues, clients or other interested persons.

However, despite the impression given by these statements that there exists a 'correct' set of terms which represent a 'correct' set of concepts, this is not the case. Indeed, a central difficulty in both the study of, and intervention in, human affairs in particular is that there is a wide range of meanings attached to even those concepts and terms which are commonly used. For example, the terms 'system' and 'methodology' do not enjoy fully agreed definitions among the academic community. Both within and between different disciplines and professions, 'system' has multiple meanings. Checkland (1981) describes his meaning of 'methodology' (p161–162) in relation to related concepts such as philosophy and technique.

The author's understanding of the term 'methodology' is a framework of principles, paradigms, methods and techniques for addressing or studying a particular subject, which agrees broadly with that proposed in Checkland (1981) and Checkland and Scholes (1990). To the author, a 'method' is an organized procedure for doing something which embodies or includes a number of practical 'techniques'. For example, a method for collecting data about a particular organization may include techniques for drawing representative samples of people for interviews, interviewing people, sampling documentation and observations of behaviour. These meanings are different from those of Checkland (1981) who equates method with technique as 'a precise specific programme of action which will produce a standardised result'.

The recursive nature of terms such as 'concept', 'theory', 'model', 'paradigm' and 'analytical framework' should be appreciated (Waring 1993). To the author, a theory incorporates relationships and this implicitly involves conceptual models. A concept implicitly involves a model of related ideas. A paradigm is a model of relationships. An analytical framework implictly incorporates one or more paradigms. However, authors use the term paradigm in various ways. For example, Burrell and Morgan (1979) refer to a world-view matrix having four quadrants or paradigms (see sections below). Johnson

(1987), however, uses paradigm as a more specific label for a 'core set of beliefs and assumptions held relatively commonly by the managers' in a particular organization. Johnson states that this core set of beliefs and assumptions has variously been called 'ideational culture, myths, interpretation schemes, or the term used here, paradigms'. The term paradigm has also been used to describe a conceptual model of cause-effect relationships as developed in conventional scientific enquiry (Kuhn 1970) and functionalist approaches to perceived problems and problem-solving. Although to some people 'model' and 'paradigm' are synonymous, confusion may arise between different senses of the terms. Therefore, the author uses 'model' when referring to a 'shorthand' *summary* of particular components and their interrelationships which are perceived to constitute a defined topic and which can often be expressed diagrammatically, and 'paradigm' to mean the *full concept* of those components and relationships. For example, the culture paradigm is complex and demands large amounts of description fully to convey this recursive concept (see for example Smircich 1983, Morgan 1986, Turner 1988), yet it is possible to reduce the paradigm to a number of (competing) models which are based on different assumptions about the nature of culture (Davies 1988, Deal and Kennedy 1986; Lundberg 1990; Waring 1992, 1993, 1994) each of which seeks to convey the essence of the paradigm. The communication paradigm provides another example. Human communication models (see Chapter 7) summarize the encoding, transmission, reception and interpretation of information. However, they do not well convey other important and often subtle aspects of the communication paradigm such as pressure, influence, threat, and deal-seeking (Vickers 1983).

The student should seek to use terminology consistently and accurately. The process of checking their use of language should also encourage the student to think carefully about the underlying concepts and assumptions which the terms enshrine. This is likely to require frequent reference to authoritative texts (see References and Further Reading).

THE WORLD-VIEW CONCEPT

One way of addressing the complexity of human existence is to consider characteristic world-views. According to Dilthey's Philosophy of Existence expounded in 1931 (Kluback and Weinbaum 1957), each person interprets the world in terms of a unique and dynamic set of experiential influences and biases. Repeated patterns of experience coalesce through reflection and lead to a complex and dynamic set of attitudes, beliefs, values, assumptions, motivations and opinions about how the world functions. Dilthey called the individual's perceptual 'window' *Weltanschauung* or world-view, a concept of importance not only in systems work (for example Checkland 1981; Davies 1988; Jackson 1991) but also in the wider literature on organization (for example Johnson 1987). For example, change processes in organizations involve people within it. The mutual influence between the world-view of an individual and the collective world-views of groups to which the individual belongs is significant in examining in particular the influences of culture and power in change processes in organizations (Waring 1993). How individuals and groups perceive reality, the social world in general, and the organizations to which they belong in particular, will affect their understanding of, and actions relating to, particular changes (see later section). Vickers

(1983) does not use the term 'world-view' but refers to a broadly equivalent 'appreciative system' by which individuals and groups appreciate or make sense of the world and their relationship with it.

SYSTEM NOTIONS AND PERCEPTIONS

The history and development of 'systems' ideas are outlined in a number of references (see for example Burrell and Morgan 1979; Checkland 1981; Checkland and Scholes 1990; Cummings 1980; Morgan 1986; Oliga 1990; Vickers 1983).

The notion of a system is inextricably bound up with an individual's world-view. Checkland (1981) poignantly adds a sting in the tail of his definition of a system: 'a model of a whole entity…(which may be) applied to human activity. An observer may *choose* to relate this model to real-world activity.' The emphasis is the author's to bring attention to the 'as if' problem and its link with world-view. According to the author's world-view, a SYSTEM is a metaphor for a wide range of topics and should refer only to a particular system as a *concept* – not as a *'thing'* which has a real-world existence. However, many concepts frequently do become reified and 'system' is a commonplace example as betrayed in everyday speech – the author is as guilty of such lapses as anyone. When some individuals refer to the money supply system, for example, they have mental images of concrete components such as the Bank of England and the Stock Exchange. To such individuals, this really *is* the monetary supply system. In order to avoid not only communication problems but also different approaches arising from different understandings of the term 'system', Checkland (1981) and Checkland and Scholes (1990) propose that it should be replaced by the term 'holon' within systems work. However, the term 'system' is now so embedded in language that it may take a long time to replace among the thousands of systems practitioners throughout the world. One way of avoiding reification or being accused (perhaps wrongly) of having a functionalist world-view (see later section) is to refer always to the 'perceived system' rather than just 'system'.

Reification and use of language are only two aspects which are problematic in systems work. Two others are world-views about the source of human behaviour and about measurement of human behaviour. When people refer, for example, to organizational systems having 'needs' and 'goals', and exhibiting 'behaviour', these are expressions of a particular kind of world-view which attributes characteristics of an individual human being to an entity that includes a number of individuals – *as if* the entity were an individual. Those who advocate measuring effectiveness of systems solely in terms of 'efficiency in use of resources', 'responses to changes in the economic and market environment', 'market share', 'survival of the fittest' and so on betray a particular kind of world-view – *as if* the system were a biological organism attempting to adapt and survive in a harsh physical environment. (see Morgan 1986 for a range of other examples of the system metaphor).

These examples illustrate some assumptions linked to particular kinds of world-view. More could have been cited. Analogies and metaphors are, of course, frequently useful provided that their limitations are known and understood. The practical problems which arise from ignoring the fact that 'as if' does not equal 'is' (Checkland and Scholes 1990; Waring 1989) can occur on many planes. A common example is to accept as given that 'the organization chart' *is* the organization. All conceptual models are reductionist. Highly reductionist models such as organization charts and 'black boxes' convey coarse-grained information about structures and processes, but little else. Less reductionist models provide fine-grained detail but may overwhelm because everything may seem to be related to everything else.

World-view as a perceptual window biases the individual's perception of systems in general, of any particular system and of approaches to understanding or improving them. The following sections seek to structure these biases.

THE NATURE OF THE SOCIAL WORLD

A number of reference frameworks have been proposed for analysing social reality. The thesis of Burrell and Morgan (1979), for example, is that all theories of organization are based upon a philosophy of science and a theory of society. They argue that social science may be conceptualized in terms of four sets of assumptions or dimensions, namely:

- ontology – the essence of the phenomenon; the degree of objectivity; is it a real object or a concept?;

- epistemology – the language of description, definition and form; meanings; the use of metaphors such as 'system';

- human nature – assumptions about the source of human behaviour; is it determined by heredity, culture, and antecedent experience, or by conscious, voluntary, self-created choice?;

- methodology – the amenability of 'variables' being measured to particular kinds of instrument; what process of enquiry is suitable for finding out which information about different kinds of perceived system?; is human behaviour a series of unique, random events or does it follow a measurable, predictable pattern?

```
                          objective
            structural/    │  radical
            functionalist  │  structuralist
            world-views    │  world-views
                           │                radical
  regulation ──────────────┼──────────────  change
            interpretive   │  radical
            world-views    │  humanist
                           │  world-views
                          subjective
```

Fig. B. Burrell and Morgan's World View Framework (simplified)

Burrell and Morgan (1979) argue that these four dimensions make up the single subjective-objective dimension of world-view i.e. at the subjective extreme an individual interprets and describes the world in a metaphorical rather than a literal way, is self-determined and measures success in qualitative terms. Conversely, at the objective extreme, an individual interprets and describes the world in a literal, concrete way, sees the role of the individual as serving 'system' interests (e.g. 'corporate man'), and measures success in hard, quantitative terms. A continuum exists between the subjective-objective extremes.

Burrell and Morgan then propose another dimension to cover the range of world-views about social order – at one extreme whether the status quo should be maintained or at the other extreme whether radical change is needed. Burrell and Morgan superimpose this regulation-radical change dimension to cut across the subjective-objective dimension to produce four quadrants which more precisely locate particular world views as in Fig. B.

The interpretive world-view fits in the subjective/regulation quadrant and is consistent with SOFT SYSTEMS analysis and other quasi-ethnographic approaches. The structural/functionalist world-view fits in the objective/regulation quadrant and encompasses scientific management, operational research, human relations models, and HARD SYSTEMS analysis. The other two quadrants on the radical side in Burrell and Morgan's paradigm are radical humanist and radical structuralist. Advocates of radical ideas regard existing social structures as fundamentally unfair. Radical humanists seek to change society by freeing the individual from all forms of oppression whereas radical structuralists seek to transfer power from those groups deemed to possess it to those groups deemed to deserve it (i.e. class-based revolution). See for example Allen (1982) and Clegg (1980).

The essence of Burrell and Morgan's argument is that the four world-view types *cannot* be reconciled, i.e. it is not possible, for example, to have a partly interpretive and partly functionalist view of society. Their argument is supported by Carter and Jackson (1991) in the modernist/post-modernist debate about organizational analysis. Astley and Van de Ven (1983), however, argue that differing world-views and analysis within one individual can be valid. Similar arguments for commensurability are made by Donaldson (1985), Reed (1991a) and Waring (1989, 1993).

Although based on different sets of assumptions about reality and cause-effect relationships, academic debate has tended to polarize the differences between functionalist and interpretive approaches to the point where they have become regarded by some as mutually exclusive (Burrell and Morgan 1979, Carter and Jackson 1991). The author argues, both from a theoretical standpoint and from empirical research (Waring 1993), that different analytical approaches and models contribute different perspectives which together enable a more complete understanding of, for example, organizational change processes. This inclusive view supports the 'new theory' commensurability of Reed (1991a). A synthesis enables multiple rationalities within organizations to be addressed in a coherent way and which in the longer term may enable organizations to be more effective and experience fewer failures (Turner 1992).

This book is a reflection of the author's world-view which he has developed over a long period of time, including several years as a lone ethnographer studying organizations as a participant observer and developing ideas about change processes in a grounded theory approach (see Bryman 1988; Denzin 1978; Jeffcutt 1991; Rosen 1991; Waring 1993). The author's world-view may be described and analysed with reference to (a) his life experience, (b) his academic research, (c) his professional career, and (d) the analytical framework of Burrell and Morgan (1979). He does not consider himself to be a devotee of any particular discipline and holds a pluralist, ordered view of society.

The author shares Reed's view (1991a) that it is possible to reconcile different interpretations of the same organizational phenomenon. In particular, Burrell and Morgan's assertion that it is not possible to hold both interpretive and functionalist world-views is challenged. The author argues that although he tends towards an interpretive view of human existence, he is readily able to adopt a functionalist perspective. The inherent ambiguities and contradictions which characterize individual thinking and action could not be explained by Burrell and Morgan's argument. Burrell and Morgan do not provide an answer to why, as they claim, an individual should always, in all cases and in all circumstances adopt only one kind of perspective. Such a claim is not borne out by common experience. Burrell and Morgan's framework also does not offer a ready fit for ideologies such as feminism, and for non-western world-views such as Islamic ideology (see Mar'ashi 1995).

It is argued that Burrell and Morgan confuse individual *preference* which, despite a prevailing tendency, can vary from one time to another according to a variety of circumstances, with an exclusive, unvarying *commitment* to one kind of outlook. The author's location on Burrell and Morgan's regulation – radical change dimension– stems from a world-view in which his preference is for order while recognizing that society is essentially unfair. His preferred location on the subjective-objective dimension is towards the subjective pole while recognizing that individual and group behaviours have a purposive or preprogrammed component. His emotional and intellectual commitments are interpretive but he values functionalist utility.

Other labels which have been applied to functionalist and interpretive perspectives are respectively 'normative' and 'descriptive' (see for example Davies 1988; ESRC 1993). The debate about the degree of commensurability of functionalist and interpretive world-views is also closely linked to the debate about the degree of commensurability between modernist and post-modernist perspectives (Carter and Jackson 1991; Jeffcutt 1991; Reed 1991a and b; Waring 1993).

The student should be wary of suggestions from academic élites that a particular systems methodology demands strict obedience to an orthodoxy laid down by them, on pain of being cast out as a 'non-believer'. For example, without acceptance of the commensurability of functionalist and interpretive paradigms a systems thinker would be confined to using methodologies which fitted his or her own particular exclusive world-view – which Burrell and Morgan and their followers insist that they must have. Reed (1991a) states that the argument about discontinuity between paradigms is false and *passé*. He suggests that 'there are very definite continuities in analytical forms and substantive themes between the "old" and the "new" organization theory'. The 'new' theory allows for uncertainty, plurality and diversity and there is now 'a much more realistic and sober assessment of the present need for mediation between conflicting paradigms or perspectives that can facilitate a *rapprochement* between competing theories and methods'. The new *real-politik* in both organizational analysis and systems thinking stresses continuity between world-view types and seeks to accommodate (but not necessarily merge, reconcile or subsume) different perspectives.

THE NATURE OF ORGANIZATIONS

How do organizations get their characteristics – to be what they are and do what they do? Some authors use a biological system metaphor in which an organization is likened to an organism competing with others in its environment for limited resources. Natural selection and macro level views (see for example Astley and Van de Ven 1983) have their uses, but as exclusive viewing instruments for individual organizations they are too coarse. All organizations will appear undifferentiated because that is what population ecology models intend.

Morgan (1986) notes the assumption of organizational homeostasis, a biological concept denoting capacity for self-regulation and maintenance of a steady state under the influence of an external environment. Biological homeostasis applied to human beings forms part of General Adaptation Syndrome (Oborne and Gruneberg 1983) whereby an individual's homeostatic control mechanisms respond automatically (R) to external stimuli (S). Thus, for example, in a moderate thermal environment, gain of heat is balanced by losses largely through radiation, convection, and conduction and also by perspiration (a passive, imperceptible loss of water through the skin). As the thermal environment strays beyond normal limits and heat loading increases, sweating (an active cooling process) is one of several homeostatic responses that enable the individual to adapt to this change in its environment. Self-maintenance is a metaphor that can be recognized in how organizations behave. In most organizations, things tick along in a habitual, predictable way; one does not usually expect to find frequent radical changes occurring at one's workplace. When things get 'hot' in the environment, however, one expects that some kind of appropriate adaptive response will be made to prevent damage to the organization.

The homeostasis metaphor is only useful up to a point, however. On the dynamics of resistance to change, Klein's thesis (1985) is that a necessary prerequisite of successful organizational change is the mobilization of forces against it. The analogy here is with a biological system such as a human being mobilizing its defensive antibodies against antigens invading from the environment. The argument suggests that social systems also exhibit defensive behaviour 'against ill-considered and overly precipitate innovations'. Klein argues that such stimulus-response (S-R) behaviour is inevitable, as indeed it would be if the biological model holds true in all cases. However, it could be argued that defensive behaviour within organisations is not automatic or purposive but is dependent upon the values of individual members. Biological homeostasis is an automatic purposive function; *organizational* homeostasis cannot be assumed to be either automatic or entirely purposive as there is a wide variety of possible responses. Some individuals may adopt a defensive role on behalf of the organization if a threat to their own value system is perceived. Others sharing those values may support them but so too may others with a variety of other motives. Thus, a biological S-R system model is not an exclusive model for all human activity nor is it necessarily appropriate in any particular case.

Morgan (1986) also discusses a number of other potential images or paradigms of organization as perceived by analytical observers or by individuals in organizations. These images include machines, brains, cultures, political systems and psychic prisons. The author infers that such images form part of an individual's world-view. Morgan stresses that many taken-for-granted ideas about organization are metaphorical. The machine metaphor for an organization, for example, conveys an image of mechanical structures, relationships and processes. Such a metaphor moulds an impression of reality in which the more the metaphor is used the more difficult it becomes to appreciate that 'as if' does not equal 'is'. Morgan also notes that a predominant image or metaphor tends to produce incomplete understanding.

How valid are the various paradigms for organizational behaviour proposed or implied in the literature? It is clear that some authors such as Mangham (1979); Morgan (1986); Pettigrew (1987); Pettigrew *et al.* (1992); and Johnson (1987) recognize the theoretical inadequacies of reductionist approaches to organizational behaviour. However, there is a continuing legacy of what has been termed 'biological functionalism' (Burrell and Morgan 1979; Korman and Vredenburgh 1984). Models for both research and managerial practice still regard individuals as passive, rational beings (either totally purposive like ants or totally purposeful and self-willed) instead of as complex psychological, social and economic beings. Organizations are still largely viewed as technical instruments with official goals, strategies, technologies and adaptation to environmental stimuli instead of having complex, dynamic cultures and interactions.

INDIVIDUAL AND GROUP BEHAVIOUR

How much of human behaviour is pre-programmed (purposive) and how much is consciously self-willed (purposeful)? Purposeful and purposive behaviour may be regarded as alternative terms for subjective and objective behaviour respectively, although Checkland (1981) and Checkland and Scholes (1990) apply the term 'purposeful' in a looser way to human activity systems to cover what is *assumed* to be purposeful activity. As discussed below, such an assumption may not be justified.

The terms 'purposeful' and 'purposive' have been used in the literature to distinguish between two different kinds of human behaviour. Pfeffer (1981), for example, uses the term 'purposive' in a sense of strategic, goal-directed managerial behaviour. However, Carter *et al.* (1984) refer to purposive behaviour as 'purpose without choice', that is pre-programmed, goal-directed actions which are likely to entail a large measure of taken-for-grantedness. Ackoff (1971) describes purposive behaviour as a characteristic of multi-goal seeking systems whose purpose is pre-determined by the goals. Carter et al. describe purposeful behaviour as 'purpose with choice' as a feature of deliberately controlled human activity, that is neither the goal nor the means to reach it are predetermined. With purposeful behaviour goals can be changed to produce different outcomes, and the same outcome can be produced in different ways, i.e. 'equifinality' (Morgan 1986).

According to Dixon (1981), a large proportion of human behaviour results from pre-conscious processing, i.e. it is pre-programmed or purposive and has a self-protective function which is unobtrusive (see also Diamond 1986). Purposive behaviour in an individual incorporates unconscious experiential features resulting from socialization, cultural norms and so on. Purposeful behaviour, however, involves creative choice. In other words, an individual is not constrained in action by antecedent behaviour or by instinct. Thus, although behaviour is partly purposive (instinct, experience and social conditioning), an individual may exert a wide variety of choice, i.e. purposefully.

Perception, interpretation and meaning involve a complex interplay between purposeful and purposive behaviours (Waring 1989, 1993). Self-definition and situational definition are partly purposeful and partly purposive in character, as are social interaction and political processes. Even habitual behaviour of interaction where situations are stable, structured and well-understood are not totally purposive. Equally, negotiation in novel, problematic circumstances is not totally purposeful.

The importance of this comes to the fore in SOFT SYSTEMS methodology in which it has been argued (Checkland and Davies 1986; Davies 1988) that the *Weltanschauung* of importance is the collective one of the social actors. The term 'organizational culture' is closely linked to the concept of 'collective world-view' and at the ideational level (Johnson 1987) may be used as an alternative term. Cultural analysis is implicitly involved in the standard form of SOFT SYSTEMS methodology (Checkland 1981) and is an explicit component in the developed form of SSM (Checkland and Scholes 1990). However, the concept of cultural analysis raises a number of problems. What, for example, is 'culture'? There are many definitions (Smircich 1983) but most relate in some way to shared ideals, values and ways of doing things. If world-view is to be defined at the level of group culture or collective consciousness, it relies on the assumption that (a) such a 'thing' has an existence independent of individuals (*cf.* public opinion), (b) the behaviour of individual actors is subordinated and pre-ordained by group culture, i.e. is wholly purposive. Clearly, this level of world-view on its own is unsatisfactory because individuals do not act solely under the influence of collective consciousness even if one accepts such a term as a metaphor for shared values, ideology, rules of behaviour etc. Individuals may agree or assume that they share such attributes, but simultaneously individuals to varying degrees influence events and sometimes contrary to what group culture would predict. It is important, therefore, to address both group *and* key individual world-views in order to avoid introducing another 'as if' problem. This is not to suggest that world-view should be used as a psychological viewing instrument on individuals selected as key figures by the analyst.

Systems texts tend to deal only very briefly with the complex inter-related topics of culture, power and political processes in relation to organizations, and do not discuss the range of different perspectives on and debates concerning them. In order to avoid addressing these topics in a narrow and naïve way, students should refer to the considerable literature on these topics for a more complete picture (see, for example, Bacharach and Lawler 1980; Clegg 1980; Deal and Kennedy 1986; Diamond 1986; Douglas 1992; Glendon and McKenna 1995; Hardy 1985; Johnson 1987, 1992; Knights and Morgan 1991; Lundberg 1990; Mangham 1979; Morgan 1986; Pettigrew 1973, 1985, 1987; Pettigrew *et al.* 1992; Pfeffer 1981, 1982; Schein 1985; Schwenk 1989; Smircich 1983; Toft 1994; Turner 1988, 1992; Waring 1993, 1994, 1996; and Westley 1990).

PARTICIPANT OBSERVATION

Debates and issues concerning systems methodologies are well covered in authoritative texts such as Checkland 1981; Checkland and Scholes 1990; Flood and Jackson 1991; Jackson 1991; and Fortune and Peters 1995. However, the student should be aware of, and think carefully about, a methodological issue which is central to systems work and particularly in soft systems methodology, namely the sense-making activity of the system analyst as observer, mediator and facilitator and his or her impact on the behaviour of those being 'helped'. SOFT SYSTEMS methodology and especially the developed form of SSM is quasi-ethnographic in its approach to human enquiry. It is therefore not sufficient simply to examine world-views or make the more elaborate 'stream of cultural enquiry' described by Checkland and Scholes (1990). The meaning systems of social actors are inextricably informing and informed by their symbolic actions, i.e. a dialectical process of action and meaning (Denzin 1978; Johnson 1987). That process involves both purposeful *and* purposive influences – it is unsafe to assume that human behaviour is only purposeful, or that people conveniently switch purposive and purposeful behaviours on and off, or that purposeful behaviour can be readily isolated. The system analyst as observer is engaged in a process of 'abduction' (Denzin 1978) whereby he or she is gaining only a partial glimpse of the process and is seeking to understand it. However, abduction necessarily involves the analyst's own action-meaning system which in turn will be interpreted and acted upon by the social actors in the setting concerned. The process of enquiry itself will therefore change the actions and meanings of those being observed as well as those of the analyst. The difficulties and consequences of this kind of enquiry, which involves participant observation, should be recognized. Suitable references are Bryman 1988; Buchanan *et al.* 1988, Clegg *et al.* 1985; Jeffcutt 1991; Rosen 1991; Turner 1988; and Westley 1990.

SUMMARY

The systems ideology is inextricably bound up with world-views and in particular assumptions about the nature of social reality, the source(s) of individual and group behaviour, the nature of organization(s) and the processes of social and scientific enquiry. Traditional HARD SYSTEMS ideas and practice, along with the physical and biological sciences and conventional managerial practice, are consistent with a structuralist/functionalist or modernist world-view that is ends-and-means dominated. They can have great practical value, but success with HARD SYSTEMS ideas in some applications may lead to false expectations for success when applied to contexts where SOFT SYSTEMS ideas may be more appropriate. Nevertheless, the three methodologies described in this book are complementary and should be viewed as such.

PART ONE
AN INTRODUCTION TO SYSTEMS THINKING

SYSTEMS IDEAS

This chapter:

- describes the concept of a 'system';
- describes the characteristics of SYSTEMS such as structures, processes, environment, hierarchy, control and prediction;
- introduces system concepts such as emergence, holism, world-view and ownership.

INTRODUCTION

This chapter aims to encourage the habit of thinking about a system more as an *idea* or metaphor for organized interconnectedness than as a *thing*. The word 'system' is used widely in everyday speech and has various meanings. Often it is used to mean something which operates in an organized way, for example a 'systematic procedure' or a 'system of work'. However, a systematic procedure is not necessarily a system. As a set of logically ordered steps for doing something, a systematic procedure may have some, but not all, of the necessary ingredients of a system. This popular confusion between system and systematic procedure explains the failure of some so-called systems to meet expectations. How often have you ended up in a mess *despite* using systematic effort?

You have probably experienced some of the unintended but none the less unwanted effects of other people's work procedures: accounting 'systems', monitoring 'systems', payroll 'systems', stock control 'systems', and so on. Essentially, such procedures take ingredients (inputs) through a procedure (process) which is expected to convert them into useful products (outputs) as expressed diagramatically in Fig. 1.1. This simple 'sausage-machine' view of a system is sometimes called a 'black-box model' – the details of the process are regarded as relatively unimportant and remain hidden in a notional 'black box'.

The input-process-output principle is essential to all SYSTEMS but it is rather weak on its own and can encourage a false sense of confidence about successful outcomes. Systematic effort alone does not guarantee success. A systematic arrangement requires a lot more before it can be fairly called a system.

NB SYSTEM, HARD SYSTEM, SOFT SYSTEM and SYSTEM FAILURE in small capitals refer to metaphorical and perceptual constructs.

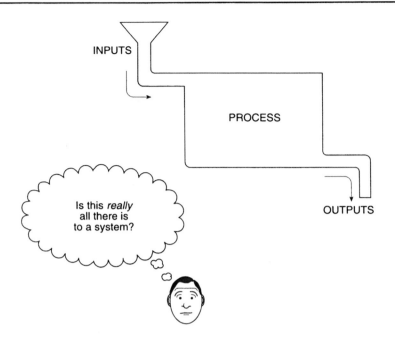

Fig.1.1 Some people's idea of a system.

The confusion between 'systems' and 'systematic effort' lies in the history of SYSTEMS work. Since the 1950s systems practice has been dominated by employer demands for greater efficiency and productivity. The effort of systems analysts, therefore, has been directed towards making the input-process-output procedure more efficient i.e. it has been ends-and-means dominated (Vickers 1983). You may be familiar with the idea of feedback, by which output is measured and compared against a reference value. Feedback loops and control typify an emphasis on improvement of system efficiency (see Fig. 5.3 in Chapter 5). If the output is too high (or too low) compared with the reference value, information is fed back to the input side to decrease (or increase) the input accordingly and so maintain control.

Such traditional systems analysis fits in the area of HARD SYSTEMS thinking and practice covered in later chapters. Most traditional systems analysts work in the related fields of computing and information technology (IT). This numerical and professional domination has had an unfortunate side effect, namely that some people see (a) computing/IT as the only legitimate application for systems thinking, and (b) the methods of computer systems analysts as the only ones of any real value. Since the mid-1980s, there has also been a steady development of systems thinking in management. The most notable application has been in the three functionally related areas of quality management, environmental management and safety management. National and international standards such as BS EN ISO 9000 Quality Management Systems, BS 7850 Guide to Management Principles for Total Quality, ISO 14001/BS 7750 Environmental Management Systems and BS 8800 Safety Management Systems have been drawn up. These standards describe *systematic* arrangements based on a process control model with feedback loops which seeks to enable users to establish a cycle of continuous improvement in aspects of management. Whatever the claims made, these standards are nevertheless limited in terms of the scope of systems thinking covered in this book.

Systems thinking and methodologies should be regarded as general approaches for use by anyone. Control-based models and systematic approaches have their place within a general systems 'tool kit' but they are not all-powerful. The student needs to develop a broad perspective of the range of systems methodologies and should not be mesmerized by what narrow sectional interests claim to be the complete answer to all systems requirements.

WHAT IS A SYSTEM?

Although there is no universally accepted definition of 'system', there are general characteristics of systems which are widely accepted as being necessary for any system. As stated above, a system is an idea or concept, even though something that may be called a system will often have a quite obvious physical substance to it. A hot water central heating arrangement for a suite of offices, for instance, includes pieces of hardware such as hot water radiators, pumps, a boiler and so on. People often refer to the 'central heating system' meaning all the hardware connected up, but is this really a system? Does it possess all the necessary ingredients?

At a simple level, a system may be described as a recognizable whole which consists of a number of parts (called components or elements) that are connected up in an organized way (the system's structure). These components interact, i.e. there are processes going on. This basic description covers the popular idea of interconnected parts and processes as in the central heating system. However, to be of real use such a definition needs amplification to include the following characteristics:

- A SYSTEM does something (there are processes and outputs).

- Addition or removal of a component changes the system.

- A component is affected by its inclusion in the system.

- Components are perceived to be related in hierarchical structures.

- There are means for control and communication which promote system survival.

- The system has emergent properties, some of which are difficult to predict.

- The system has a boundary.

- Outside the boundary is a system environment which affects the system.

- A system is owned by someone (See 'System Ownership' below).

These characteristics are an amalgam of those quoted in Carter *et al.* (1984), Checkland (1981), Checkland and Scholes (1990), Morgan (1986) and Open University T301 material.

The reasons for this expansion of the definition will become apparent as the book progresses.

Exercise 1.1

Taking the office central heating system as an example, (a) identify the outputs, (b) predict the likely effects of removing a room thermostat (temperature controller), and (c) say how the system's environment might affect the system. You might want to consider not only obvious but also less obvious outputs.

The answer to Exercise 1.1 shows that there are subtleties to consider. When people think of system output they usually do so in terms of the expected or desired output. Nevertheless, all SYSTEMS have multiple outputs, some of which may be of little interest or even undesirable.

Just as the addition of a component changes the SYSTEM, the component itself is also affected. For example, the central heating pump receives electrical power and should respond to control signals from the thermostat. The pump will get warm during use and undergo wear and tear. To widen your thinking, pause to consider the SYSTEMS in which you could be considered to be a component and how your presence in or absence from them could affect them and you.

STRUCTURES AND PROCESSES

There are two kinds of system component – structural and process components. A systems structure is represented by relatively stable, lasting components which either carry out processes or are acted on by processes, i.e. the 'doers' and the 'done-to'. For example, in the central heating case structural components include:

- boiler;
- pump;
- thermostat;
- pipes;
- radiators.

Fig 1.2 shows these structural components linked up. The processes within a SYSTEM are represented by transient, changing components, i.e. action, change, growth, decline or 'doing' of some kind. For example, in the central heating system, processes include heat generation, pumping, heat transmission, temperature control, flow control, and time control.

A SYSTEM encompasses more components than the immediately obvious ones. But who is to say which components are correct and how will you know when you have included all the relevant ones? There are no easy answers to these questions. A SYSTEM includes necessary components (i.e. those which are essential to any system of its type) and additional components which vary according to the situation and the view

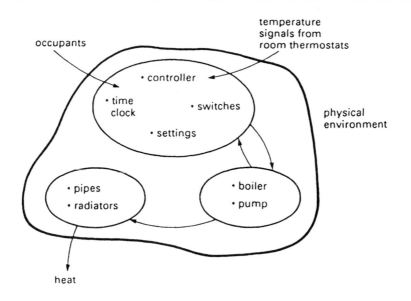

Fig 1.2 Office central heating system.

of the analyst. Clearly, the hot water central heating system would not function at all without a boiler and a pump. These are essential components. However, the number, kind and location of thermostats depend on the analyst's viewpoint and purpose. Knowing when to say 'enough is enough' is a matter of experience, systems skills and purpose. The process of iteration or repeated refinement until you decide enough is enough is central to the methodologies in this book and is described more fully in Chapter 2.

System components are usually organized by the analyst into groups which are closely related in terms of function and which represent an identifiable sub-system. A SUB-SYSTEM is part of a SYSTEM which itself has all the general characteristics of a system. For example, in Fig. 1.2 the boiler and pump are the two main components of the heat generating and pumping sub-system as perceived by the author. The central heating system shown in Fig. 1.2 could be depicted as in Fig. 1.3.

SYSTEM ENVIRONMENT

The concept of a system environment is important as it determines where the analyst sets the boundary between what is inside the SYSTEM and what is outside. There are no absolute rights and wrongs and analysts often disagree about where a boundary should be set. The system environment comprises components which affect the SYSTEM but which the system is unable to control directly and is unable to affect to any significant extent. For example, the environment of the overall management system of an organization is likely to include public policy, legislation, the economy, technology, product markets and so on. Although many organizations do seek to influence such external matters (e.g. through trade associations, lobbying etc.), they cannot control them and are able only to influence some of them.

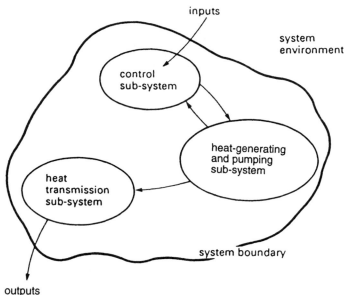

Fig 1.3 Office central heating system in sub-system format.

The central heating system is a little unusual in that it is designed specifically to affect a particular aspect of its physical environment, i.e. the air temperature, and so prevent thermal discomfort among the occupants of rooms served. However, this system does not exercise control over its physical environment.

To use a different kind of system as another example, the environment of a bridge building SYSTEM might include:

- financial restrictions;
- legislation;
- local authority planning committee;
- Department of the Environment;
- weather;
- geological conditions;
- local conservationists.

These components affect the system rather than the other way round.

Exercises 1.2
In addition to the physical environment, what other components might be present in the environment of a central heating system? Consider, for example, people who have specific responsibilities, financial factors etc.

HIERARCHY AND RESOLUTION

The sub-system concept introduced above broached the subject of focus, resolution and hierarchy which concern the level of detail appropriate to the analyst's task. Setting a boundary is also part of the process of bracketing-off those components deemed to be important for the analyst's particular purpose. In Fig. 1.3, for example, the three identified subsystems are considered by the author to be at the same level of resolution. Going down a level of detail to examine one of these SUB-SYSTEMS would require identification of lower order sub-systems, for example the boiler and its components. It is common in systems practice to adjust levels of resolution up and down as the work progresses.

Hierarchy is allied to resolution in that some components are considered by the analyst to be subordinate to others in terms of authority, time, sequence or some other characteristic. For example, policy-making in an organization is usually regarded as a higher order function than operational activities. The board is usually regarded as being at the top of the organization. Even with a vogue for smaller, leaner, flatter organizations and looser hierarchical reporting relationships, there will always be discernible hierarchies. Hierarchy and resolution are discussed further in Chapter 2 and other chapters.

PREDICTION AND CONTROL

Prediction and control relate to the SYSTEM's ability to head off dysfunction and survive when things go wrong. Knowledge of a SYSTEM's structure, processes and control characteristics enables its behaviour to be predicted in a range of circumstances. However, the more complex the SYSTEM and the factors which influence it, the less likely that predictions will always be accurate. SYSTEMS have a mixture of predictable properties and properties which are difficult to predict. Predictable properties are often desirable, but many undesirable predictable properties are often overlooked. In man-made SYSTEMS, the job of system specifiers and designers is to look beyond the expected, desirable outcomes and try to identify undesirable possibilities so that they can be designed out or their consequences mitigated.

Monitoring of system performance against criteria or reference standards is a key control requirement and, in principle, enables the SYSTEM to correct deviations from desired outputs. Fig. 5.5 (in Chapter 5) is a representation of the general control model. However, as discussed in later chapters, it should be appreciated that some assumptions about control which fit 'engineered' and other HARD SYSTEMS well are less satisfactory when applied to groups of people and organizations perceived as 'human activity' systems.

EMERGENT PROPERTIES

A system is not just a collection of interconnected components. Their interaction as a whole, or 'synergy', produces emergent properties or behaviour which could not readily be predicted simply by examining each component in isolation or even some of the components together. For example, examination of a microchip does not enable prediction of all the functions of a complete computer system. Examination of a company's production department (a SUB-SYSTEM of the formally organized system of the company) does not enable prediction of the company's corporate image in the eyes of its customers. Emergence is consistent with holism or, in popular speech, 'the whole is greater than the sum of its parts'. Scrutiny of individual components and sub-systems may provide some useful information about the SYSTEM as a whole, but it will be limited.

Prediction of adverse properties is especially important where harm could result. Some components can often work together counter-intuitively or do the opposite to what might be expected. For example, power presses ('powered metal pressing systems') have a habit of operating unexpectedly, and numerous cases of power press operators having fingers amputated are on record. SYSTEMS designed with noble intentions, such as social aid schemes and housing corporations, sometimes can have devastating consequences for those who were meant to be helped. Examples of such SYSTEM FAILURES are described in Chapters 5, 10 and 11.

SYSTEM OWNERSHIP

System ownership does not necessarily refer to persons who are the title owners in the 'goods and property' sense. The term refers to those persons who are interested in the particular SYSTEM for the purposes of design, improvement, implementation, problem-solving, study and so on. Ownership implies a perception that it is worthwhile viewing a particular set of components as a SYSTEM.

The concept of system ownership is important because it relates to who controls and maintains the SYSTEM. In some areas of management, 'system owners' have come to mean those who have responsibility for a SYSTEM and those who are internal 'customers' or beneficiaries of it. However, a distinction needs to be drawn between system owner and stakeholding beneficiary. The system owner or owners are likely to be particular managers, possibly at a senior level, who can cause the SYSTEM to change significantly or cease to exist, whereas stakeholding employees throughout the organization, or individuals with an operational role in the SYSTEM, cannot.

TYPES OF SYSTEM

For the purposes of this book, SYSTEMS may be classified under four main headings (Carter *et al.* 1984; Checkland 1981):

*   natural systems (e.g. biological systems, disease, the weather);

*   designed abstract systems (e.g. computer programming languages, simulatory models, signing systems);

- engineered or designed technical systems (e.g. process plant, computer systems)

- human activity systems (e.g. work organizations, a department, a committee).

This classification enables some kind of sense to be made of the enormous number and range of things which could be described as systems. Although all four types share common features, each also has its own characteristics. Sometimes it can be convenient to regard particular SYSTEMS, such as manufacturing organizations or companies in the process industries, as combining aspects of both human activity and designed technical systems – so called socio-technical systems. The complex system of human factors which permeates an organization and influences the management SYSTEM is sometimes referred to as a socio-political system. Information systems are often classified separately from the four types listed above, although they are likely to combine aspects of abstract, engineered and human activity systems.

Exercises 1.3
Allocate each of the following to the most appropriate system type (natural, abstract, engineered/designed technical, or human activity):

- nuclear reactor;

- Burmese teak forest;

- strip steel mill;

- company marketing department

- taxation;

- AIDS (Acquired Immuno-Deficiency Syndrome);

- warehouse;

- central heating system;

- housing association

Some people, particularly those having functionalist leanings (see Some Perspectives on p 5) also classify systems as either HARD or SOFT. Engineered systems, natural systems and designed abstract systems are perceived by them to be HARD. From a functionalist perspective, the properties of HARD SYSTEMS typically have (or are perceived to have) a high degree of predictability and attributes which are readily quantifiable and measurable. Compared with those SYSTEMS classified as SOFT, HARD SYSTEMS are assumed to have fewer unpredictable properties, but even if one takes this view their possibility should always be borne in mind.

Those systems perceived as SOFT have a much higher degree of assumed unpredictability because they involve (or are perceived to involve) people's values, attitudes and behaviour which are complex and variable. SOFT SYSTEMS are perceived typically to have properties which are difficult to quantify and measure e.g. viewpoints, conflicts, vested interests and other qualitative characteristics.

Although it can be convenient to use such a classification, there are dangers, in that it suggests some mutually exclusive properties as if in each case only one classification is correct.

Exercise 1.4

For each of the following examples, provide counter-arguments as to why the perceived system could be classified as both HARD and SOFT depending on one's view:

- container truck (a motor vehicle system for transporting heavy goods containers?);

- computer steering committee (a system for guiding the introduction and implementation of computers?);

- parent-teacher association (a system for enabling parents and teachers to co-operate to improve children's education?);

- a trout farm (a system for rearing trout for profit?)

WORLD-VIEW

World-view, also called *Weltanschauung* (Dilthey 1931) (See some perspectives p 7), represents the complex set of perceptions, attitudes, beliefs, values, assumptions and motivations which characterize an individual or a group of people. World-view is a kind of perceptual window or 'tinted spectacles' through which each person interprets the world and his or her relationship with it. It is a SOFT mental phenomenon which cannot be measured as such, only inferred from what people say or do. It has immense importance in systems work because it concerns characteristic biases, not only of key figures and other owners of the particular SYSTEM but also of the system analyst. Because world-views affects SYSTEM behaviour and outcomes, the world-views both of the social actors in the setting being examined and the analyst need to be identified.

It should not be taken for granted that in a given setting everyone holds the same views about problems, issues, solutions and priorities; this important point is often overlooked. In systems work it would usually be impractical to consider the world-views of hundreds of individuals but it is important to identify the world-views of key individuals who appear to exert particular influence.

Of course, many people in organizations do have similar world-views. Such collective world-views form a major part of organizational cultures. Shared world-views are important for the integration and stability of the organization. However, sometimes a shared world-view held by one group clashes with that of another group. Some examples are given in Table 1.1.

Table 1.1 Examples of different world-views in organizations

Organization	Group A	Group B
Political parties	pro-Europe	anti-Europe
Health service	holistic medicine	surgery and drugs
Trade journal publishers	editorial content takes priority	advertisements take priority

---

Exercise 1.5

World-views need to be considered in analysing any situation under investigation. What sort of situation would warrant a deeper examination of world-views?; explain why.

Sometimes world-views differ so much that either a clash occurs or people part company. In boardrooms blood is sometimes said to 'gush under the doors'. In industry, managements and unions fight or manoeuvre to secure advantage in the play for valued resources. The battles between political parties and between trades unions and employers provide classic examples of views that are often 'worlds apart'.

On a grand scale, differences in political and religious ideologies result in conflicts and wars between peoples and countries – the Middle East, Afghanistan, Bosnia, Chechnia, and Rwanda providing recent examples. Until 1993, Albania had effectively shut out the rest of the world for over 40 years – an example of a state-controlled world-view which resisted potential contamination by foreign ideas.

In all systems work the analyst has to try to identify explicit and implicit world-views in the situation. World-views are especially important in soft systems methodology because they are usually at the heart of the 'messy' problems being examined.

C. West Churchman (1985) tells a fable about an aircraft hijacked to Cuba while *en route* to New York. On board the hijacked plane three passengers pass the time discussing the nature of reality and how to improve things. They are a hard systems expert, a senior executive and a philosopher. Each argues that his profession has the best approach to social problems. A fourth passenger sitting alongside gets steadily drunk and ignores the debate other than swearing occasionally.

The debate gets heated with no one prepared to give ground. Each is convinced that his profession's world-view is superior and enables problems to be solved more effectively. After hours of argument, the pilot announces that the hijackers have ordered him to fly to New York and release the passengers. The three experts demand to know why.

At this point, the fourth and rather drunk passenger interjects that he is one of the hijackers who had intended to kidnap these high-powered experts. After listening to their endless argument and debate about the merits of their respective world-views he felt the revolution would be best served by returning them home. As the hijacker disappears, the stewardess apologizes for his outburst and adds: 'He had a point you know. After all, none of you men ever once included a woman in your elegant and comprehensive systems.'

Activity
As Churchman's story shows, the world-view of a particular profession creates a tendency towards a biased view of issues, problems, solutions and priorities. Spend some time thinking about your membership of groups and your world-view. How does your world-view affect your capacity to 'put yourself in other people's shoes'? Describe world-views which may differ considerably from your own; for example, contrast the likely world-views of a social worker, business tycoon, engineer and nurse. In developing systems skills, you will need to try to discard the notion that your world-view is 'good/correct' whereas others are 'bad/incorrect'. Systems work frequently requires seeking *rapprochement* and accommodations between differing world-views relevant to the particular situation, and the analyst as facilitator both affects and is affected by this process (see Some Perspectives p 5). World-views therefore need to be judged as relevant and appropriate to the particular context.

SUMMARY

This chapter has sought to describe the concept of a system, key characteristics of SYSTEMS and how systems may be classified.

Systems do not exist in an absolute sense. A system is an idea or convenient metaphor for a wide range of things. A system as a concept is a recognizable whole which consists of a number of parts that interact in an organized way. Specifically:

- A SYSTEM does something (there are processes and outputs).
- Addition or removal of a component changes the system.
- A component is affected by its inclusion in the system.
- Components can be arranged in hierarchical relationships.
- Means for prediction, control and communication promote system survival.
- There are emergent properties, some of which are unpredictable.
- A system has a boundary.
- Outside the boundary is a system environment.
- A system is owned by someone.

The world-views of key individuals and groups who are in or who affect a SYSTEM are very important in understanding how that system behaves, and therefore must be identified and examined before attempting to change the system. The analyst must always consider his or her own world-view and how it contributes to an analysis.

SUGGESTED ANSWERS TO EXERCISES

1.1 (a) The main output of a hot water central heating system is convective heat from the so-called 'radiators'. The radiator warms the air which rises and moves around the room (less than 25% of heat output is actually radiated in the scientific sense). Other outputs include sound (e.g. pump noise, vibrations, air locks) and waste gases from the boiler flue.

(b) A room thermostat contains a device designed to monitor air temperature in the room and to switch the boiler on or off. If the temperature is higher than a set value, the boiler is switched off; if lower, the boiler is switched on. Removing the thermostat would make it difficult for the air temperature to be controlled; removal of a component *changes* the SYSTEM.

(c) The air temperature itself would affect the system provided that a thermostat was operating. So also would the presence or absence of people in the environment, whether in the offices or in the boiler room. People may open or close windows. They may alter the positions of local control valves on radiators. Building services engineers and maintenance staff may adjust the equipment.

1.2 Other possible components in the environment of a hot water central heating system:

- electricity supplies;
- gas supplies;
- boiler operatives;
- maintenance engineers;
- statutory boiler inspectors;
- insurance surveyors;
- energy conservation and safety legislation;
- company budgets.

1.3 Natural systems: Burmese teak forest, AIDS

Abstract systems: taxation

Engineered/designed technical systems: nuclear reactor, strip steel mill, warehouse*, central heating system

Human activity system: company marketing department, housing association.

1.4 (a) container truck:

HARD SYSTEM classification: a designed technical system of hardware having relatively predictable properties;

SOFT SYSTEM classification: human activity of driver, driver's mate and significant others e.g. fleet manager, maintenance department.

---

*This classification holds if you view 'warehouse' as an engineered system of premises and equipment (racking, fork lift trucks, conveyors etc.) and processes (goods inwards, outwards, rack allocation, record-keeping etc.) However, a warehouse could also be regarded as a socio-technical system in view of the human activity elements. How you name your system is therefore important (see the questions in Exercise 1.4, for example).

(b) computer steering committee:

HARD SYSTEM classification: formally organized group functioning according to a formal constitution, terms of reference, agendas;

SOFT SYSTEM classification: human activity involving political interaction and debate as essential processes.

(c) parent-teacher association:

HARD SYSTEM classification: formally organized group functioning according to a formal constitution, terms of reference, agendas;

SOFT SYSTEM classification: human activity involving political interaction and debate as essential processes.

(d) trout farm:

HARD SYSTEM classification: biological system manipulated and controlled by humans with relatively quantifiable and predictable attributes;

SOFT SYSTEM classification: human activity in managing and operating the farm, involving culture, power, management-staff relations.

Remember, you as observer decide whether to view a particular system as predominantly HARD or SOFT.

1.5 SOFT SYSTEMS require a deeper examination of world-views because the world-views of particular actors or groups forming the human activity SYSTEM are likely to be at the heart of any actual or potential malaise in the situation.

2 Developing systems thinking

The objectives of this chapter are to:

- introduce categories of system diagram;
- describe a range of diagramming techniques for visualizing SYSTEMS or aspects of them;
- outline diagramming rules and conventions;
- outline the pre-analysis technique of system description.

INTRODUCTION

In Chapter 1, you were introduced to the concept of a system. In this chapter, the aim is to develop your systems thinking and, in particular, introduce you to techniques for describing and visualizing SYSTEMS. A variety of source material has been used, largely but not exclusively from the Open University. This chapter contains a lot of material and there are numerous exercises and activities. It is suggested, therefore, that you take a fairly relaxed approach to it and perhaps revisit the chapter a number of times.

DIAGRAMMING TECHNIQUES

Diagramming techniques are essential to good systems practice because they:

- require the analyst to think clearly about the topic of interest; often they cause the analyst to revise his or her thoughts on the topic;
- form a permanent record of the analyst's thoughts on the subject at the time, and are useful for future reference;
- facilitate communication of information between the analyst and others.

NB SYSTEM, HARD SYSTEM, SOFT SYSTEM and SYSTEM FAILURE in small capitals refer to metaphorical and perceptual constructs.

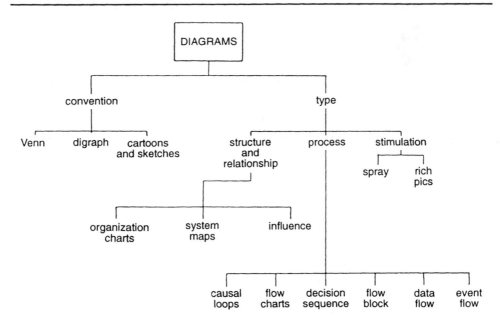

Fig. 2.1 Organization chart of diagramming techniques.

The author offers a word of comfort to readers who are not good at drawing and who may be anxious about drawing system diagrams. Artistic talent is definitely not required, and sketching and scribbling skills will be adequate for most needs. Only if and when you have to present diagrams in reports or to meetings will you need to tidy them up.

There are many diagramming techniques used in systems work and these are summarised in Fig 2.1. This figure represents diagramming techniques in the form of an organisation chart and so is itself an example of a system diagramming technique (i.e. a structure and relationship diagram).

Some techniques are usually associated with particular kinds of work. However, these industry-specific techniques such as data flow diagrams and entity-relationship diagrams as used in information systems development are variations and adaptations of the more general techniques shown in Fig. 2.1.

ORGANIZATION CHARTS

Activity 2.1
Sketch an organization chart for an organization that you know, e.g. your department, your employer, a club, your family.

Organization charts introduce two concepts which are important in all systems work. First is the concept of relationship. For example, Fig. 2.1 indicates that flow block diagrams are a type of process diagram; flow block diagrams relate to process rather than to structure-and-relationship. As another example from Fig 2.1, Venn diagrams, relate to conventions or rules for drawing diagrams rather than to types of diagram.

The second concept is that of hierarchies in relationships – the idea that one item is subordinate or junior to another or that one item is a more specific example of another. Very often you will be in possession of a jumble of information. By drawing up a list of topics and then putting like with like, you can readily construct an organization chart (or other structure and relationship diagram) which summarizes and clarifies that information.

Exercises

2.1   Look at Fig. 2.1 again. Assuming that there is nothing missing from the organization chart itself, is there anything else that such a diagram ought to have in it?

2.2   It was stated above that an organization chart helps to summarize and clarify relationships. This can be very useful in analyzing a business organization. Can you foresee a downside to such use?

SYSTEM MAPS (see for example Open University T301 1984, 1993)

A system map is often drawn according to the Venn convention. This convention is consistent with the theory of 'sets' whereby sets of like components are bound together and boundaries overlap where some properties of two or more sets are shared, as shown in Fig. 2.2.

The following examples show how the Venn convention has been used to construct system maps. Fig. 2.3 is a simple map of a school and Fig. 2.4, which concerns a typical local authority housing department, may look daunting but bear in mind that it started out as a simple rough-and-ready diagram like Fig. 2.3. You do not need to make the components in your system maps look as regular as they do in Fig. 2.4 - using straight lines rather than blobs is a matter of preference, purpose and perception of the situation. Indeed, neatness and straight lines can often convey a false picture of order and control when the reality may be chaotic.

Exercises

2.3   In Fig. 2.4, how would you interpret the relationship between the assessments function of the housing department and the customers?

2.4   How would you interpret the relationship between the department's system for building new houses ('new build') and external suppliers of services?

2.5   How would you interpret the relationship between the Government and the housing department?

Fig. 2.4 also introduces the concept of a wider system. A housing department does not enjoy an independent existence; it operates entirely within and under the control of the local authority. The limits of the local authority itself are shown as the wider

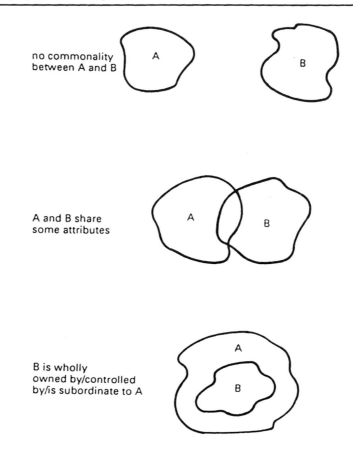

Fig. 2.2 Conventions in Venn diagramming.

system boundary outside which the SYSTEM environment affects both the wider system and the system of interest. If the focus was on the accounts sub-system of the housing department, this could be regarded as existing within a wider system represented by the housing department. Expenditure control could be seen as a sub-system of accounts if *accounts* is the main focus, or as a system within the wider accounts system if *expenditure control* is the main focus. Thus, any particular SYSTEM may be regarded as part of a hierarchy or nest of systems and the setting of boundaries (sub-system, system, wider system) is determined by your focus of interest.

Systems work requires the analyst to make a judgement as to what level he or she is working at, i.e. the resolution or level of detail. During iterations, the resolution often has to be adjusted so that all the components (areas) are at the same level. To aid both thinking and visual communication, the general rule is that a system diagram should not contain more than a dozen components and ideally between five and nine i.e. the 7 ± 2 rule (Miller 1956; Checkland and Scholes 1990; Turner 1988; Waring 1989). Fig. 2.4 is therefore stretching this rule to the limit. The practical significance of this rule is that it allows you to adjust the work to manageable levels in terms of conceptual complexity and your resources available.

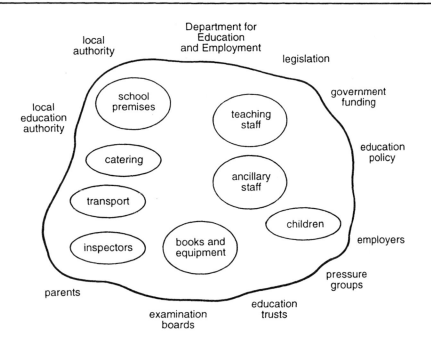

Fig. 2.3 System map of a school.

Exercise 2.6

Imagine that you work for a company that runs management training courses. Draw a simple system map of your market.

SPRAY DIAGRAMS (see for example Carter *et al.* 1984; Open University T301 1984, 1993)

Spray diagrams (or 'spider-grams') are useful for loosening up your thinking in the early stages of problem solving or analysis. Typically, in the early stages the analyst's thinking is dogged by partial images of 'the problem' and of possible solutions based on past experience. Systems thinking tries to break out of this serial, 'vertical' approach by forcing an expansion of thought, i.e. 'lateral thinking'. Alternate expansion and contraction of focus is a common feature of systems work.

FREE CAR PARKS TO GO!

'A minimum fee of 20p per car is soon to be levied on motorists who presently use six free car parks in Blogton, according to the local council. The council's Finance & General Purposes Committee approved the scheme last week and it is to be considered again by the full council next Wednesday.

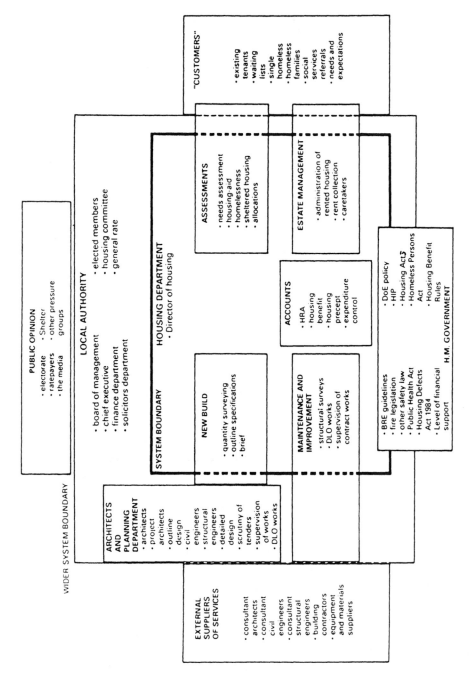

Fig. 2.4 System map of a typical local authority housing department. (Note purpose is to clarify relationships between components and adjust resolution to a manageable level).

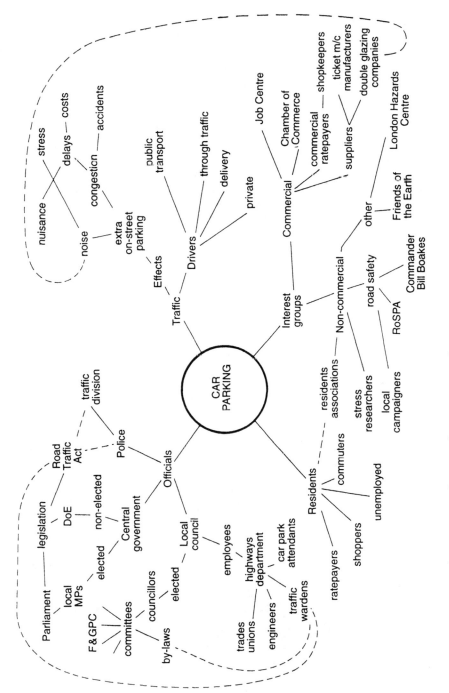

Fig. 2.5 Spray diagram of components relating to car parking situation (first iteration).

A one-month experiment will be conducted initially to see what level of takings result. The six car parks have already been assessed with regard to use, size and likely transfer to on-street parking if the charges are introduced. Experimental charging will initially cost £1,000 per site plus wages of about £150 per week per site. If successful, the experiment will lead to 'pay-and-display' ticket machines. Local shopkeepers and union officials representing traffic wardens are thought to be against the new proposals'.

(The Blogton Advertiser, 1990)

The reasons for the car park levy proposal are not stated, but what could the effects be? Who could be affected? The knee-jerk response of vertical thinking is to focus on the obvious effects – car drivers having to pay or park elsewhere. But introduction of a levy represents a new component in the road traffic SYSTEM of Blogton and, as discussed in Chapter 1, a new component will *change* the SYSTEM. Will the new system behave differently?

Fig 2.5 shows a spray diagram which opened up the author's thoughts on the subject. He pursued particular lines as indicated but you might have chosen other lines of enquiry. It is also possible to draw spray diagrams in a more structured way as in Fig 2.6 which relates to asbestos.

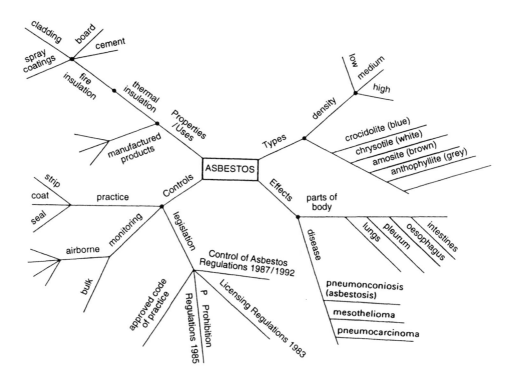

Fig. 2.6 Spray diagram of the absestos situation.

INFLUENCE AND CAUSAL DIAGRAMS (See for example Carter *et al.* 1984; Roberts *et al.* 1983; Open University T301 1984, 1993)

The digraph convention employs linked boxes or blobs, although many analysts do not bother to enclose components in circles or blobs. At the simplest level, the lines between components show only that a relationship exists but indicate nothing about the direction of influence as in Fig. 2.7.

Arrowheads can be used to indicate direction of influence as in Fig 2.8. Double-headed arrows indicate mutual influence.

Influence means that one component affects another but that does not necessarily mean that a *causal* relationship exists between them. For example, a person's height influences their weight but weight is not caused by height. Causal diagrams are used where evidence suggests a causal process. For example, there is evidence to suggest that an increase in accident prevention activity causes a reduction in the number of accidents, as depicted in Fig. 2.9a.

In Fig. 2.9a, the minus sign at the arrowhead indicates a reduction. However, there is also evidence to suggest that as the number of accidents increases so does the amount of accident prevention activity, depicted in Fig. 2.9b.

The plus sign at the arrowhead in Fig. 2.9b indicates an increase. These two causal diagrams can now be combined into a single causal loop diagram (Fig. 2.9c).

Fig 2.9c is read thus: 'as the number of accidents increases, the amount of accident prevention activity increases; as the accident prevention activity increases, the number of accidents decreases'. The minus sign in the middle of the loop indicates control, and the arrow shows the direction. The net effect of this causal loop is the tendency to limit, or control, the number of accidents (i.e. it is a negative feedback loop). Fig

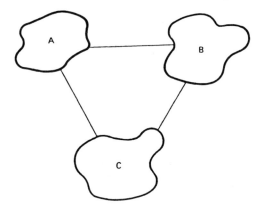

Fig. 2.7 Simple influence diagram (digraph convention).

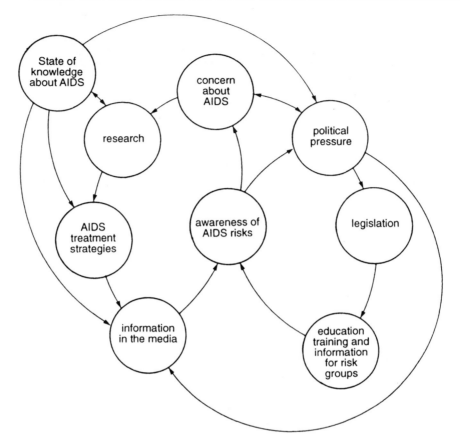

Fig. 2.8 Influence diagram relating to awareness of AIDS risks (digraph convention).

2.10 shows an expanded version with several causal loops. Thicker lines indicate what the analyst considers to be the main causal links. A plus sign in the middle of a loop indicates that it is self-enhancing or self-maintaining (i.e. overall growth or overall decline). A positive loop contains either none or an even number of minus arrows. A negative loop contains an odd number of minus arrows. Fig. 2.10 is in effect a multiple-cause diagram which incorporates several causal loops.

Exercises

2.7. In Fig. 2.10, give your interpretation of loop A (shaded area).

2.8. It is generally recognized that inflation leads to an increase in wage demands; successful wage demands in turn increase the costs of production, and fuel inflation. This is, of course, a very naïve explanation. Wage demands are stimulated by inflation and in particular by many other factors such as house prices. The demand for housing, availability of mortgages, movement of skilled people, and availability of jobs are other factors. Draw a causal loop diagram to help explain the economic dependency of people, housing and jobs.

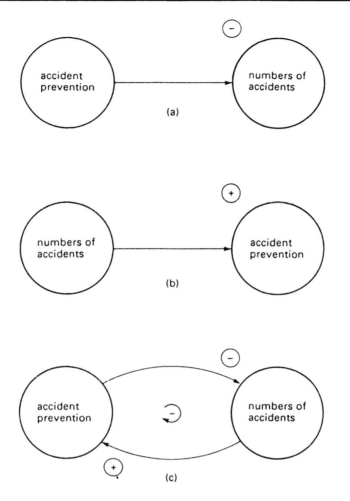

Fig. 2.9 Example of how to develop a causal loop diagram.

Generally, control loops which are negative are classified as adaptive. In other words, the system tends to respond to changes in the loop variables by counteracting those changes and maintaining stability. Typically, biological systems are self-maintaining or homeostatic, i.e. they tend to resist and adapt to changes in their environment (Morgan 1986; Oborne and Gruneberg 1983). Control loops which are positive are classed as non-adaptive. They tend towards either rapid increase or rapid decrease. Such processes result in system instability, for example uncontrolled money supply in the economy leading to hyper-inflation.

Causal loop diagrams are at the heart of simulatory models used to predict the effects of changes in particular variables, i.e. system components. They are used

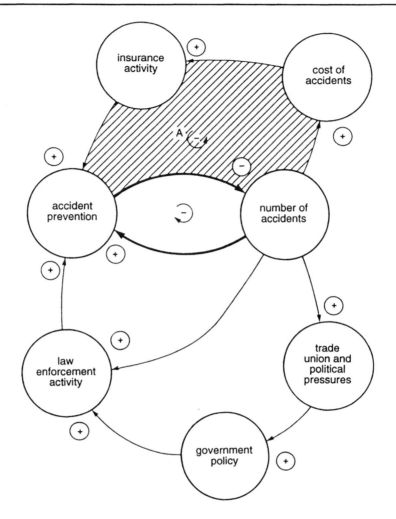

Fig. 2.10 Causal loop diagram of processes involved in accident prevention (digraph convention).

widely by economists, engineers, biologists, environmental scientists and others. They are often computerized. However, even highly sophisticated models are still only rather pale shadows of complex behaviour which they are intended to represent. Note how the above descriptions used qualified language: 'tendency to limit' rather than 'it will limit'. So long as the limitations of simulatory models are borne in mind, the analyst can get a lot of value out of using such models. However, if you fall into the trap of regarding the model as near-perfect, you will run the risk of blaming reality for failing to fit the model when it is the model which is not accounting for all aspects of reality!

FLOW CHARTS (See for example Lewis et al. 1967; Layzell and Loucopoulos 1987; Open University T301 1984, 1993)

A flow chart is a summary means for expressing any well-defined set of operations for carrying out a task. Such a set of operations is called an algorithm, which could be expressed solely in words but is easier to follow in flow chart format. Fig. 2.11 is a simple flow chart for adding up a VAT (Value Added Tax) bill. With a few modifications it could be used as the basis of a computer program for a programmable calculator or point-of-sale terminal, although generally in computing such flow charts have been superseded by other techniques.

Activity

Flow chart algorithms appear in many guises. For example, written procedures have been at least partly converted into a flow chart in such things as tax return forms, passport application forms, instructions in telephone kiosks. Find another example of a written procedure and convert it to a flow chart.

DECISION SEQUENCE DIAGRAMS (See for example Open University T301 1984, 1993)

A decision sequence diagram is a special kind of flow chart which relates to rational decision-making. The contents of each box or blob relate to choices or decisions, and the connections between them represent either a logical sequence and/or actions. Fig 2.12 shows a decision sequence diagram for a product promotional campaign.

FLOW BLOCK DIAGRAMS (See for example Carter *et al.* 1984; Open University T301 1984, 1993)

Flow block diagrams are flow charts which depict blocks of actions in a practical procedure for doing something. Resource input requirements are identified at relevant blocks. For example, Fig. 2.13 summarizes the sequence of things that a management auditor would have to do.

EVENT FLOW DIAGRAMS (See for example Waring 1993)

An event flow diagram shows the flow of events over time. Such diagrams are useful in systems analysis for summarizing the sequence of events leading to the current position and how the latter relates to projected future developments. An example is provided in Fig. 2.14 which shows the sequence of events in the development of an organization's IT strategy over several years.

DATA FLOW DIAGRAMS (See for example Clare and Loucopoulos 1987; Cutts 1987; Layzell and Loucopoulos 1987)

As the name suggests, data flow diagrams depict the flow of information in an information system. An example is given in Fig. 2.15.

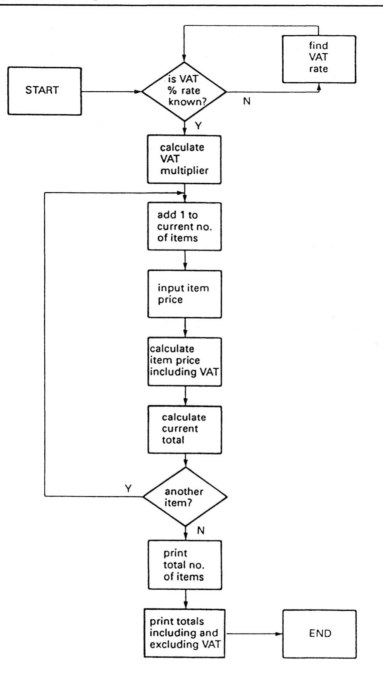

Fig. 2.11 A simple flow chart for adding up a VAT (Value Added Tax) bill (error traps omitted).

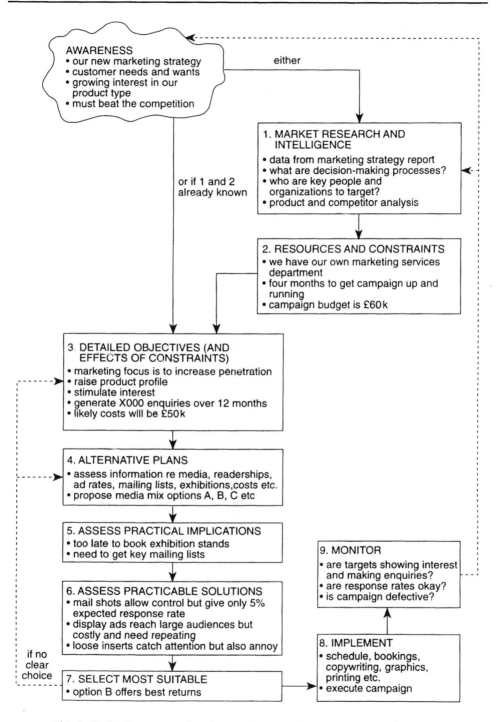

Fig. 2.12 Product promotional campaign as a decision sequence diagram.

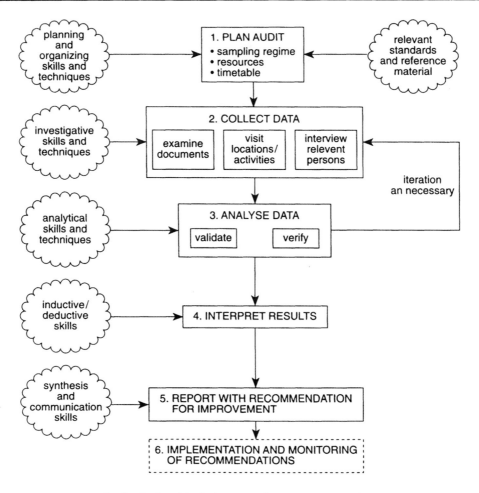

Fig. 2.13 Flow block diagram of management auditing.

RICH PICTURES (See for example Checkland 1981; Carter *et al.* 1984; Checkland and Scholes 1990).

A 'rich picture' is an evocative visual summary of complexity perceived by the analyst in a situation involving human activity. See Fig 2.16 as an example.

PREPARATORY SYSTEMS DESCRIPTION IN HARD SYSTEMS AND SYSTEMS FAILURES METHODOLOGIES

The antithesis of systems work is to jump to conclusions about the nature of the problem and its solution on the basis of past experience. However, latching on to

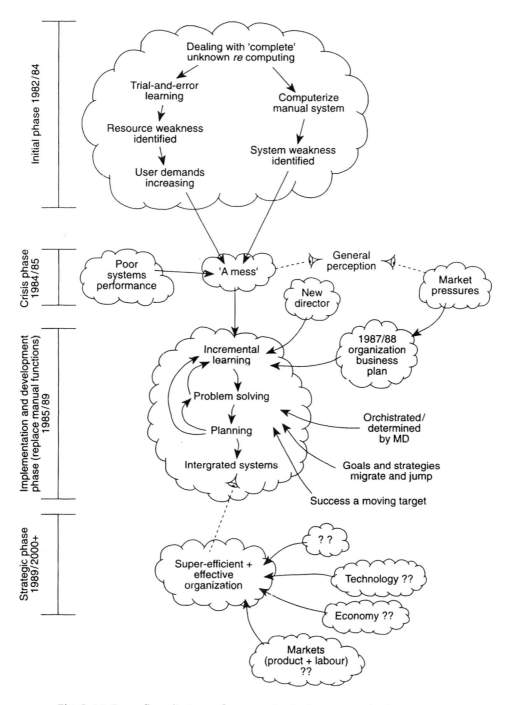

Fig. 2.14 Event flow diagram of an organization's computerization process.

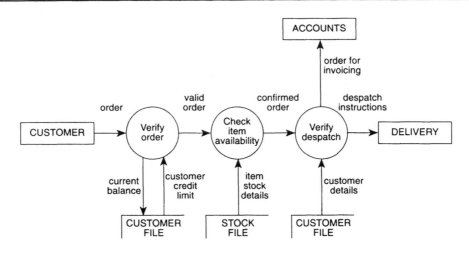

Fig. 2.15 Example of a data flow diagram for order processing.

what is already known is much more comforting than delving into murky, uncharted waters. As any researcher, particularly in the social sciences, knows, dealing with uncertainty and the unknown can be stressful. As self-maintaining systems, humans tend to avoid the unknown unless they have the capacity to withstand or adapt to new discoveries and experiences. Therefore, any tool which can clarify the murky waters before the analyst begins the voyage of discovery is to be welcomed. 'System description' is such a pre-analysis tool which may be used in both the HARD SYSTEMS and SYSTEM FAILURES methodologies as described by the Open University. System description is an analytical framework which enables you to identify some key systems for detailed analysis.

In the approach described in Carter *et al.* (1984) and Open University T301 (1984, 1993) there are five stages of pre-analysis, leading to detailed analysis as the sixth stage:

(1)   awareness/consciousness of problems/issues;

(2)   your commitment;

(3)   testing of whether analysis is warranted;

(4)   separation of a few relevant SYSTEMS;

(5)   selection of one or two key SYSTEMS;

(6)   detailed analysis and full description.

System description examples are included in the case studies in Chapters 7 and 11. To show how pre-analysis works, the car park levy case from (p. 36) will be used as an example. Imagine you have been called in by the chairman of the council's Finance and General Purposes Committee (F&GPC) who is concerned that their proposed decision may have unforeseen adverse effects.

(1) AWARENESS/CONSCIOUSNESS

You have expanded your own awareness by listing topics and constructing a spray diagram (Fig. 2.5). However, these structural components tell nothing of the issues or feelings in the community about car parking. The 'messy' situation can be portrayed more evocatively by a rich picture as in Fig. 2.16. The rich picture technique is described in detail in Chapter 4.

(2) COMMITMENTS

Your own commitment to analysis is clear: you are being paid as a consultant. The rich picture, however, enables you to identify relevant persons or role figures who might also be committed to finding out more about the situation because the proposals raise problems for them. For example, the chair of the F&GPC is definitely com-

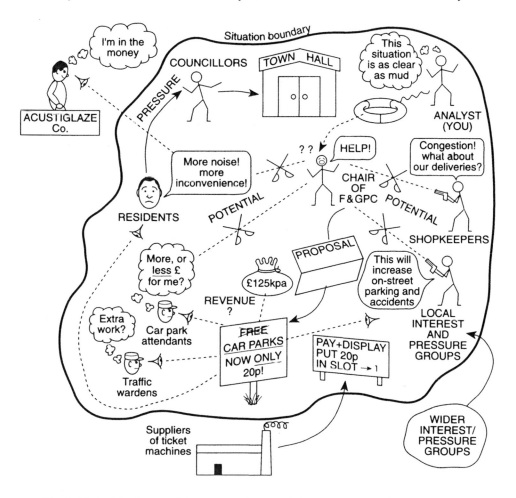

Fig. 2.16 A rich picture of the proposed car park levy situation outlined in Fig. 2.5

mitted. A road safety campaigner would have a commitment too, as would a traffic warden. There are others who could be identified.

As a consultant, you would normally be interested only in your own and your client's commitments. In the car park case, the client is the chair of the F&GPC. For study purposes, however, the analyst could also construct commitment statements for other problem owners. Such a statement does not have to be literally what they have said but can be a mixture of fact, deduction and induction. The aim is to put the analyst in their shoes and capture the essence of what someone in their role would be committed to. For example:

CHAIR OF FINANCE AND GENERAL PURPOSES COMMITTEE:

'Our car parks are not paying their way. A 20p levy seems a modest charge which will offset costs and should not encourage drivers to park in the street. However, I can foresee opposition from some quarters and I am concerned about unforeseen knock-on effects. The community expects us to get it right. I need to know far more about the likely implications.'

ROAD SAFETY CAMPAIGNER:

'Putting a levy on car parks is bound to increase on-street parking. The more cars and congestion on the streets, the greater the potential for accidents. We have a duty to improve road safety. I would like to know more about how the proposal came about and what evidence there is that road safety will not suffer.'

TRAFFIC WARDEN:

'On-street parking will probably increase. That means more illegal parking and more parking tickets to issue. Will we get extra resources to cope? I need to know if my job will suffer.'

(3) TESTING

Each commitment statement (and as a consultant you would have only your client's) is then tested to see whether it reveals sufficient content to warrant a systemic analysis. For example:

- Will success be recognizable?
- Is analysis the most effective way of getting results?
- Would analysis be purposeful or simply be indulging someone's idle curiosity?
- Is the client's or problem owner's goal important enough to warrant systems analysis?

For systems analysis to continue, positive answers to each of these questions would be needed.

(4) SEPARATION

Separation involves first teasing out areas of concern from the successful commitment statement(s). For example:

Different problem owners	*Potentially fruitful areas*
Chair of F&GPC	A: Traffic management
	B: Road safety
	C: Financial policy
Road safety campaigner	D: Social behaviour of drivers
	E: Council consultative processes

For each fruitful area, a trial definition and description of a SYSTEM is set up. Thus, for area A, a relevant SYSTEM might be: 'The Council system for managing traffic on and off the highway'. The likely components of this SYSTEM, both within the system and in its environment, are listed below. This early separation reduces the uncertainty and nervousness often felt by analysts in setting the system boundary.

Within the SYSTEM	*In the environment*
Chair, F&GPC	police
F&GPC	drivers
councillors	public transport
highways department	residents
traffic wardens	ratepayers
car park attendants	shopkeepers
trade unions	local newspapers
car parks	safety and environment bodies
road markings and signs	local campaigners
parking meters	
pay-and-display machines	
levies	
resources	

This process would be repeated for the other areas identified. Each description would then be assessed to see whether as a potential system it could be described as a key system, i.e. is it essential to making sense of the situation and to helping the problem owner's task? In the present example, system A appears to satisfy both criteria.

(5) SELECTION

Several key systems may have been separated out. The decision as to how many are carried forward for detailed analysis depends on the analyst's resources. Often only one or two are given the full treatment. You must use your own judgement about which one(s) you select for detailed analysis.

Activity
Separate another SYSTEM from the list of fruitful areas (B to E) in the car parking case. Give it a title in the form 'a system owned by......... for.........' and separate out its likely components. Consider whether it would be a key system which would warrant detailed analysis.

SUMMARY

The objectives of this chapter were to (a) introduce categories of system diagram, (b) describe a range of diagramming techniques for visualizing SYSTEMS or aspects of systems, (c) outline diagramming rules and conventions, and (d) outline the pre-analysis technique of system description.

Diagramming is the major tool in systems work. Techniques are many and varied. The three main types of diagram are (a) structure and relationship (organization charts, system maps, and influence diagrams), (b) process diagrams (flow charts, decision sequence, flow block, event flow, and data flow), and (c) thinking aids (rich pictures and spray diagrams). The main conventions or diagramming rules are Venn and digraph. To avoid confusion, different types and conventions should not be used by unskilled analysts in one diagram.

Diagramming techniques need to be used within a framework for describing and analysing systems. In both the HARD SYSTEMS and SYSTEMS FAILURES methodologies, 'systems description' provides an invaluable way of examining a situation before committing yourself to a full-blown analysis. Systems description as a pre-analysis consists of awareness (spray diagrams, rich pictures), commitments (of you and the client), tests (for SYSTEMS), separation and trial boundaries, and selection of key systems.

SUGGESTED ANSWERS TO EXERCISES

2.1 In addition to a title, every diagram should indicate the analyst's name and date. The state of iteration (see Glossary) should also be indicated. It is not uncommon for diagrams to be developed through many iterations.

2.2 An organization chart of a 'human activity' SYSTEM usually describes only the *formal* structure and relationships, i.e. the official view. It gives no indication of informal aspects which usually are at least as influential on what occurs as are the formal aspects.

2.3 Since the assessments sub-system overlaps customers in the environment, it suggests that customers are outside the SYSTEM for the most part, but are part of the SYSTEM when one looks specifically at housing. For example, the assessments function determines who customers are, how they are defined, waiting list criteria etc.

2.4 Usually housing departments do not deal directly with external suppliers on 'new build' but arrange for the architects and planning department to get the work done for them. The architects and planning department may do so through its own construction workforce (the DLO, direct labour organization) and/or through external consultants and contractors. In contrast, housing departments usually organize their own maintenance and improvement work, with or without the assistance of external suppliers. Thus, in Fig. 2.4 the maintenance and improvement sub-system reaches across to the external suppliers.

2.5 The Government through legislation, grants, benefit rules etc. takes precedence over and limits what a housing department can do. Fig 2.4 shows this by the Government overlapping the housing department system boundary.

2.6 The author's suggestions are shown in Figs. 2.17 and. 2.18.

2.7 As the number of accidents increases, so does the cost of accidents. As the cost of accidents increases, insurers (who foot a large part of the bill) increase their pressure on employers. With an increase in insurance pressure on policy holders (e.g. premium increases, capping introduced in 1994), accident prevention activity should increase. As accident prevention increases, in principle the number of accidents should decrease. Loop A is therefore a control loop,

2.8 The causal loop diagram for the economic dependency between people, housing and jobs is shown in Fig. 2.19.

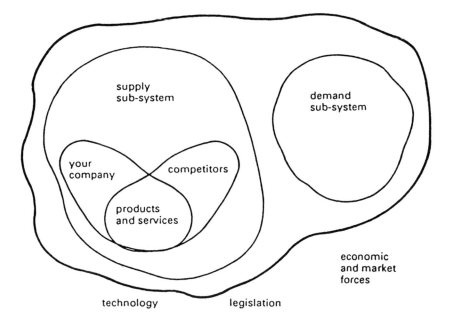

Fig. 2.17 A system map of the management training market (first attempt).

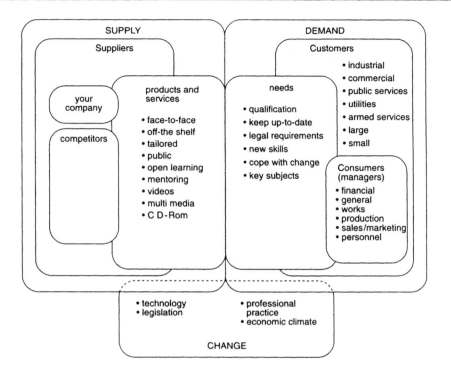

Fig. 2.18 A system map of the management training market (after several iterations).

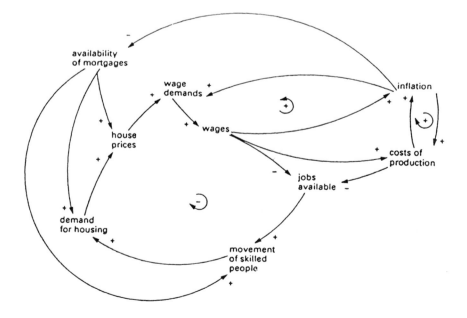

Fig. 2.19 Causal loop diagram of the economic dependency of people, housing and jobs (*Note*: diagram incomplete and assumptions are debatable).

INTRODUCTION TO HARD SYSTEMS THINKING

The objectives of this chapter are to:

- expand upon the concept of HARD SYSTEMS thinking introduced in Chapter 1;

- develop the themes of engineered, abstract and natural systems;

- discuss quantification;

- discuss the nature of problems;

- discuss the analyst-client relationship;

- outline a particular approach to HARD SYSTEMS analysis;

- consider a range of HARD SYSTEMS methodologies for different uses.

INTRODUCTION

Chapter 1 discussed briefly some criteria for classifying SYSTEMS as either HARD or SOFT. HARD SYSTEMS may be regarded as relating to those situations in which human behaviour is perceived to play a minor role, even though many people may be involved in the SYSTEM. The adjective 'hard' does not imply situations which are difficult to understand, although they often are. Rather, 'hard' refers to attributes perceived to be quantifiable, predictable and relatively undisputed, such as when someone says 'give me the hard facts'.

This chapter opens up the HARD SYSTEMS concept and gives some graphic examples of situations in which HARD SYSTEMS attributes could be perceived. A formal methodology for HARD SYSTEMS analysis is then described with the aid of a case study.

NB SYSTEM, HARD SYSTEM, SOFT SYSTEM and SYSTEM FAILURE in small capitals refer to metaphorical and perceptual constructs.

ENGINEERED OR DESIGNED TECHNICAL SYSTEMS

An 'engineered' or 'designed technical' system is one that is perceived to incorporate hardware, equipment or technical processes of some kind, and has been designed to achieve certain desired goals. The central heating system in Chapter 1 (see Fig. 1.2) is an example. People may also form part of such a SYSTEM to a greater or lesser extent, but usually it is taken for granted that they are only functionally important. For example, the driver is functionally important to the effective operation of a car (a small self-driven passenger transport system?) but motor manufacturers used to consider the driver's world-view to be largely irrelevant to the car's design and efficient working. Similarly, computerized data processing and information systems are usually designed in functional terms. Those who make the computer systems work are often assumed to be little more than functional appendages who, if they feature at all, can be reduced to single matchstick figures on systems diagrams. Such assumptions may be unwarranted. Although world-views are not central to a HARD SYSTEMS approach, they should *always* be considered throughout any analysis.

Fig. 3.1 shows a data flow diagram of a typical computer SYSTEM in, say, a newspaper or popular magazine publishers. Fig. 3.2 shows a diagram of a metal power press SYSTEM. In the latter diagram there is both flow within the power pressing process (e.g. blanks, power) and flow of information about the process (e.g. quality control).

Exercises

3.1 Where would you place the system boundary in Fig. 3.1?

3.2 What kind of printouts (outputs) would you expect in Fig. 3.1?

3.3 In Fig. 3.2, what kind of feedback would production control be giving the operator?

3.4 Assuming the system boundary envelopes the whole of Fig. 3.2, what components would you expect to find in the system environment?

NATURAL SYSTEMS

Natural systems are those which are not man-made, for example biological systems, the weather, the oceans, and volcanoes. Some apparently natural systems may also be regarded as 'engineered' systems because they are designed, operated and controlled by humans e.g. a trout farm. The life cycle of the trout, however, is part of a natural system.

Other natural systems include micro-organisms. Controlling the spread of infectious diseases in man, animals and plants is a major concern of all governments. Such concern extends beyond humanitarian issues. If the population is debilitated by disease, for example, it will be less able to work efficiently to produce goods and so a whole economy may be weakened. The problems of bilharzia and 'river blindness' in parts of Africa are examples. A weak economy, in turn, may be unable to fund a

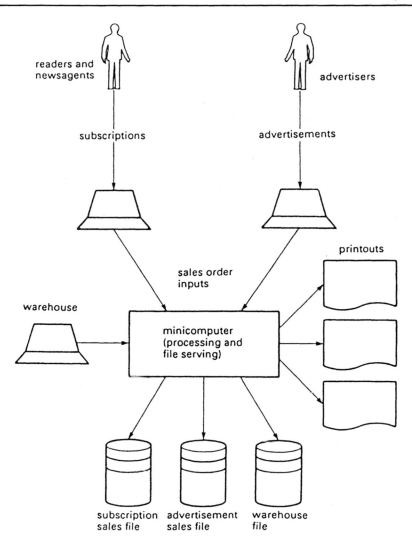

readers and
newsagents

advertisers

subscriptions

advertisements

printouts

sales order
inputs

warehouse

minicomputer
(processing and
file serving)

subscription
sales file

advertisement
sales file

warehouse
file

Fig. 3.1 Diagram of computer system in a popular magazine publishers.

health service capable of effectively combatting disease. Thus, failure to control the spread of an infectious disease may lead to a 'snowball effect' (an epidemic) which in turn may lead to instability in non-biological systems. The fact that these kinds of problem lend themselves to quantitative modelling and a degree of prediction and control explains their inclusion in the HARD SYSTEMS area.

Exponential growth is a characteristic of epidemics, i.e. the number of new cases reported for each successive period continues to increase. Thus, the total number of cases and the number of new cases per unit of time (i.e. the rate of growth) are important measures of an epidemic's progress. However, such measures do not offer a clue as to the causes, transmission and spread of the disease. In order to predict

Key

——▶ = information
━━▶ = mechanical
      operations

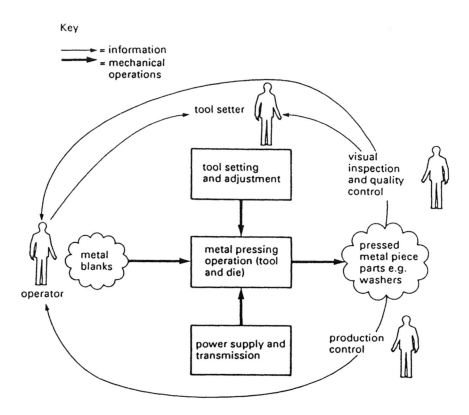

Fig. 3.2 Diagram of a metal power press system.

and then control an epidemic's progress you would need to know all the disease vectors (i.e. the dynamic variables) and their rates of change which characterize the epidemic.

Exercise 3.5
Intravenous drug abusers who have become infected with the AIDS viruses are said to be a key vector in the spread of AIDS. Identify other dynamic variables thought to contribute to the spread and draw a plausible causal loop diagram to simulate the disease pattern.

Of course, many micro-organisms are relatively harmless. For example, humans have used natural systems such as yeast colonies for thousands of years in the production of bread and wine. In this century, micro-organisms have been used on a large scale to produce antibiotics. More recently, third generation biotechnology is being used to synthesize high purity organic chemicals on an industrial scale. In all these examples, humans have been able to harness natural systems as part of their own 'engineered' systems. Such control requires the ability to predict what the natural system will do under defined conditions. Prediction requires detailed knowledge of the dynamic variables which affect growth and product yields. For example, yeast growth depends on the temperature and acidity of the medium. It also depends on the number of cells in the colony and their age. From causal loop models and numerical data, it is possible to construct a numerical model which simulates the SYSTEM's behaviour. As the numerical values of dynamic variables are changed, the model predicts the numerical values of the product yields, for example. If those predictions match what are measured in reality, then the model is reliable and has great practical value in production management.

ABSTRACT SYSTEMS

Abstract systems are those created by the human mind. They have no physical reality although humans may create physical representations of them and they may be incorporated within 'engineered' or 'designed technical' systems. Abstract systems may also incorporate symbolic systems which comprise symbols organized by rules. For example, a natural language such as English comprises vocabulary and punctuation (symbols) organised by the rules of English grammar. Mathematics with its symbols and rules is another example. Commonly accepted symbols and rules confer predictability in interpretation. Computer languages and programs (lists of instructions) written in them may also be thought of as abstract systems. They represent a means of communication between humans and computers.

Exercise 3.6
In what ways are abstract SYSTEMS important to the conduct of human affairs?

QUANTIFICATION

Quantifiable measures are the information source used to predict and control the behaviour of HARD SYSTEMS. They are thus vital in determining whether the SYSTEM is operating as its owners and operators intended, i.e. is success being achieved? People often use such measures of performance in a taken-for-granted way or may even fail to monitor them at all. Common examples are car fuel consumption (miles per gallon or kilometres per litre) and domestic electricity consumption (kilowatt hours). The latter measure is a level of consumption whereas the former is a rate. Both levels and rates may be used to ascertain whether a SYSTEM is functioning efficiently, i.e. whether the system's desired outputs are matching expectations for a given level or rate of inputs. If an electricity bill is higher than expected it may be simply a case of greater use. However, greater use of electrical heating may have been stimulated by faults or lack of control in system components or sub-systems; e.g. heat loss from a poorly insulated building, or badly adjusted boilers and central heating units.

Often, a number of different measures are available for particular kinds of HARD SYSTEM. With computers, for example, a key structural measure is the amount of memory or storage capacity available to a user, either in main memory (RAM) or in backing store (floppy or hard disk or CD). Computer storage is measured in bytes, one byte being equivalent to one character input from the keyboard. A byte is a small unit and so storage capacity is usually measured in thousands (kilobytes – Kb) or millions (megabytes – Mb). However, system efficiency is usually measured by a series of speed 'benchmarks' – how fast the computer system processes data. The performance of large computers is often measured in mips (millions of instructions per second). Although modern computers process data rapidly, a computer with a poor benchmark can result in perceptible and sometimes lengthy delays during processing.

Computer programs, too, can be designed to be more or less efficient in the way they run. A poorly designed program can take hours to sort or search through a file of records that a well written program would tackle in seconds or minutes.

Exercise 3.7

For the following SYSTEMS, suggest suitable measures of performance: ventilation system, a business quoted on the Stock Exchange, an hotel, a company PR department, a chemical reactor system.

THE NATURE OF PROBLEMS

A large part of human endeavour is directed at solving problems and at constructing practical 'things' to meet unfulfilled needs. Most formal problem-solving activity involves a tacit set of assumptions on the part of problem-solvers, namely:

- The existence of the problem may be taken for granted.

- The structure of the problem can be simplified or reduced so as to make its definition, description and solution manageable.

- Reduction of the problem does not reduce the effectiveness of the solution.

- An optimal or superior solution exists.

- Selection of the optimal solution is a rational process of comparison (measures of performance against criteria).

The formal problem-solving procedure may be expressed as a decision sequence diagram as in Fig. 3.3.

Although such a formal procedure is obviously systematic, it is not really a 'systems' approach. A 'HARD SYSTEMS' view of problem-solving, while accepting most of the assumptions listed above, makes a more detailed and probing examination of the SYSTEM experiencing the problem. Whereas formal problem-solving starts to focus early on finding a solution, a HARD SYSTEMS approach does not. (see 'Hard Systems Methodology' below).

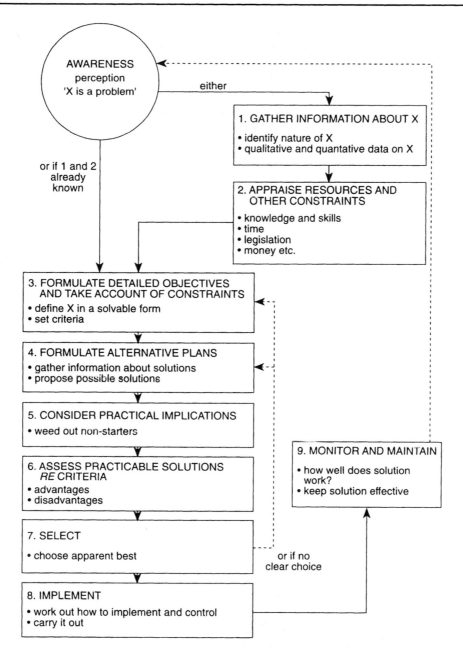

Fig. 3.3 Formal problem-solving procedure as a decision sequence diagram.

An important question to ask is 'who says that X is a problem?' A problem does not actually exist outside an individual's mind, even though many people may agree that X is a problem. Problems do not have a physical existence. Thus, it should not be taken for granted that a particular problem exists, for what one person regards as a problem may be thought of differently by other people. Some may regard it not as a problem but as an opportunity to fulfil a need or achieve a goal. Others may have no particular opinion about it.

A HARD SYSTEMS approach to problem-solving requires the analyst to check that there is a large measure of agreement among the 'client set' (see the following section on Analyst – Client relationship) as to what the perceived problem or opportunity is. For HARD SYSTEMS analysis to be effective there will also have to be a large measure of agreement about the overall goal. This does not mean that everyone has to agree literally about everything; any group of people is likely to hold a range of opinions about matters of fact and to have differing interests. For example, the interests of the marketing department may be different from those of personnel. However, a fundamental assumption of HARD SYSTEMS analysis is that differences in *values* do not form part of the client-set's perception of the problem or opportunity. In other words, the analyst has to check early that there is a shared world-view about the present situation, the nature of the problem or opportunity, and the future situation (the goal to be reached).

Fig. 3.4 is a simple model of problem/opportunity perception. Assuming that there is general agreement about the present and desired situations, the analyst's task becomes one of devising ways of getting from S(now) to S(future) (i.e. strategies to reach objectives) and deciding which is likely to be the most effective option. (Checkland 1981)

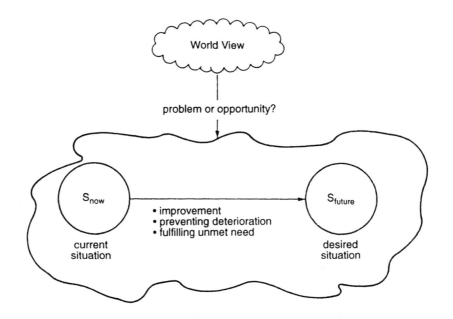

Fig. 3.4 Problem perception.

> **Activity**
> For a situation you are familiar with, where change is being discussed or planned, examine the world-views of those involved for agreement about the nature of the problem/opportunity and the goals to be reached.

ANALYST–CLIENT RELATIONSHIP

The analyst does not have to be an external consultant called in as an expert to provide a solution. As stated in earlier chapters, this is a DIY guide and there is no reason why the HARD SYSTEMS analyst should not be a manager or adviser within the organization. The analyst's client-set is one person or a number of people for whom the systems study is undertaken, but not necessarily those to whom the analyst reports. Remember, in HARD SYSTEMS work the system owner, the problem owner and the client-set may be all different people or just one person. Indeed, the analyst can undertake the study on his or her own behalf. The client-set may be defined as all those with whom the study seeks to gain *credibility*, for if the study and its results lack credibility among key decision-makers and implementers then proposals for change may be rejected.

As part of the initial groundwork on problem/opportunity perception and gaining awareness and understanding of the system, the analyst has to decide who the client-set is, what their interests are, and what their shared world-view is. This is important because the analyst's definition of the overall goal and the objectives to be reached must reflect those of the client-set. The analyst needs to accept the client-set's world-view, otherwise there is no point in continuing the study. However, the analyst may have good reason to modify the objectives, and the client-set may well be expecting guidance. The early stages of a HARD SYSTEMS study will probably involve some negotiation between analyst and client-set towards an agreed set of objectives.

HARD SYSTEMS METHODOLOGY

Looking back at Fig. 3.3, you can see that formal problem-solving is a relatively straightforward procedure. It can be used where problem-solving is felt to require more thought than simply relying on past practice, experience or intuition e.g. because the consequences of a poor solution may be serious. However, it is fairly prescriptive and, because of its assumptions, leaps quickly into 'devising solutions'. Where the perceived problem is complex or involves many interwoven variables, a more powerful method may be needed. HARD SYSTEMS analysis provides such a tool.

A variety of HARD SYSTEMS methodologies is described in 'Different kinds of hard systems thinking', below. However, they share a common approach to problem-solving that has evolved since the 1950s through cross-fertilization of ideas and practice stemming from such experts as Ackoff, Churchman, de Neufville, Stafford, Jackson, the Open University Systems Group and many others. The approach developed by the Open University Systems Group (1984, 1993) comprises the following nine stages:

1. *doing the groundwork* (identifying the client-set and its world-view, and establishing communication and mutual confidence – see above);

2. *gaining awareness and understanding of the perceived problem* (the current position; systems description – see Chapter 2);

3. *establishing overall goal and set of objectives* (the position to be reached; constraints to be contended with);

4. *finding ways to reach objectives* (creative, divergent thinking followed by structured focusing on a range of practical possibilities);

5. *devising assessment measures* (quantitative and qualitative measures of performance);

6. *modelling* (techniques to test possible options against measures of performance);

7. *evaluation* (assessing the likely outcomes of each option under a range of possible conditions; testing credibility with client-set);

8. *making a choice* (selecting the route that best meets the objectives, given the constraints and prevalent world-view);

9. *implementation* (putting the solution into effect; may require further systems design work).

The nine stages of this approach are not serial; some may be carried out in parallel. As with all systems work, there will be iterative loops as later stages highlight defective understanding, woolly objectives, inadequate measures of performance etc. Fig. 3.5 summarizes the approach.

TECH-ABS PUBLICATIONS – A CASE STUDY

Tech-Abs Publications Ltd specializes in producing weekly reports and bulletins comprising sets of abstracts of articles from scientific and technical journals. The company subscribes to some 2000 journals covering medicine, pharmacy, veterinary practice, plastics, engineering etc. Articles are selected to be abstracted by technical abstractors. Abstracts are written according to guidelines: a maximum length of 1200 words plus title and classification details. Abstracts are then edited and details checked before passing to the production department.

Tech-Abs has a high proportion of science graduates in all departments and most of the senior managers have worked their way up through departments from junior positions. A large multinational corporation now has a controlling interest in Tech-Abs and is exerting its influence, e.g. seeking greater professionalism in business strategy, increased efficiency etc.

The market for abstract bulletins has been growing rapidly. Tech-Abs has, over 30 years, built up a commanding position in the market with its weekly bulletin service. Typical subscribers are large organizations throughout the world who wish to monitor not only technical developments in their field but also the activities of competitors

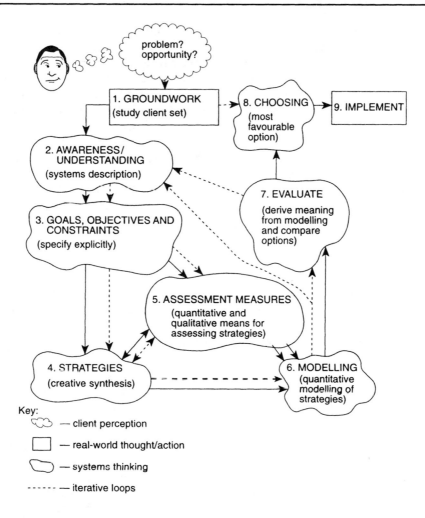

Fig. 3.5 Hard systems methodology (Adapted from: John Hughes and Joyce Tait, *The Hard Systems Approach*, Open University T301 Course Material, 1984 revised 1993).

and to spot market opportunities. Particular subscribers are increasingly demanding more specialized abstract services, e.g. articles relating only to particular classes of psychotropic drugs, or articles relating only to the design of direct broadcasting satellites.

Until 1985 batches of abstracts were sent daily to typists working at home who would re-type the abstracts on master sheets. A smaller number of internal typists also typed up master sheets and corrected those from the external typists. The master sheets were then available as camera-ready copy for the printers. Prior to being sent to the printers, the master sheets were passed through an OCR (optical character recognition) scanner which created corresponding computer files for subscribers requiring them as an extra service.

The experience with the OCR scanner was bad; files were frequently corrupted and a lot of the computing department's time was diverted to trying to sort out one mess after another. The sales department were having to field an increasing number of complaints from dissatisfied customers. In any event, customers were beginning to demand a complete on-line computer-searching facility whereby they could dial up abstract files and search for abstracts according to whatever their current need was. For example, a customer might want to find all abstracts originating within a defined period of time on substituted benzodiazepine psychotropics published in West German journals. Such precise searches could not be done on the OCR files.

By 1988, there was general agreement among marketing, sales, production and computing departments that a better system was needed to improve production efficiency, to make it easier to produce printed bulletins tailored to individual subscriber needs, and to provide a fully searchable on-line database (computerized abstract files) which was reliable.

Exercises

3.8 Imagine you were in Tech-Abs management services department in 1988 and were asked as a systems analyst to help solve the problem. Who is the client-set?

3.9 Does the position in 1988 represent a problem or an opportunity? Explain your answer.

3.10 Summarize the client-set's world-view in so far as you can judge from the information provided. Are there other world-views that need to be considered?

Fig. 3.6 was produced by one of the client-set to summarize the production position as she saw it. This helped the analyst at the systems description stage.

The overall goal was to introduce flexibility by adapting the SYSTEM of data handling which was dominated by manual methods (typing, hard copy corrections, hard copy masters etc.) so that the abstracts could be captured electronically at an early stage in the publishing cycle. Once stored in a reliable computerized form, the abstracts could be searched, sorted, categorized and used quickly and in a wide variety of ways.

A number of objectives were identified, such as:

* speed up entry of abstracts on to computer;

* introduce computer-searchable indexes on each abstract;

* speed up error corrections;

* maintain current weekly publishing schedule and four-weekly production cycle;

* individualize bulletins for customers.

Fig. 3.7 shows the objectives in the form of an objectives tree or hierarchy.

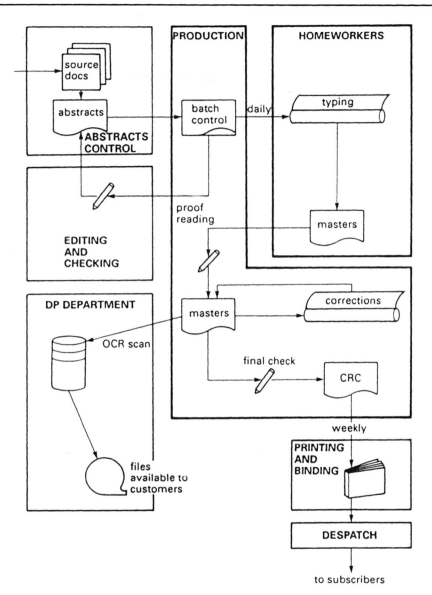

Fig. 3.6 Flow block diagram of Tech-Abs production run superimposed on system map of departments/functions (1985).

Constraints included the need to introduce changes without disrupting a tight publishing schedule and production cycle. Any new SYSTEM which required substantial staff training would be likely to be disruptive.

A number of possible routes were considered. One was to have the abstractors key their abstracts directly into a microcomputer, thus removing the need for typists and

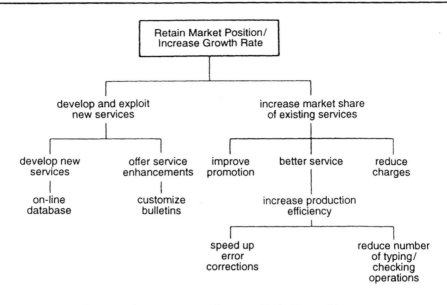

Fig. 3.7 Objectives tree relating to Tech-Abs problem.

two keying operations. This was rejected, however, because the abstractors were not 'computer literate', would require training, and had indicated a reluctance to change their way of working.

The route that was eventually chosen involved the replacement of the typist's typewriters by microcomputers and a special word processing package. Keyboard entry of abstracts was faster than before and the typists-turned-word-processing operators could produce 1000 abstracts plus searchable indexes on disk in the same operation. Corrections could be done quickly on-screen before any hard copy printouts were made. The corrected files on floppy disks were then 'dumped' into a main file on the company's main computer. Once a week, indexed files were passed to a phototypesetting computer which printed out camera-ready copy according to subscriber requirements. The main indexed database file was now also available for on-line searching by subscribers.

Fig. 3.8 shows the production system in 1990, a year after the implementation of the revised system (as summarized by the production manager). In the period 1993–94 production efficiency was improved further by providing abstractors with mainframe terminals for both text entry of their abstracts as they created them, and subsequent editing (a solution rejected in the 1988–90 changes). A number of features of the old SYSTEM disappeared, such as the homeworkers and generation of handwritten abstracts which previously were handled and copied a number of times. CD-ROM abstracts also became available as a new subscriber service. Fig. 3.9 shows the present arrangement.

DIFFERENT KINDS OF HARD SYSTEMS THINKING

Historically, two branches of HARD SYSTEMS thinking have grown in parallel: systems analysis for decision support (DS) and systems engineering (SE) (see Checkland and Scholes 1990). Open University T301 course materials (1984, 1993) refer to aids-to-decision-making (ADM) rather than decision support. In some respects, ADM is a

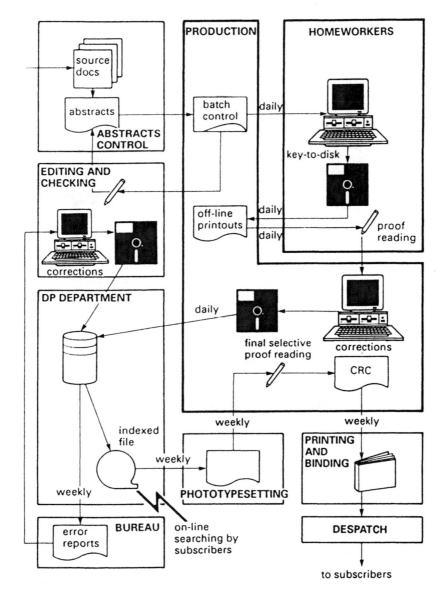

Fig. 3.8 Flow-block diagram of Tech-Abs production run superimposed on system map of departments/functions (1990).

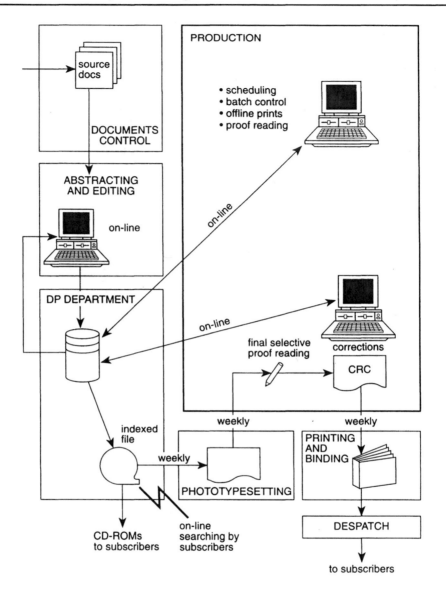

Fig 3.9 Flow block diagram of Tech-Abs production run superimposed on system map of departments/functions (1994).

better label since it is less likely to confuse decision support with Decision Support Systems (DSS), a specific kind of designed SYSTEM (see for example Finlay and Wilson 1991; Arinze 1992; Sarma 1994; Ho and Sculli 1994). Both DS/ADM and SE employ the general framework of HARD SYSTEMS analysis as outlined above and in Fig 3.5 but their emphases are different. The DS/ADM approach emphasizes problem-solving at strategic and tactical levels in organizations. It provides a rationalistic tool for mapping a way forward from the current position. Typically, perceived problems and opportunities concern marketing strategies, business development, product development etc.

Whereas a DS/ADM study may conclude that a new networked computer SYSTEM is required, systems engineering emphasizes design of such technical systems. SE translates decisions into working SYSTEMS; for example, practical options to reach objectives would have to consider several network configurations available, their specifications, advantages and disadvantages, and their costs.

In practice, HARD SYSTEMS studies often incorporate aspects of both DS/ADM and SE at the same time. A lot depends on the perceived problem. The Tech-Abs case provides an example of both DS/ADM and SE considerations.

There are a growing number of HARD SYSTEMS methodologies. Usually, these have been developed for application to particular kinds of perceived problem. The computing and information technology fields in particular have spawned a large number of methodologies which are mostly variations on a theme, for example:

- JSD   Jackson structured design

- SSADM   Structured systems and design methodology

- SASD   Structured analysis and systems design

- YSM   Yourdon structured method

In the production and mechanical engineering fields, one of the best known SE methods is MRP-II (manufacturing resource planning).

Once you have grasped the ideas presented in this book, you should have little difficulty in learning the characteristics of these variants.

SUMMARY

The objectives of this chapter were to:

- expand upon the concept of HARD SYSTEMS thinking and develop the themes of engineered/designed technical, abstract and natural systems;

- discuss quantification;

- discuss the nature of problems;

- discuss the analyst-client relationship;

- outline a particular methodology for HARD SYSTEMS analysis;

- consider a range of HARD SYSTEMS methodologies for different uses.

So-called HARD SYSTEMS have assumed characteristics such as clear structures and well-defined processes which are readily measurable. Such quantifiable attributes enable a SYSTEM's behaviour to be predicted, monitored and controlled. The world-views of people who 'own' or operate HARD SYSTEMS must be taken into account but are usually not considered by the system analyst to be of *central* importance. The use of HARD SYSTEMS ideas implies a particular view of the nature of problems and implicitly of the nature of reality, human nature, and methodology. The HARD SYSTEMS approach described in this book is a specific methodology comprising nine stages which are based on the ideas and assumptions about HARD SYSTEMS.

It could be argued that the Tech-Abs 'problem' could have been solved without recourse to HARD SYSTEMS analysis. For example, it is easy to see that direct data entry onto computer is very appropriate. The case study was greatly condensed and simplified as a means of introducing a number of aspects of good practice that should typify HARD SYSTEMS analysis (e.g. consideration of world-view, objectives hierarchies, quantification). In particular, HARD SYSTEMS analysis seeks to avoid the pitfalls of solving the effects of *symptoms* rather than the *causes* of the symptoms.

Examples of knee-jerk solutions which merely treat symptoms are countless. Just one will suffice as a reminder. Sales were dropping in a car dealership. The solution tried was to install bigger, better and brighter showrooms. This failed because the owner did not appreciate that the main cause of poor sales was the dreadful reputation they had for after-sales service, i.e. an *emergent property* of that dealership as a SYSTEM.

Compared with formal problem-solving, HARD SYSTEMS analysis provides a greatly enhanced approach to solving complex 'problems' which are perceived to be readily structured and which can be reduced to a quantifiable model. The approach and its limitations are examined in more detail in Chapters 6 and 7.

SUGGESTED ANSWERS TO EXERCISES

3.1 The boundary would go around all the components but between 'readers/ newsagents' and 'subscriptions' and between 'advertisers' and 'advertisements'. Readers and advertisers are in the environment. It is not unusual to see data flow and other system diagrams presented without a system boundary.

3.2 Obvious printouts would include invoices to customers (newsagents, individual subscribers and advertisers), sales ledger, stock lists, despatch lists, address labels. This diagram does not show various other likely functions such as purchase order inputs, and invoices received and payable. It also does not show what software (programs of instructions) would be used in processing. NB 'software' and 'soft systems' are entirely different things and should not be confused.

3.3 Production control would be relating the quantity of washers actually produced per shift to the quantity required. If the output is too low then the operator may be required to increase the rate at which blanks are input. This quantification of performance is characteristic of HARD SYSTEMS thinking. Quality control may also include quantified measures of quality e.g. numbers of misshapen washers per 1000. Production control, quality control and tool setting are all part of this SYSTEM's monitoring and control sub-system.

3.4 Typical components in the environment would be: production management, stock control, finance, accounts, payroll, personnel, sales, marketing, safety

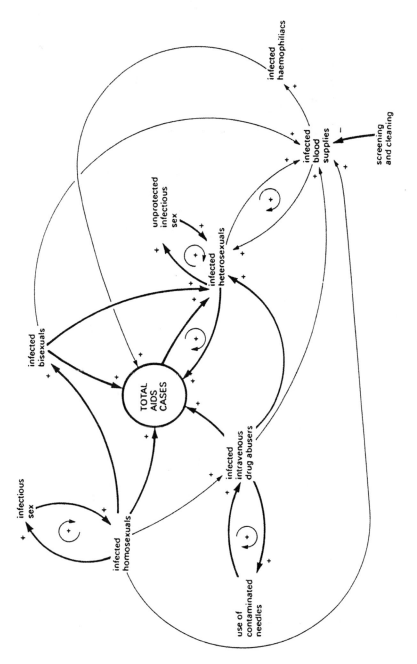

Fig. 3.10 Causal loop diagram of the AIDS epidemic.

department, trade unions, customers, safety regulations etc. Of these, production management represents the wider SYSTEM of the metal power press SYSTEM.

3.5 Other dynamic variables are: use of contaminated needles, infected homosexuals, infected heterosexuals, infected bisexuals, infected haemophiliacs, infectious sexual activity, infected blood supplies. Fig. 3.10. shows their relationship as a causal loop diagram at first iteration.

At present the greatest prevalence of AIDS cases, including HIV infection, is among male homosexuals, bisexuals and intravenous drug abusers, and these categories together represent a tiny fraction of the population. However, as Fig. 3.10 shows, the worry is that the majority heterosexual population will become infected. Since sexual activity is a normal and frequent human function, an epidemic would then be difficult to control; at present there is no cure for AIDS. Fig. 3.10 is, of course, inadequate. For example, no distinction is made between AIDS and HIV infection; no account is taken of educational and other efforts which might modify human behaviour and introduce control loops.

3.6 Many abstract SYSTEMS are vital to human communication. Failure to use the correct symbols or to follow the rules may result in communication failure, with possibly dire consequences. National and international conventions and agreements seek to minimize such problems; for example, road traffic signs and signals and hazard warning pictograms on containers of dangerous substances.

3.7 Suitable measures are:

Ventilation system: number of air changes per hour, linear flow rate (metres per second), volume flow rate (cubic metres per second).

Business quoted on the Stock Exchange: earnings per share, net profit before tax, stock turnover, profit as percentage of sales, return on capital employed (%), ratio of current assets to current liabilities.

Hotel: room occupancy rate, staff turnover, net profit before tax, stock turnover, profit as percentage of sales, return on capital employed (%), ratio of current assets to current liabilities.

Company PR department: enquiries per 1000 mail-shot letters, feature articles placed per month, product write-ups per month, enquiries per display advertisement inserted, enquiries per £1000 of advertising expenditure, sales conversions per enquiry (%).

Chemical reactor SYSTEM: percent theoretical yield, tonnes of product per hour, ratio of market value of product to cost of reactants, power consumption per tonne of product.

3.8. The client-set must include departments which have already expressed a clear interest in the 'problem', namely marketing, sales, production and computing. You may decide that only the heads of those departments are key decision-makers, but you may well decide that the study will also have to gain credibility with some of their subordinates. The client-set may also have to include other key figures not yet mentioned, for example those who will have the power to allocate or withhold financial or other resources, the managing director who has to keep within policy guidelines laid down by the parent company, and so on. You must decide who the client-set is.

3.9. The client-set in 1988 saw the situation as a problem that needed to be resolved (poor OCR performance, wasted time of computing staff, customers' needs not being met). However, routes to objectives might be devised that not only solve the current 'problem' but also create 'opportunities', for example the creation of new products and services.

3.10. Scientists tend to be fairly serious and rationalistic in their approach to things, and the client-set is dominated by science graduates. They are not likely to favour flamboyant or 'risky' solutions. Tech-Abs is a company which rewards dedication and loyalty, as evidenced by senior managers having worked their way up; the client-set cares about the company, the products and the customers. Therefore the objectives and routes to them would have to be feasible within the culture which characterizes Tech-Abs in general and the client-set in particular. They are likely to value an improvement in the existing SYSTEM rather than to replace it with a radically new one.

Of course, in describing the SYSTEM it is not just the world-views and commitments of the client-set that you will have to make explicit. What is *your* world-view and commitment? Do they accord with the client-set's?

4 INTRODUCTION TO SOFT SYSTEMS THINKING

The objectives of this chapter are to:

- expand upon the concept of SOFT SYSTEMS introduced in Chapter 1;
- discuss the nature of SOFT SYSTEMS;
- describe the rich picture technique for preparatory analysis;
- discuss the role of the analyst;
- outline a particular methodology known as SOFT SYSTEMS methodology (SSM) in its basic form.

INTRODUCTION

From previous chapters you will have learned that 'hard' in systems terminology does not mean 'difficult'. Similarly, 'soft' does not imply SYSTEMS that are easy to deal with – usually quite the reverse. With HARD SYSTEMS, it is often assumed that human beings form only part of the SYSTEM in a simplified and predictable way – as if they were simple inanimate components of a machine or other engineered system. The features of HARD SYSTEMS are assumed to be readily capable of being measured and quantified. Their behaviour is assumed to be relatively easy to understand and to predict.

THE NATURE OF SOFT SYSTEMS

Of course, in many ways human beings are anything but predictable in the way they behave. Each individual is unique, not only physically but also in the way they think, act and feel about things. Each person's world-view, as described in Some Perspectives p 5 and in Chapter 1, is made up of a complex set of attitudes, beliefs, values, opinions and perceptions. Each of us reveals only a glimpse of our own world-view in

NB SYSTEM, HARD SYSTEM, SOFT SYSTEM and SYSTEM FAILURE in small capitals refer to metaphorical and perceptual constructs.

our relationships with others – and this may lead to misunderstandings and conflicts. Each of us is constantly guessing at what other people *really* mean, what they *really* intend, and *really* believe. When the general manager announces his intention to reorganize a department, some people likely to be affected may read into the announcement all sorts of ulterior motives which may or may not be correct. In human relationships it is perhaps easy to see how disputes and strikes start, how marriages break down and how wars break out. Part of a manager's job is to anticipate misunderstandings and to aim for better communications, but even with the best of efforts sometimes 'wicked', 'messy' situations may result.

SOFT SYSTEMS are perceived as those concerned with human activity of some kind and Checkland's original SOFT SYSTEMS methodology (SSM) (Checkland 1981) described in this book is specifically intended for use where a situation is perceived to exhibit crisis, conflict, uncertainty or unease in relationships among the human 'actors'.

LUCRATIVE PUBLICATIONS – A CASE STUDY

The following description of Lucrative Publications illustrates a typical soft 'problem situation'. Whatever your views on the uses and abuses of English, in SOFT SYSTEMS thinking it is conventional to refer to a problem *situation* rather than the idea of 'the problem to be solved'. The reasons for this subtle and important difference will become clear as you proceed through this chapter.

THE UNSTRUCTURED PROBLEM SITUATION

Lucrative Publications Ltd is a small company of about 100 staff based in Central London and specializes in publishing yearbooks and reference handbooks for professional and trade associations. The company has existed for 20 years and has always been located at the same four-storey converted Victorian premises. Originally, the company was owned by three brothers who were ex-advertising space salesmen. In 1994 the brothers sold out to an entrepreneur who wanted to move into publishing.

The company ethos prior to the acquisition was that of a conventional small commercial publisher, namely maximization of advertising revenue coupled with minimization of overheads and production and sales costs. Total staffing had been held at about 40 to 45 for some five years, the nominal breakdown being 30 telephone sales people, 5 sales administrators, 5 accounts and payroll staff, 5 typists, and the three brothers as publishers and editorial directors.

The company's policy was to pay outside subject specialists to act as consultant editors rather than to employ full-time editors. Production editing, layout and paste-up were all handled by a freelance editor in Peterborough. The printers were in Gloucester. The editorial content typically comprised a mix of informative articles and reference sections, since experience had shown that readers wanted this. The viability criterion for publishing any book was the projected ratio of advertising pages to editorial pages. However, provided that a reasonable balance was reached publication would continue. With some books a cover charge would also be made.

In 1992 the company's gross advertising revenue began to level off. The number of readers willing to purchase books also began to fall. The recession was blamed. The brothers decided to sell the company to someone who would inject capital and who had ideas for expansion.

The new owner, as managing director, began to 'sweep clean' quickly. The major changes were:

- Two full-time editors were appointed to handle list-building, commissioning, text editing and production (so replacing the consultant editors and the freelance production editor).

- New computers were introduced into the accounts section and new word-processors into the typing pool. No additional typists or operators were appointed and no special training was thought necessary for the changeover; the new editors were also provided with word-processors for the first time.

- The sales department was enlarged by the appointment of a 'dynamic' sales manager and a doubling of the telephone sales staff. The new owner decided that advertising revenue was still top priority and the sales manager was given authority to overrule editorial decisions if he felt it expedient e.g. he could substitute editorial advertisements (revenue) for commissioned articles (costs).

- Physical reorganization of the staff and offices was carried out so as to accommodate the new staff; the premises became even more cramped than before; there was a rumour that the company might move to larger premises in Northampton, some 80 miles away.

SIGNS AND SYMPTOMS OF ORGANIZATIONAL DISTRESS

Ever since the introduction of the new VDUs, there were complaints from the typists and the new editors that these were dangerous and that their health was being damaged. A long list of alleged illnesses had been logged, yet investigations by expert ergonomists and safety specialists failed to substantiate any of the allegations. Still the allegations persisted and staff relations fell to a low ebb. The word-processing operators said that they were being forced by the editors and sales staff to work at sweat shop rates on equipment that was dangerous. The editors said that they were being forced to work as skivvies for the sales department and, to cap it all, they were having to work with hazardous equipment. Several of the word-processing operators and editors joined trade unions in order to pursue their fight against using the new VDUs. In addition to the company's internal problems, purchasers of the books had, for the first time, complained about the quality of editorial content. In desperation, the managing director has called you in as a systems consultant.

Exercise 4.1
Justify describing the Lucrative Publications setting as a 'soft' problem situation rather than a 'hard' problem to be solved.

BEGINNING YOUR ANALYSIS – THE RICH PICTURE

The rich picture or situation summary (Carter *et al.* 1984; Checkland 1981; Checkland and Scholes 1990) is one of the most delightful aspects of SOFT SYSTEMS work. Rich pictures can also feature in SYSTEMS FAILURES work and so you will meet them again in following chapters. One of the centres of apparent conflict in the Lucrative scenario, namely the editors versus the advertising staff, will be used to show how to construct a rich picture. The editors' grievance has already been outlined, but words can be much more evocatively portrayed in picture form. Fig. 4.1 depicts how the author sees the conflict.

This cartoon (rich picture) captures the *essence* of the conflict perceived by the analyst (the author) between the editors and advertising staff and it readily conveys the story to others.

Activity
Take another centre of apparent conflict in the Lucrative story – the word processing operators' grievance – and construct your own rich picture. Remember, artistic talent is of little importance here, whereas some imagination is necessary.

BUILDING UP A RICH PICTURE

Suppose you wanted to create a rich picture summary of the whole Lucrative scenario. Obviously, both the sketches developed so far would feature in it. To create a rich

Fig. 4.1 A rich picture of the conflict between editorial and advertising staff at Lucrative Publications.

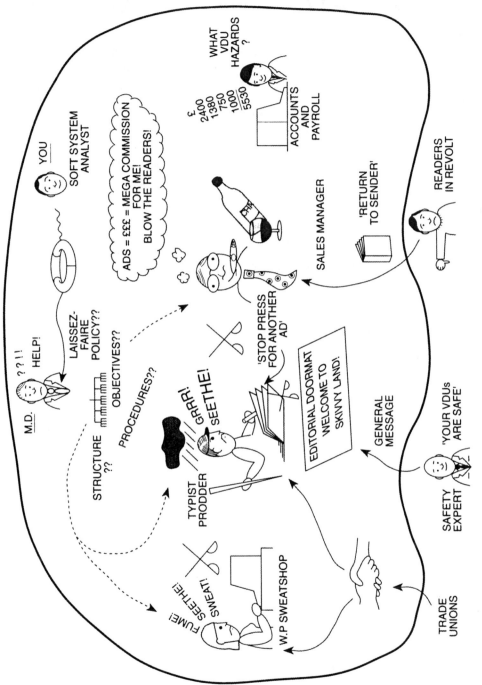

Fig. 4.2 A rich picture of the 'mess' at Lucrative Publications (at first iteration).

picture of the whole setting, get a large sheet of drawing paper and draw the pictures conjured up in your mind's eye by the description you have. The result, probably after several improvements, should be a mixture of 'structural components' or things which are relatively stable in the setting such as editors, Sales Manager, Managing Director, accounts section, and 'processes' or activities, transient relationships, and connections of some kind as in Fig. 4.2.

Your own rich picture of Lucrative might bear only a passing resemblance to Fig. 4.2; if so, it does not matter. Remember, it is *your* understanding of the situation which you are trying to capture. Note that you can use whatever symbols you find convenient. The table in Fig. 4.3 lists some of those which are often used.

Notice in Fig. 4.2 that a boundary is drawn around the situation. Although some people argue that rich pictures must not include such a boundary, the author is more flexible on this point where different aspects or contexts regarded by the analyst as relevant to the situation are deemed by the analyst to be distinctive in some way, or 'outside' the immediate situation (as in 'outer context' Pettigrew 1987, Pettigrew *et al.* 1992; Waring 1993, 1996). Although the setting of boundaries is important in all systems work, a rich picture is *not* a system diagram – it is a visual summary of the human activity situation that you are concerned with at the *start* of your enquiry. The reasoning of SOFT SYSTEMS thinking is that the sheer complexity of human behaviour will defy superficial attempts at rationalizing. Thus, by setting down a *system* boundary on a rich picture you would be rationalizing (i.e. trying to make sense of it according to previous knowledge) which at such an early stage would be self-defeating. You would be superimposing and locking your thinking into a prejudicial framework which suggests 'answers'. Some politicians may be able to get away with 'instant judgements' and 'instant solutions', if only because they may soothe public anxieties. You, however, are seeking to facilitate effective and long-term improvements. So, if you choose to draw in a boundary make sure that it is not a SYSTEM boundary but a 'context' boundary.

The style of your rich pictures reflects your personality and your world-view in general. Those having vivid mental imagery tend to draw them on the rich side, like those in this book. Bear in mind, however, that you may wish to show your rich pictures to other people, and especially to 'actors' in the problem situation. You can avoid possible offence by having two versions – one for your own reference and a cleaned-up version for showing to other people.

SOURCES OF RICH PICTURES

Where does the information come from which indicates a SOFT SYSTEM problem situation and from which you can construct a rich picture? Within an organization there may be many sources, for example reports, memoranda, minutes, interview notes, meetings and chance encounters that to varying degrees betray disharmony or dysfunction. Interviews with a selection of the 'actors' are really a necessary requirement but many people are ill-equipped to conduct an interview to best effect. Just because most individuals have been talking to people throughout their lives does not mean they are all good at interviewing. Knowing how to approach people, how to

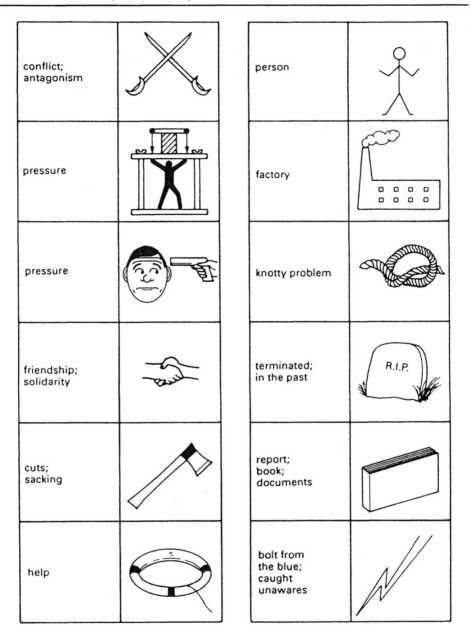

Fig. 4.3 A selection of visual symbols for use with rich pictures.

phrase non-directive questions and how to respond to answers are most important. A detailed description of interviewing technique is beyond the scope of this book, but some training videos on the market concerning recruitment and selection offer some useful guidance on interviewing technique.

HINTS ON INTERVIEW PROGRAMMES AND TECHNIQUE

Although some interviews are likely to take place informally and *ad hoc*, a programme of formal interviews is usually required as a part of the process of enquiry. The analyst will therefore need to organize and plan the programme within usually limited resources. Important questions to be addressed will include:

- who should be interviewed? how will they be identified? what kind of sampling techniques will be used?;

- why will they be interviewed? what are the purposes?;

- how will they be interviewed? what sort of interview style? what schedule of questions will be used? how long will each interview last?;

- when and where will they be interviewed? what schedule of dates, times and locations will be appropriate?

For more detailed coverage of interviewing as part of human enquiry processes, see Reason and Rowan (1985) especially Massarik, chapter 17.

As an interviewer, you need to establish rapport at the start of each interview. Rapport is a state of mutual confidence and harmony. Talking briefly and casually about neutral topics such as the weather and sport is one way of developing rapport before getting down to the subject of the interview. In summary:

- make sure you have got the right person;

- interview on a one-to-one basis wherever possible;

- avoid interruptions (telephones, visitors etc.);

- establish rapport;

- state your purpose clearly, however diplomatically it is wrapped up;

- ask open-ended questions (why was that? could you tell me more about...?);

- avoid superimposing your own biases on questions and responses;

- get the interviewee to do most of the talking;

- make notes;

- avoid interrupting to clarify (leave it till later);

- check through your notes at the end and then clarify points;

- have you forgotten anything?

- thank interviewee for assistance

- close interview but mention the possibility of follow-up if there are any points to clarify.

Newspaper reports and journal articles may also be a useful source of initial indications, especially if you are hired as an external consultant to the organization in question.

Exercise 4.2
Read the following newspaper report, in which names and details have been changed to disguise identities. Identify clues to the soft nature of the situation. Construct a rich picture.

While negotiations on their reinstatement founder, sacked workers at a local cigarette factory have received backing from Lord Ted Grimbal. Six women were dismissed two weeks ago when they stopped work to support a colleague suspended for refusing to operate a new machine at the Acme Tobacco Company. They have set up picket lines and have appealed to other workers not to cross until they have been reinstated.

The National Joint Council of the Tobacco Industry met yesterday and heard from both management and unions. It ruled that the six had been wrongly dismissed and that the two sides should negotiate their reinstatement. But management refused to budge and the meeting was adjourned for two weeks.

Lord Ted praised the 'principled' stand of the strikers and their supporters when he made a surprise visit to their picket line. 'I am shattered to learn of the breakdown in industrial relations', he added. 'These workers are not militants or troublemakers. The grievance they sought to raise was legitimate. If they were to reinstate these six, the company would restore its previous reputation for fair play'.

The Tobacco Union branch secretary claimed that management wanted to 'smash the union at the factory' and said that the six were paying an enormous penalty for a principle.

THE ANALYST'S ROLE

This is a convenient point to pause and consider your role as analyst. The question arises as to how far an analyst dare assume that he or she is a neutral observer, like a scientist observing things under a microscope. The assumption of neutrality is open to challenge and, indeed, the soft systems methodology explicitly requires the analyst to recognize his or her contribution to the setting under examination and the impossibility of strict neutrality or true objectivity in the analyst's interpretations (see discussion in Some Perspectives p 5).

It is important in soft systems work to try to avoid passing judgement on the rights and wrongs of the situation of interest. The tobacco factory example was chosen because it involves matters about which many people hold strong views. For example, some people argue that it is management's job to manage and that trade unions often create a lot of fuss about nothing. Other people argue that workers are inherently at a disadvantage and are vulnerable to exploitation by 'macho' employers. Both values are symptomatic of different world-views about power, authority, order and many other things. Neither value is open to objective scrutiny and value-free testing because no observer (e.g. systems analyst) comes to the situation with a mind empty of knowledge, beliefs, opinions, prejudices, motivations etc.

Most people do not question or probe their own set of values and assumptions which amount to systematic biases. There are two implications arising from this fact. First, to be competent in SOFT SYSTEMS analysis and systems work generally, you must try to be frank about your own values, assumptions, prejudices and motives. Include an explicit statement on them in your reports so that others may judge what influence they may have had on your line of enquiry and its outcome. Second as noted in Some Perspectives, you as analyst will both affect and be affected by the situation under examination. Your world-view through your behaviour will be interpreted by others, and their behaviour will be modified as a result - and vice-versa. If the 'problem' is perceived to be soft in character and you are, say, a manager in the situation who is attempting to analyse and remedy the 'problem', you may find it difficult to disentangle yourself from the 'mess'. As an 'actor' already in the setting, you would be as much a part of the problem situation as anyone else. You would be affected by the organization's culture, customs and social interactions to an extent that you may be unaware about. You would have a stance towards, and opinions about, the 'problem' and its solution.

Such immersion may cause the analyst difficulty at two levels in 'seeing the wood for the trees'. At one level there may be perceptual failure due to familiarity whereby work practices and social behaviour hallowed by the passage of time become almost ritualistic. Few people in the setting may be aware of just how absurd it might appear to an outsider. If asked for explanation, an insider would probably be reduced to an answer such as 'Well, it has always been done like that'.

At a more insidious level, acts or omissions (so-called 'blind spots') which appear to contradict official statements or policy, or which flout procedures, may occur over considerable periods of time. Blind spots may be deliberate and are heavily value-laden, especially where they reflect protection of vested interests. Values and vested interests may be shared implicitly by one group and not by another. The gulf between the value sets and the actions they inspire may be such as to create issues, i.e. bones of contention which may fester and create the crises, conflicts, unease or uncertainties which characterize SOFT SYSTEM problem situations. Even in situations where issues have been stated, or appear, to be obvious, apparent explicitness can be misleading. People are naturally guarded and are unlikely to reveal the true reasons for their dissatisfaction or what they regard as the issues at stake. If expressions are made at all, they are likely to be muted or 'dressed up' in coded language which they deem to be politically safe and publicly acceptable. For example, expressions such as 'feeling our way' and 'the time is not yet ripe' are coded language for 'we are deliberately avoiding doing it'. Table 4.1 gives some further examples.

To emphasize the importance of appreciating the frequent differences between what is said and what is meant, consider the following. Imagine you are the data processing manager of a company which is experiencing difficulties in staff accepting the introduction of new computers into offices. You attempt to identify the causes of dissatisfaction by visiting users and discussing their perceived problems. You discover that users are unhappy about 'unfriendly' software and manuals. It is relatively safe for them to be frank about whether or not the computer and its software does its

Table 4.1 Examples of coded language

Expression	Coded meaning
Some cause for concern	People are hopping mad
The time is now ripe	It should have been done ages ago
Within the resources available	Our resource estimates were too low
We need a balanced view	We want our view to prevail
This report covers familiar ground and reveals no new problems.	We do not want to tackle these longstanding problems.

job and whether or not the manuals are understandable. However, they are most unlikely to reveal that their underlying dissatisfaction is with what they regard as the unwarranted power which your department exercises over them in such matters as computer selection and access to computer facilities. Unless you are particularly per-ceptive and sensitive, you are likely to remain ignorant of this issue. Users may be more willing to reveal their concerns to an outsider who may also be able to notice clues that you would fail to spot because you are too close to the setting.

Identification of world-views, vested interests and issues that actors in the setting would prefer remained hidden is difficult for any analyst. For the insider who is a working member of the situation he or she wishes to analyse, these difficulties are often compounded by familiarity with the setting and other actors' sense of self-preservation. Although such difficulties are relative and dependent on the particular situation, in order to avoid them the use of an external SOFT SYSTEMS analyst is gener-ally preferable to an internal analyst (so-called Mode 1).

However, in the developed form of SSM (Checkland and Scholes 1990), the inter-active nature of the work of the analyst and other social actors throughout SSM is emphasized (i.e. Mode 2).

SOFT SYSTEMS METHODOLOGY

Having established some of the characteristics of SOFT situations in the preceding sec-tions, the remainder of this chapter outlines the SOFT SYSTEMS methodology (SSM) pio-neered by Checkland (see References and Further Reading.) SSM provides a means of action for change in situations that are perceived to be 'messy'. The methodology is capable of being used to tackle situations where a HARD SYSTEMS approach would be inappropriate and would be unlikely to produce expected results. The original Checkland methodology is represented diagrammatically in Fig. 4.4. SSM differs markedly from HARD SYSTEMS approaches in that it does not focus on finding a solution to a pre-defined, structured 'problem'; the purpose is not to devise ways of reaching objectives. With SSM, problem solving in a practical sense only comes (possibly) at the *end* of a process of enquiry. To those who are used to *starting* by focusing on problem definition, setting objectives and a creative search for solutions, SSM may be somewhat disconcerting.

It should be noted that Checkland and colleagues have developed SSM beyond the original seven-stage approach which now forms an ingredient in a broader approach

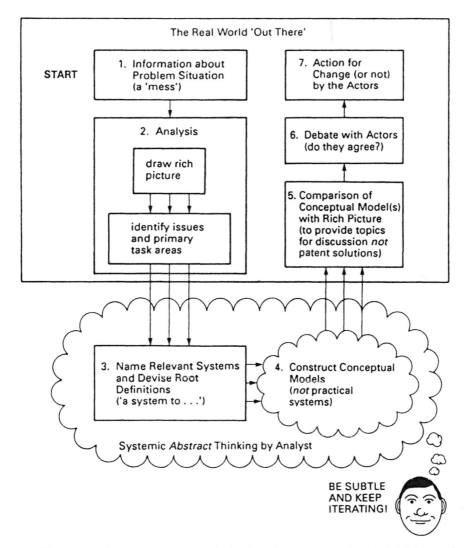

Fig. 4.4 Diagrammatic representation of the basic soft systems methodology. (Adapted from P. Checkland, *Systems Thinking, Systems Practice,* John Wiley & Sons, 1981).

to the subject. Coverage of the developed version of SSM is beyond the scope of this book and is best obtained by reference to Checkland and Scholes (1990). To fully appreciate the developed version of SSM, however, understanding of concepts from organization behaviour such as inner and outer contexts, strategy, culture and political processes would be needed. For these topics, reference should be made to Professor Andrew Pettigrew's various books, for example, and to the literature listed in Some Perspectives (p 5) and in References and Further Reading.

In this book, the original SSM is addressed to provide a basis of understanding for the developed version of SSM, which is intellectually much more demanding.

ISSUES AND TASKS

SOFT SYSTEMS problem situations are often referred to as 'messes'. Ackoff's definition of a mess may be paraphrased as 'a system of problems which defies resolution simply by solving the constituent problems'. Solving individual 'problems' would, of course, merely change the SYSTEM of problems. SSM starts by collecting information about the unstructured problem situation or 'mess' and creating a rich picture as described in earlier sections. Having drawn your rich picture, the next stage is to study it in order to identify parts of the picture which appear to be important or relevant to the overall problem situation. In searching for clues there are useful guidelines as outlined in the following activity.

Activity
Examine some of the rich pictures developed so far in this book. Look for symbols of conflict (e.g. crossed swords), someone under pressure (e.g. man in a wine press) and uncertainty (e.g. question marks). These are usually good clues to stimulate your thinking. Also, do not stifle your own hunches that, for example, apparent harmony in part of the picture is really masking deep seated antagonism or mistrust which may be relevant.

The aim of searching the rich picture is to make explicit your perception of what is causing so much trouble. In addressing yourself to what appears to be wrong, two kinds of 'wrongness' may be discernible – problems which are based in the primary task and problems which are issue-based. 'Primary task' refers to the overall objective purpose(s) of the human activity SYSTEM, or the part of it which is being examined. For example, the primary task of a manufacturing concern is to make marketable goods. The primary task of a furniture manufacturer is to convert wood into furniture. If the company stopped this primary activity, it would no longer be a furniture manufacturer.

In order to carry out a primary task, sub-SYSTEMS may be required for such things as:

* production;

* provision of customer spares;

* sales;

* stock control;

* finance.

For example, in a particular case the analyst may identify that the causes of dissatisfaction lie in the sales function not fulfilling one of its objectives, such as meeting sales revenue targets. Although no obvious reason may be discernible, the analyst's hunch is that the SYSTEM for meeting that objective is defective. The analyst might then conclude that a 'system for maximizing sales revenue' is a relevant system for further examination.

In a hospital plagued by organizational malaise, the staff might all express a commitment to the primary task of patient care (i.e. everything that is done to and for a patient). However, the analyst's observations that some administrators behave as if the hospital is an 'administrator career benefit system'. In the Lucrative case, it appears that the sales manager regards the publishing house as a 'sales commission maximizing system'. In other words, an apparent mismatch between the goals of different groups or individuals and their perceptions of the primary task is leading to disaffection.

Focusing on primary tasks is tempting because primary tasks deal with aspects of organizational life which are relatively concrete and unambiguous. However, primary tasks tend to avoid underlying causes of the 'mess' and so may not always produce an effective outcome. For example, a primary task SYSTEM may be defective *because* of unresolved issues.

An issue is something which evokes emotional responses such as frustration, anger, despair and resentment and which may lead to conflict, disaffection or poor performance. For example, in the hospital example above, one issue might be the way in which management decisions are made which affect patient care. Another might be the role of administrators in ensuring patient care. Generally, the analyst should try to identify several issues and perhaps one or two primary task areas for consideration.

Whether particular problem situations are issue-based or primary task-based is often debatable. For example, an analyst might perceive the primary task of a hospital as being to cure sick people and that 'patient care' is a subsidiary welfare issue. If, however, the analyst perceives patient care in a holistic way (i.e. everything that is done to and for the patient), then patient care is the primary task.

Exercise 4.3

Identify some possible issues in the Lucrative Publications story and the tobacco factory story (Exercise 4.2 above).

FROM ANALYSIS TO SYSTEMIC THINKING

With reference to Fig. 4.4, the next two stages of basic SSM require a certain amount of mental agility. The aim is to think not in terms of 'what is' or 'what ought to be' or 'what will be' but in terms of 'what *might* be'. In other words, the focus is a notional SYSTEM. Further, the line of thinking should be at a purely *logical* level of what the notional SYSTEM would have to include for it to be functional. In particular, the components of this SYSTEM have to be framed in terms of *functions* and not practical choices.

The emphasized words above were deliberate, since experience shows that many people find it difficult to think in such abstract terms. Thinking in terms of familiar, tangible choices (e.g. container lorries) may be more comforting than abstract concepts such as goods transportation. In the latter example the choice of container lorries is a specific real-world example of how goods could be transported, and tends to block off consideration of many other possible ways of transporting goods. Such considerations come at the end of SSM whereas a HARD SYSTEMS approach considers practical solutions and strategies to meet objectives at an earlier STAGE.

Practical solutions should not be in the analyst's mind when drawing up a short-list of issues and/or primary tasks. This list forms the seeds of SYSTEMS which appear to be relevant to the problem situation in the real world. The next stages, 3 and 4, are in the abstract world of systemic thinking in which relevant SYSTEMS are fleshed out and tightly defined as 'root definitions' i.e. the roots of notional SYSTEMS.

RELEVANT SYSTEMS AND ROOT DEFINITIONS

In the Lucrative case, one of the relevant SYSTEMS might be entitled 'an editorial and advertising reconciling system'. A first attempt at the root definition of such a system might be: 'a system to ensure that editorial decisions reflect the best interests of the publishing house'.

An examination of this root definition reveals some rather woolly and vague wording. For example, what are the 'best interests'? 'Best' in whose terms? Who is operating the system? A second attempt might be: 'a system to be operated by the managing director to ensure that editorial decisions reflect the objectives of the publishing house in terms of financial viability and profitability and in terms of reputation in the marketplace among purchasers and advertisers'.

Notice how this first refinement or 'iteration' has made the root definition much less ambiguous, although it still needs to be tightened. The title can also now be modified to reflect more accurately its root definition: 'a system for making cost-effective editorial decisions'.

Exercise 4.4
One of the difficulties in the Lucrative 'mess' is the growing dissatisfaction among book purchasers about quality and value-for-money. Write a root definition for a notional 'system to satisfy the needs of customers'. Make one iterative refinement to your root definition.

Iterative development of the root definition continues until the analyst is satisfied that it is adequate. A good test for adequacy is the CATWOE, a mnemonic which stands for:

- customers: (beneficiaries or victims of the SYSTEM; not necessarily customers of the company);

- actors: (those involved in operating the SYSTEM);

- transformation: (the essential process);

- *weltanschauung(en)*: (world-view(s) of the actors);

- owner(s): (power figures who control the existence of the SYSTEM; not necessarily owners of the company);

- environment: (constraints on the SYSTEM).

The essence of the test is to see whether the CATWOE elements are explicit or implicit in the root definition and whether any omissions are critical. In the Lucrative example, the notional editorial decision-making system is subtle. The transformation or essential process is not taking editorial copy plus advertisements and converting them into marketable books as outputs. The essential process is editorial *decision-making* – a process essential to Lucrative regardless of whether it was publishing books, boys' comics or electronic news-sheets, and whether or not advertisements were carried. Editorial copy, advertisements and marketable books are all concrete options from the real world.

The *Weltanschauung* (W in CATWOE) is the world-view which relates to the essential transformation process (T) and makes it meaningful to the social actors, i.e. the underlying valuation. For example, the essential transformation process of a mass transport system might be 'to convert passengers with travel requirements into satisfied, transported passengers'. This (T) is tied to a valuation (W) that mass transport is a social and economic necessity.

CONCEPTUAL MODELS

Having satisfied yourself with the adequacy of a root definition, the next stage is to construct a conceptual model of what the SYSTEM *logically* would have to comprise in order for it to work. At this stage, you are still working with notional systems and not solutions, and so practical elements such as 'word-processing facilities' or 'fleet of container trucks' must not appear in the conceptual model.

The root definition already drawn up from the Lucrative case forms the basis of an illustration of how to develop a conceptual model, i.e. 'a system for making cost-effective editorial decisions'. The root definition itself does not include the essential components for such a SYSTEM. Start by considering what the input(s) and output(s) of the SYSTEM would be then identify the 'activities minimally necessary' (Checkland 1981) or 'front-line activities' (Open University T301). Fig. 4.5 is a suggestion in which the essential activities or 'verbs' would be:

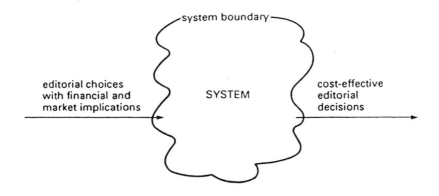

Fig. 4.5 The beginnings of a conceptual model for a notional system for making cost-effective editorial decisions.

- *determine*: market needs and wants;
- *formulate*: policy and objectives of publishing house;
- *allocate*: resources;
- *set up*: communication and control procedures;
- *operate*: communication and control procedures;
- *establish*: criteria for editorial decisions;
- *decide*: on editorial questions;
- *monitor*: performance

The conceptual model based on the expansion of Fig. 4.5 now looks like Fig. 4.6. This is no more than a first attempt and is likely to be inadequate. Tests for adequacy

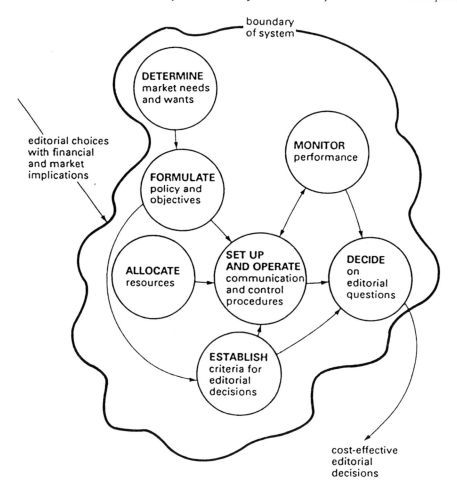

Fig 4.6 A conceptual model of a notional system for making cost-effective editorial decisions (at first iteration).

of the conceptual model should be applied, and these are described in Chapter 8. Also, each of the activities or verbs in the model needs to be expanded to describe the essential process more fully. Development and testing is an iterative process.

COMPARING 'WHAT MIGHT BE' WITH 'WHAT IS'

Stage 5 represents a return from abstract, systemic thinking to the real world. A comparison is made between the conceptual model and the rich picture, with the purpose of identifying discrepancies. The comparison can be done in a number of ways ranging from intuitive inspection to more structured assessment. For example, each activity in the conceptual model could be examined in turn to check whether it does happen in the real world. If it does not happen, why not? If it does, why? Probing questions need to be asked. Alternatively, the whole conceptual model could be envisaged as a SYSTEM in operation, and a comparison made with what actually happens.

The aim of the comparison is to draw up a list of activities or topics which are either missing or unsatisfactory in the real-world situation. Having emerged from an uncomfortable journey through abstract thinking and having started to make comparisons with the real world, it is tempting also to think of real-world practical 'solutions'. Such temptation should be resisted, as the comparative list is really an agenda for discussion with the actors in the situation. You, as analyst, identify *functional* deficiencies but it is up to the actors to decide how, if at all, practical changes should be made.

Do not pre-empt stage 7 of the basic SSM by offering patent solutions. For example, in the Lucrative case various back-up activities to communication and control procedures might be missing, such as apparent gaps in management structure, unclear division of responsibilities, lack of agreement on authority etc. These are items for discussion. The agenda should therefore not include statements loaded with practical direction such as 'general manager needed', 'needs an editorial manager', 'sales manager should have no editorial remit' and so on.

In common with other systems approaches, iteration is a permanent feature of SSM. The comparison stage could well suggest that there are aspects of the problem situation which remain opaque, and so more information may have to be gathered in order to sharpen up the rich picture. This in turn may cause reflection on, and modification of, the relevant system(s), root definition(s) and conceptual model(s).

DISCUSSING THE AGENDA

To reiterate, in stage 6 of the basic SSM the analyst should not be providing practical or prescriptive solutions in the way that a conventional management consultant might do. The analyst's role in the discussion is that of a skilled facilitator who is able to draw on his or her knowledge of SYSTEMS and of the situation. The aim is to encourage the actors to reach agreement about which activities are functionally deficient and require attention. Some, and perhaps all, the analyst's suggestions may get turned down. Whatever the case, those which are accepted as requiring action will have to be valid in systemic terms and feasible within the culture of the organization. For example, many large organizations have divisions or departments which are run semi-autonomously by their particular directors. A suggested change which would, or would appear to, upset the *status quo* and their jealously guarded power would probably not be culturally feasible. However, since conceptual models from two or three root definitions will probably have been developed, the analyst should not have to rely on just one agenda for discussion.

Agreed changes typically fall into one or more of the following categories:

- structural changes (organizational and/or physical);
- process changes (activities and procedures);
- policy changes (overall objectives, criteria and strategies);
- cultural changes (characteristic attitudes, values, behaviours).

Cultural changes are fashionable in management rhetoric but are the most difficult to achieve. Culture change programmes typically involve a mix of visionary statements from company leaders, education and training about the vision and the strategy to realize it, as well as structural and process changes. There are a number of reasons why culture change programmes are unreliable. A main reason is the assumptions about the nature of culture upon which such programmes are based (see Some Perspectives p 5). The culture of an organization (i.e. unwritten and usually unadmitted rules of behaviour, ideologies, language, rituals etc. which characterize the set of people) continually reaffirms the identities of its members. Any proposal or action to change the culture is likely to be perceived as a threat to identity as well as possibly to more mundane, but none the less important, matters such as job security. To be effective and to avoid resistance from people in the organization, culture change programmes need to ensure that the sense of identity is maintained. This requirement dictates that such change programmes are gradual rather than rapid. It is generally accepted that culture change in an organization will take years, typically five to ten years, to become recognized as complete. Short-term prescriptive approaches which expect culture change to be a 'quick fix' are unlikely to be successful. Considerable skill, commitment and time are needed to effect culture change. For research findings on this topic, see Beer, Eisenstat and Spector's article in *Harvard Business Review* (1990), 'Why change programmes don't produce change'.

ACTION FOR CHANGE

Specific actions, in terms of how to implement agreed changes, are matters for the actors in the setting. However, an agreed change may well point to a HARD SYSTEMS study as a desirable way of planning the change. For example, if an agreed change is 'an improved information processing and handling facility', this might be achieved practically in a number of ways, such as various kinds of computerized data processing, microfiche, videodisk, CD, or even improved manual methods. A range of HARD

SYSTEMS methodologies (e.g. SSADM) might be appropriate for detailed design, planning and implementation of the most suitable change.

SUMMARY

The objectives of this chapter were to (a) expand upon the concept and nature of SOFT SYSTEMS problem situations, (b) describe the rich picture technique for preparatory analysis, (c) discuss the role of the analyst, and (d) outline basic SOFT SYSTEMS methodology (SSM).

Situations amenable to SSM concern human activity and especially hard-to-quantify aspects such as attitudes and relationships between one group of people and another. When such situations exhibit crisis, conflict or unease, it may be inappropriate to use a HARD SYSTEMS approach to try to solve such a 'mess'. The analyst's role is not to solve the 'problem' but to provide insights to the actors in the setting, and to facilitate their understanding of 'what is' and 'what might be'.

Basic SSM starts with a rich picture or situation summary which serves to capture the analyst's various, and probably somewhat jumbled, mental images of the unstructured problem situation from which issues and primary tasks areas are identified. Consideration of these areas leads to selection of relevant systems and framing of root definitions. These must be notional and not drawn from, or offer real-world solutions. They relate to what 'might be' rather than what 'ought to be' or 'will be'.

A root definition is converted into a conceptual model showing the relationship between this notional system's essential processes or 'verbs'. Comparison of the model with the real-world problem situation enables an agenda of topics to be drawn up for discussion. Only if aspects of the conceptual model are agreed by the actors does consideration of practical requirements occur.

Chapters 8 and 9 provide more detailed coverage of SSM.

SUGGESTED ANSWERS TO EXERCISES

4.1. The Lucrative setting is soft in character because:

(a) Although there are apparently elements of both FAILURES (e.g. the possibility that the company had failed to protect its workers) and HARD problems (the possibility of a demonstrable cause-effect relationship between VDUs and the alleged illnesses), these had been rejected by the expert investigations.

(b) The managing director is at a loss to know why there appears to be so much staff discontent and he does not know how to proceed. This lack of clear objectives, coupled with no general agreement within the company about what is wrong, suggests that a HARD SYSTEMS approach would be inappropriate.

(c) There are clear indications of overt discontent about alleged hazards. However, there is also a suggestion that other more subtle and hidden values are operating. For example, the word-processing staff feel that they are getting a raw deal – more work, cramped conditions, no training – as exemplified by expressions such as 'sweat shop'. The editors feel that their professional status and independence is being undermined (e.g. expressions such as 'skivvies for the advertising staff'). The fact that the accounts and payroll staff have *not* complained may be significant.

(d) The current situation is confused with suspicions of further undercurrents such as:

- For whose benefit is the current policy on advertising and editorial content – the purchaser? the editors? the sales manager?
- What do the staff feel about the rumoured move to Northampton? Are people worried about losing their jobs?
- There seems to be some personal antagonism between the sales manager and the editors.
- Various world-views appear to be clashing in the new organization.
- There is an underlying issue of control over jobs, tasks etc. which has become focused through the discontent about VDUs as the presenting problem.

4.2 Clues to the 'soft' nature of the situation: breakdown in industrial relations; escalatory spiral of action and reaction; entrenched views. The problem situation in rich picture form is shown in Fig. 4.7

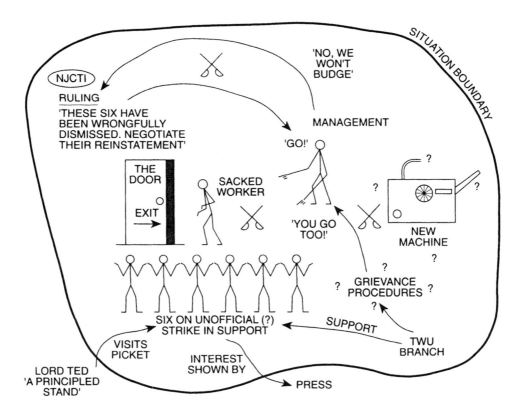

Fig 4.7 A rich picture of the problem situation at the Tobacco Company (at first iteration).

4.3 *Lucrative issues*: how editorial decisions are made; relationship between editorial and advertising staff; the move to Northampton.

Tobacco factory issues: industrial relations machinery; grievance procedures; trade union and management power relations

4.4 Root definition of a 'system to satisfy the needs of customers' in relation to Lucrative: 'a system owned by Lucrative which aims to satisfy the needs of purchasers of its range of books, coupled with a return on investment to Lucrative commensurate with at least maintaining its share of the yearbook/handbook market'.

INTRODUCTION TO SYSTEMS FAILURES THINKING

The objectives of this chapter are to:

- introduce and discuss the concept of system failures thinking;
- discuss the implications of SYSTEM FAILURES;
- describe the Formal System Model and its applications;
- describe various models for control, communication, engineering reliability and human factors and their applications.

INTRODUCTION

Any SYSTEM is capable of failure. Perceived failure in systems i.e. SYSTEMS FAILURES can be dramatic and sometimes the consequences can be very serious. Study of SYSTEM FAILURES enables a great deal of value to be learned for the improvement of SYSTEMS and the prevention of future FAILURES.

WHAT IS A FAILURE?

Most people would claim to recognize a failure when confronted with one. The car will not start; the company's latest product meets only a quarter of projected sales; the power failure which wipes all your data off the computer; the breakdown in pay negotiations between management and unions. Presented in this way, failures may seem obvious. However, just as SYSTEMS and problems only really exist as ideas, so too do failures. You cannot touch a failure, You can only perceive something to be a

---

NB SYSTEM, HARD SYSTEM, SOFT SYSTEM and SYSTEM FAILURE in small capitals refer to metaphorical and perceptual constructs.

failure, i.e. see it as a failure in your mind's eye. Just as 'hard' and 'soft' are used in systems terms differently than in everyday speech, so too is 'failure'.

Failure is a device of definition. What one person may regard as a failure may be considered as a success by someone else. At a personal level, if your car breaks down you are likely to regard this as a failure (e.g. mechanical failure, personal failure because you ignored the oil light flashing, servicing failure at the garage). However, suppose you were in the lead in a car rally – your rivals might regard your car breakdown as a success. Most people regard wars as failures, but arms dealers and black marketeers who profit from wartime economies see the breakout of peace as a failure. World-views and vested interests play a large part in perception of success or failure.

Perception of failure is fairly easy to detect. Expressions in conversation, in reports and in the media such as 'it's a failure', 'an absolute disaster', 'heads must roll', 'crisis must be resolved', 'what went wrong?' all betray a failure to achieve something which someone thought should have been achieved.

Exercise 5.1

In 1979, the Three Mile Island nuclear power station at Harrisburg in the United States suffered a LOCA (loss of coolant accident). Sifting through evidence from official investigations, the following points emerge:

- No major radioactive release occurred.
- There was disruption of normal life on a massive scale over a wide area
- The plant safety systems proved largely effective.
- Public confidence in nuclear power was severely damaged.
- No one was injured.
- The emergency was badly managed at every level.

In your opinion, was this a failure or a success?

Because a failure is a product of a person's perception it is always preferable to refer to an *apparent* failure. However, the more predictable and certain the properties of a SYSTEM are, the more likely people are to agree about whether or not a failure has occurred. Failures of HARD SYSTEMS, especially engineered or designed technical systems, fall into the latter category.

The effects of spectacular failures of SYSTEMS may be on such an immense scale as to warrant the label 'disaster' or 'catastrophe'. Major accidents which result in large-scale injuries, loss of life or material destruction provide dramatic examples: the cyclohexane explosion at Nypro's Flixborough plant (1974); the release of toxic substances into the atmosphere at Seveso (1976) and Bhopal (1986); the Zeebrugge ferry disaster (1987); the Kings Cross fire on London Underground (1987); the Piper Alpha offshore rig explosion (1988); the Boeing 737 crash on the M1 motorway (1989); and many more. Failures in natural systems can also be catastrophic: the Sahel drought and crop failures in the Horn of Africa leading to widespread famine, floods in the Sudan and the Indian sub-continent, and earthquakes in Japan are examples in recent history. According to some scientists, the world's climate is getting warmer as a result of man-made atmospheric pollution and this could lead to a future catastrophe.

Economies are very complex systems, and failures in them often affect many people. They are perceived to involve socio-technical and other designed systems (e.g. the stock markets, industries, agriculture etc.), human activity systems (e.g. government policy making, trade unions, consumer activity etc.), natural systems (e.g. weather, pests etc.), and abstract systems (e.g. supply and demand formulae, planning models to reduce inflation, computer programs to simulate and predict effects of changes in exchange rates etc.) Depending on your point of view and purpose, you could choose to regard the economy as occupying any of these four categories. When a national economy fails, the effects can be catastrophic. The Stock Market Crash of 1929 and the worldwide slump which followed it still hold bitter memories for those who experienced hunger and deprivation as a result. Since the 1930s, the world economic SYSTEM has been gradually modified so as to better withstand 'snowball' shocks. However, better SYSTEMS have not prevented persistent or recurrent economic difficulties in individual countries, such as recession and inflation.

Most FAILURES do not occur in such an awe-inspiring public way as some of the disasters cited above. Nevertheless, the consequences of 'lesser' failures can be serious for many individuals.

Exercise 5.2
In what ways could the failure of a business affect a large number of people?

IMPLICATIONS OF SYSTEMS FAILURES

When an apparent failure is detected, there is a great temptation to indulge in 'instant diagnosis'. The apparent failure is attributed to a single cause on the basis of a quick reading of the situation. In some cases, experts can be given licence to do this because of urgency and their own wealth of experience. For example, an accident investigator arriving at the scene of an explosion has to make some preliminary informed guesses as to the cause, if only to ensure that there is no risk of further explosion.

However, non-experts and those assessing the situation from afar frequently do make pronouncements about the causes of apparent failures which are little more than guesswork inspired by their own interests, values and prejudices. The two causes typically cited as the cause of a particular accident are 'human error' and/or 'technical failure'.

Exercise 5.3
What is so unsatisfactory about attributing the cause of an accident solely to human error or technical failure?

The answer to Exercise 5.3 challenges conventional and often received wisdom on the subject. After all, when someone makes a mistake and an accident occurs, surely that is 'human error'? If sprinkler systems do not operate during a fire, surely that is 'technical failure'? The author has long contended that, in the main, human error and technical failure do not simply come out of nowhere as if they were not preventable. For example, inadvertence is a kind of human error to which everyone is subject, e.g. inadvertently putting your foot on the accelerator instead of the brake. However, many human errors occur as a result of receiving inadequate information, instruction and training. Latent defects do occur in 'engineered systems' but many defects would be patently obvious from routine inspection and testing. Organizational, and especially managerial, functions such as selection, training, design engineering, maintenance and others need to be examined. Thus a *systems* approach to apparent failures of whatever kind probes not only the technical and individual human aspects but also the *organizational* and *cultural* precursors to signs and symptoms of failure.

There is growing support for a more systemic and holistic view of accident causation, and therefore accident prevention. Following two explosions at BP's Grangemouth plant in 1987 which resulted in fatalities and much damage, BP were fined £750 000. Mr Basil Butler, BP's managing director, later confessed to a British Institute of Management meeting in London: 'Incidents and accidents cost industry dearly in injuries, lives lost, shutdowns, and business interruption. It is now apparent (that) poor safety management can be as much to blame as human error or plant failure.' In major accident inquiries since 1989 it has become commonplace for official reports to cite management failures and cultural characteristics as underlying causes. Examples include the Kings Cross fire and the Piper Alpha disaster. A range of cases are described in detail in the author's book Safety Management Systems (1995).

COMPARATIVE MODELS

Anticipation and prevention of an apparent failure requires understanding of one or more SYSTEMS conceived to be relevant to that apparent failure. Models (sometimes called paradigms – see Some Perspectives p 5) are useful tools for gaining understanding. There are many models which can be applied to an apparent failure situation. A selection of some particularly useful models are described in the following sections.

By comparing various aspects of the apparent failure situation with appropriate models it is possible to discern whether discrepancies or agreements occur and whether these are significant. For example, if characteristics of a particular paradigm are usually considered desirable (e.g. control) but are absent in the apparent failure situation this discovery may be significant in understanding the apparent failure. Such comparisons can be very illuminating.

Fig 5.1 depicts an organization chart of some important models or paradigms.

THE FORMAL SYSTEM PARADIGM

The formal system model or paradigm (FSP), as described in Open University T301, is essential to any systems failure study of a situation in which human activity forms a part. The FSP should always be the first model used for comparison. It addresses the question: was there a SYSTEM *at all* immediately before the apparent failure in the situation being examined? Use of the FSP can also often point towards other models

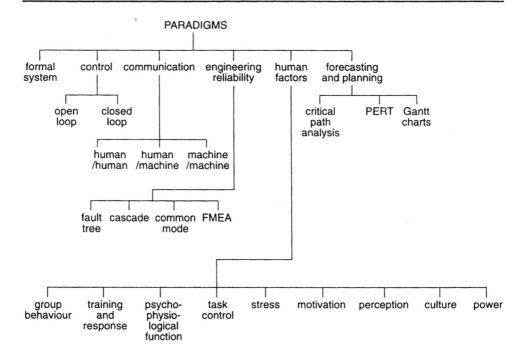

Fig. 5.1 Organization chart of useful paradigms.

that would be useful for comparison. For example, an apparently defective control element implicated by FSP comparison could then be compared with the control paradigm to elicit more detail. Fig. 5.2 shows the FSP.

As Fig. 5.2 shows, the FSP requires the presence of the following components within the SYSTEM:

- a control (or decision-making) sub-system;
- one or more operational (or executive) sub-systems;
- a performance monitoring sub-system;

The control sub-system tells each operational sub-system what is expected of it, and requires the performance monitoring sub-system to monitor the operational sub-systems and report back. For example, a board of directors (control) issues overall instructions and costs and revenue targets to production, warehousing, marketing and sales (operations) as appropriate. The finance department (monitoring) monitors the performance of departments in meeting those targets and feeds data to the board. If targets are not being met, the board has the opportunity to take control action to remedy the situation.

By comparing a particular situation with the FSP, discrepancies will be highlighted. Omissions such as no performance monitoring sub-system (a structural omission) or no control action (a process omission) are classic indicators of SYSTEMS FAILURES. The FSP also requires the identification of a wider system which legitimizes both the existence of, and activities within, the SYSTEM being examined. For example, the board

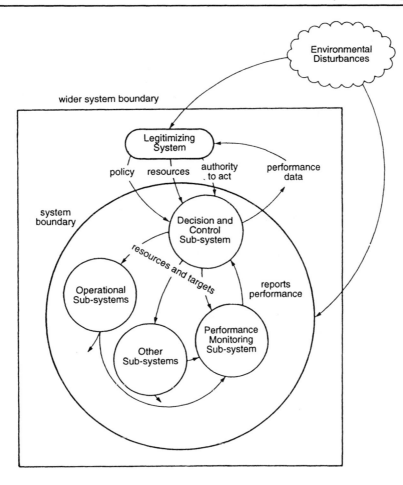

Fig. 5.2 The formal system paradigm (source: adapted from P. Checkland, *Systems Thinking, Systems Practice*, John Wiley & Sons, 1981; and L. Watson, *Systems Paradigms*, Open University T301 Course Material, 1984 revised 1993).

of a parent company might be regarded as the *wider* SYSTEM in the example in the previous paragraph. The wider system:

- issues policy decisions and directives;
- provides resources;
- gives authority to act;

} to the control sub-system.

The wider system also receives performance data from the control sub-system. The analyst has to make a judgement in each case as to where the boundary lies between the SYSTEM and its wider system. Both WIDER SYSTEM and SYSTEM are likely to be affected by environmental influences and disturbances.

Activity

For a situation that you know about which has been described as a failure, compare it with the FSP. You may find it helpful to list out the essential FSP features first and then check their presence/absence/quality in the situation. Then superimpose what you obtain on to the FSP diagram. Consider what understanding you gain about the system and its failure.

THE CONTROL PARADIGM

An initial comparison with the FSP may suggest a lack of control. Comparison with the control paradigm should then provide greater detail of the inadequacy and confirm initial findings. Even if FSP comparison does not indicate lack of control, a comparison with the control paradigm is always worthwhile. Fig. 5.3 depicts the control paradigm in a simple form, and Fig. 5.4 shows an application.

CHARACTERISTICS OF CONTROL

Control *per se* is an action or process which a system or subsystem applies to itself so as to reach and maintain a desired state. Control processes may be differentiated by

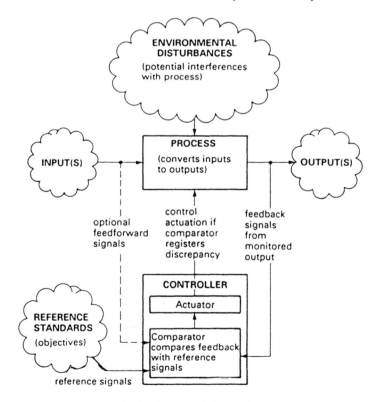

Fig 5.3 The control paradigm.

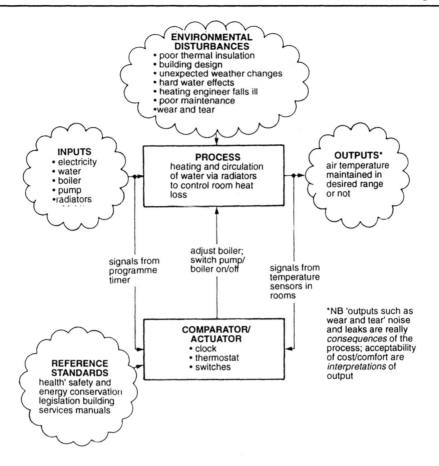

Fig. 5.4 The control paradigm with the office central heating system superimposed to show both feedback (adaptive) and feedforward (non-adaptive) loops.

the frequency with which monitoring occurs – either continuous or as discrete samples at preset or irregular intervals. Control processes also differ according to how they function. Linear control processes are those in which control action is proportional to the discrepancy between the actual state (i.e. output) and the desired state (i.e. reference value). With non-linear control, however, no control action occurs until a predetermined discrepancy is encountered.

Exercises

5.4 Give some examples of (a) continuous monitoring, and (b) discrete or discontinuous monitoring.

5.5 Give some examples of (a) linear control, and (b) non-linear control.

Effective control requires certain conditions to be met:

- The process to be controlled must be understood.

- Inputs and outputs must be capable of being monitored reliably and at suitable frequency (e.g. with suitable measuring devices).

- There must be an adequate communication link between monitor and controller.

- Reference standards must be compatible with outputs being monitored.

- Time delays between control action and control effect should be within tolerable limits and there should be no overshoot.

ENGINEERING AND OTHER CONTROLS

The origins of the control paradigm lie in engineering, and most of the preceding examples relate to designed technical SYSTEMS. There are, however, other kinds of control which relate to *people*, such as:

- managerial controls;

- organizational controls;

- procedural controls;

- behavioural controls.

Managerial controls refer to decisions and actions of management which seek to assist in attaining and maintaining desired outputs of a particular SYSTEM. Examples are: policy changes, strategies and responses to information received from: sales figures, audit reports, quality data, trade unions etc.

Organizational controls refer to structural arrangements within the organization which seek to ensure that a particular SYSTEM is achieving, or is capable of achieving, desired outputs. Examples are: functions such as audit departments, IT steering committees, maintenance departments, board review teams.

Procedural controls refer to sequences of actions designed to enable people to carry out tasks to meet predetermined standards or outcomes. Examples are: plant start-up and shut-down procedures, accounting procedures, staff selection procedures, computer log-on procedures.

Behavioural controls refer to actions which seek to modify the behaviour of individuals or groups of people so as to achieve a desired outcome. Examples are: training, motivational techniques, stress control, empowerment techniques, rewards and punishments.

Discussion of the strengths and weaknesses of different controls is beyond the scope of this book. However, it is important to appreciate that although all types of control share the general characteristics of the engineering control model (Fig. 5.3), controls relating to people and human activity SYSTEMS are different in two significant ways. First, provided they have been designed, constructed and maintained correctly, engineering controls tend to be relatively reliable and predictable. Second, engineering controls generally operate quickly or as predetermined. In contrast, human activity SYSTEMS, however well conceived, organized and resourced in real-world manifestations, are much less reliable and predictable. They often experience time delays between control decision, control action and control effect.

A common failing in organizations is to assume that control SYSTEMS and control actions aimed at people will operate reliably and quickly by analogy with engineering control. The implication of such an approach is that people are regarded as little better than programmable robots. Standards for quality management SYSTEMS are often misapplied in this way. The complexities of human beings are overlooked. It is therefore important to use the control paradigm wisely.

Exercises

5.6. The rate at which chemical reactions progress increases disproportionately with a rise in temperature i.e. for every 10°C rise in temperature the reaction rate roughly doubles. Some chemical reactions are prone to cause 'runaways' i.e. the reaction itself releases heat which, if not dissipated, speeds up the reaction which in turn releases even more heat and so on. If temperatures and pressures were monitored as outputs from such a chemical reactor by discrete sampling every 15 minutes, what problems could arise?

5.7. Give an example of technical overshoot.

5.8. Give an example of the kind of organization which typically experiences time delays between control decision and control effect.

THE COMMUNICATION PARADIGM

Communication FAILURES are characteristic of apparent failures in human activity SYSTEMS but they may also occur in other types of SYSTEM. There are three kinds of communication to consider: human-human, human-machine, and increasingly machine-machine.

HUMAN-HUMAN COMMUNICATION

A frequently quoted example of communication failure between humans concerns the story of the telephone request from a frontline army commander to his headquarters: 'Send reinforcements, we're going to advance' which the young corporal taking the call understood as 'Send three-and-fourpence, we're going to a dance'. Although the originator's message was obviously received it was misinterpreted by the receiver. In a communication process, there are numerous opportunities for interference, as shown in Fig. 5.5.

The two main kinds of interference are language difficulties and system noise. Communication obviously becomes more difficult if the language of the receiver

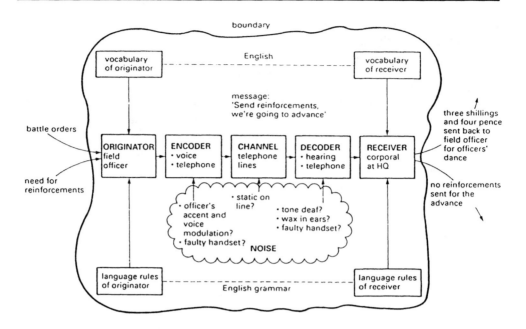

Fig. 5.5 The human-human communication paradigm with example superimposed.

differs from that of the originator. Even people apparently using the same mother tongue can run into difficulty if one person is using special vocabulary which the other does not know. This latter phenomenon is sometimes called 'blinding with science'. Christopher Rowe (1985) in a case study of failure in computerized stock control quotes a company manager:

> *I remember we were presented with this big orange folder, all about the computer we were going to get. I must confess it didn't mean much to me: it was all in computer jargon. But I didn't want to look daft so I didn't say anything. They explained it and it seemed reasonable, but I didn't really understand it. Of course it was decided by then that we were going ahead with it.*

More recently, during research into the introduction of computers, the author has been told by a number of experienced users about their communication difficulties with computer departments. Some have referred to computer staff as 'speaking computerese'. The opening sentence of one computer manual reads 'Boot up your system in the normal way' which, if taken literally by a naïve user, could lead to interesting effects!

Most trades and professions use their own special language. Sometimes terms are identical with words used by the general public, but with quite different meanings.

For example:

Term	Specialism	Meaning
gutter	printing	where facing left and right hand pages join (not the road/pavement junction)
liquor	brewing	water (not alcoholic spirit)
detect	policing	solving a crime (not uncovering it)
HARD SYSTEMS	systems	a style of systems thinking related to structured and quantifiable characteristics (not necessarily a system which is difficult to understand)

Misunderstandings of vocabulary can have important safety implications; an accident may be considered to be a SYSTEM failure and quite often apparent communication failures are involved. For example, chemicals may have similar looking and sounding names but quite different chemical and toxicological properties. The term 'on-line' is used widely in computing, manufacturing and the process industries to mean connected and powered up for processing. When disconnected or shut down, processes are said to be 'off-line'. However, some chemical processess which are assumed to be complete and off-line may contain residual reactants which may continue to react and cause a runaway. If off-line is understood to mean that temperature monitoring is not required then a dangerous situation could develop unnoticed.

Referring to Fig. 5.5, encoding includes such things as voice, pen, and keyboard. Channels include the post, telephone, electronic mail etc. Decoding refers to the receiver's processes of vision and hearing. With written communications, encoding and decoding are more structured and formal than with oral communication. In this context, 'noise' refers not just to unwanted sound but to anything which interferes with or stops communication.

Exercise 5.9
Give examples of communication noise.

As noted in Some Perspectives p 5, the communication paradigm applied to human-human communication cannot readily convey subtle characteristics of meaning and intent such as pressure, deal-seeking, body language, fear etc.

HUMAN-MACHINE COMMUNICATION

Encoding and decoding are also features of the human-machine communication model depicted in Fig. 5.6. Noise can interfere with the process. For example, in the Three Mile Island nuclear power station accident, an indicator light in the control room was

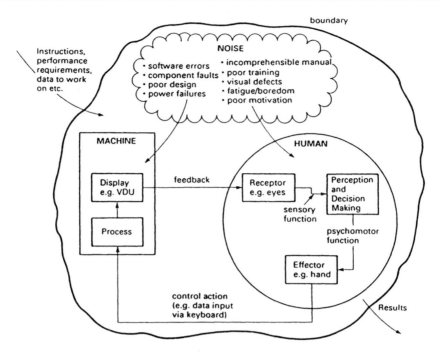

Fig 5.6 The human-machine communication paradigm with example superimposed.

masked by a caution tag. When a temperature indicator read 285° F, the control room operators misread it as 235° F because that is what they expected to see. However, not only does noise which interferes with the human sub-system need to be considered but also noise which affects the machine. For example, machine noise may arise from:

- failure to validate data input (e.g. computer data);
- failure to provide internal error checks (e.g. in system software);
- damage to remote sensors causing false display;
- corruption of signals;
- component wear or failures.

MACHINE-MACHINE COMMUNICATION

Communication between machines usually entails electronic signals passing between two or more computers or machines which are computer-controlled. The distinctions between computer technology and telecommunications is rapidly blurring as more and more computers send data to each other via the telecommunications network, and telephone products are given features of computer terminals. The possibilities of communication failure as a result of 'noise' are as described in the previous section. Some of the more common ones are component failures, faults at exchanges and channel interruptions such as telephone lines cut or shorting out.

Information overload is another source of failure for machine-machine communication, which also can occur with human-human and human-machine communication. When this occurs, the originator is encoding and sending more data more rapidly than the receiver can cope with. An evocative example of this was provided by the so called 'big bang' in the City of London in 1986 when the Stock Exchange was deregulated and an on-line computerized information system called SEAQ was introduced. Previously, brokers and traders relied on various different information systems to guide their transactions, which were done mainly over the telephone. SEAQ provides a much faster monitoring of deals and thus requires much faster decisions and responses from users. Transactions are intended to be made through SEAQ rather than on the telephone. As SEAQ is an integrated system aimed at replacing several others, the number of users at any one time is high. In order to make SEAQ easy to use, SEAQ data are fed to the TOPIC computer which displays SEAQ data in Viewdata format on users' terminals. In the early days of 'big bang', so many users were sometimes on-line that SEAQ was overloaded and TOPIC could not keep up with SEAQ. Users were unable to rely on share data displayed on their TOPIC screens. It should be added that lessons were learned and improvements were made.

ENGINEERING RELIABILITY PARADIGMS

Engineering reliability seeks to ensure that there is an acceptable period of time before failure occurs in 'engineered systems'. In addition to engineers, any reader potentially involved in the design, manufacture or supply of products will need to consider this section carefully. Legislation designed to protect consumers and users of products, coupled with increases in product liability claims, will require a greater emphasis on system reliability.

MEASURES OF RELIABILITY

The term 'reliability' in an engineering sense refers to the degree of confidence which can be placed in a component (or SYSTEM of components) fulfilling its duties in service. In other words, reliability is more concerned with success than with failure. Engineering reliability is a numerical concept and is usually quoted as a probability value in the range 0.0 to 1.0. A reliability of 1.0 means that it is expected never to fail in service whereas a reliability of 0.0 predicts certain failure. The period of time over which the component or SYSTEM is expected to operate is called the mission time.

Exercise 5.10

If an insurance engineer carried out a thorough six-monthly examination of a powered lift and stated in his or her report that the overrun device had a reliability of 0.4, what would you conclude from this?

Component failures do not occur at a uniform rate. For example, if a batch or sample of new components was tested under service conditions, there would be a relatively high number of failures early in the test period. These systematic failures are usually due to poor manufacturing methods and lack of quality control. This high initial rate is followed by a rapid falling off to a more or less constant failure rate for a long period. At the end of this stable period, i.e. useful life, the failure rate rises again as components wear out. Plotting failure rate against time gives the well-known 'bathtub' curve.

It is possible to estimate the number of failures likely to occur in a component's service life from the formula $R = e^{-\omega t}$ where e = the exponent (2.718), ω = constant failure rate (i.e. the flat part of the bathtub curve), and t = operating time in hours. For example, an electric pump has a stable failure rate of 0.001 per hour and operates for a period of 18 hours. Therefore, $\omega t = 0.001 \times 18 = 0.018$. Referal to published exponential tables gives a value of 0.98 or 98% reliability. Thus, if 100 similar pumps each operated for 18 hours, two of them would be expected to fail.

Another measure of reliability is the mean time between failure (mtbf) which is an estimate of component life and is usually derived from testing to destruction a sample of components. A safety factor can then be applied, with the intention that in service a wide enough safety margin will exist between operating conditions and failure conditions. For example, the maximum service load might be chosen to be one quarter of the destructive load found in a laboratory test. This gives a safety factor of 4 and, in theory, a four-fold safety margin. Thus, a maximum safe working load of 2.5 tonnes might be set based on the assumption that failure will occur at 10 tonnes. Similarly, a maximum service life of 5 years might be set, based on an mtbf of 20 years.

Exercise 5.11
On what main assumption do safety factors rely? What adverse consequences of this assumption could arise?

OUTCOMES OF COMPONENT FAILURE

Since a system comprises interconnected components, it is easy to see that component failure may lead to SYSTEM FAILURE. In other words, system reliability is a function of component reliability. However, although each component's reliability may be regarded as constant, the way in which they are interconnected may have a profound effect on system reliability. Also, failure of one component may accelerate the failure of another e.g. fan belt failure may lead to radiator failure.

In order to increase system reliability and reduce the effects of component failure on the SYSTEM, it is common practice to introduce redundancy, i.e. duplication or triplication of critical components. In space craft, for example, it is usual to have three identical computers running in parallel. The idea behind redundancy is that component failures are independent and if one fails then one or more redundant partners are available to take over its function.

If a critical component fails under redundancy conditions, the SYSTEM continues to run and is deemed safe to do so. This is a fail-run condition. Without redundancy, other possible failure conditions of the SYSTEM are fail-safe, fail-soft and fail-danger which are described in more detail in the author's book *Safety Management Systems* (1995).

TECHNICAL FAILURE CATEGORIES

Typically, component failures occur owing to discrepancies between actual and expected service conditions (Booth et al. 1988). Such discrepancies may be categorized as:

*   The design is inadequate for the expected forces and environmental conditions in service.

*   The component or structure is not made to the design drawings or specification.

*   The loading or environmental conditions in service are greater than those assumed in the design specification.

*   Maintenance and inspection procedures are faulty or absent.

There are many cases of catastrophic failures where some or all of these categories were involved. Examples are:

*   Brent Cross crane failure 1964 (Overload; design specification for a critical component was not followed).

*   Flixborough Nypro explosion 1974 (Temporary bypass design did not follow relevant British Standard and was inadequate for stress conditions; inadequate testing).

*   Littlebrook 'D' hoist failure 1978 (Overload; corrosion; poor state of repair; inadequate inspection; design faults) – see case study in Chapter 11.

*   Piper Alpha offshore installation fire and explosion 1988 (Design weaknesses in emergency shut-down valves, fire precautions, escape routes).

*   British Adventure flash fire at Jurong 1994 (Compression couplings not according to specification; uncertified modifications; no pressure test; valve lever wrongly fitted).

Design and construction procedures to prevent such disasters should include:

*   performance standards;

*   estimation of component failure characteristics;

*   estimation of knock-on effects of component failure;

*   monitoring performance levels against standards.

Four paradigms are particularly useful in failure analysis: fault trees, cascade, common cause or common mode, and failure modes and effects.

FAULT TREES

Fault trees chart the conditions necessary for a particular apparent failure and are used to identify or predict how such a failure might occur. Although fault trees can be used to address apparent failure of purely engineering components and designed technical systems, they may also incorporate elements relating to human activity.

Each tree is built up as a series of levels or hierarchies as in an organization chart. Levels are linked by logic gates as in Fig. 5.7. Starting at the top with the failure event 'application software fails to run', this could arise from one or more of three conditions – hardware fault, OR software fault, OR user error. Lower down the tree, a hardware fault may arise from lack of power if a unit is not switched on AND routine checks are omitted.

Activity
On a civil engineering site a particular diesel vehicle is failing to start in the mornings. The cause could be mechanical or use of wrong procedures. Construct a fault tree showing the possible causes of the apparent failure.

CASCADE PARADIGM

The cascade models a chain of failures – the so-called 'domino effect'. However, in its simple domino form, the cascade paradigm is not very useful because so few failures occur in a simple linear way.

A more useful cascade model incorporates multiple and looping failures in which the SYSTEM of failures enhances itself in a chain reaction or 'snowball'. A runaway chemical reaction is an example of a cascade. Fault trees are unable to show the presence of self-enhancing processes, and cascades are typically depicted as causal loop diagrams which include positive loops. (see Fig. 2.10 in Chapter 2 and further examples in Chapter 11).

COMMON MODE

Common mode or common cause failures occur when all components of a specified kind have a common fault. Systematic faults such as this are usually a result of poor design, or manufacturing faults which have not been identified by quality control procedures. Typical examples are whole batches or models of car being recalled after the manufacturer has discovered a design or manufacturing fault. Sometimes common mode faults are only discovered as a result of a number of similar accidents.

Exercise 5.12
Redundancy is an effective way to increase system reliability against component failure. How would system reliability be affected if redundant components possess common mode faults?

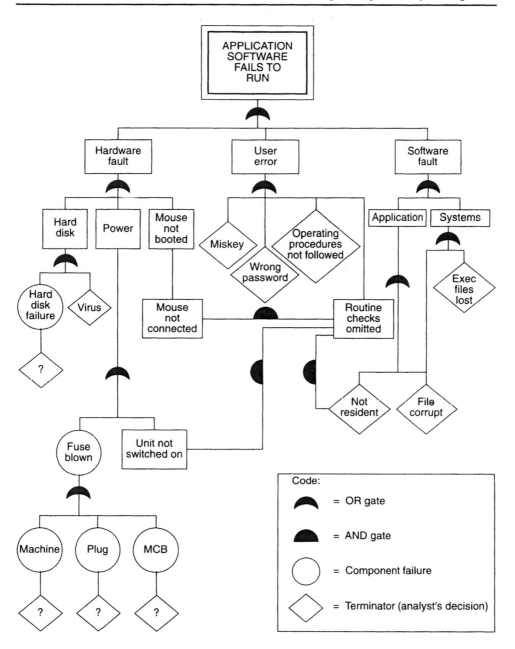

Fig. 5.7 Fault tree analysis of application software failure.

FAILURE MODES AND EFFECTS ANALYSIS (FMEA)

Rather than showing *how* failures might arise, which is the main use of fault trees and cascades, FMEA seeks to predict *what* failures might occur and what their effects might be. FMEA provides a systematic method for examining each component in a technical SYSTEM, its function(s), what kinds of failure it might experience, how such failures might arise, what effects they could have on the system, failure detection methods, and so on. The starting point is an inventory of all components which are then tabulated and examined as described.

Typical applications of FMEA are in detailed planning, design, construction, commissioning and in-service monitoring of safety-critical SYSTEMS such as nuclear plant, chemical and petrochemical plant, aircraft, and spacecraft.

HUMAN FACTORS PARADIGMS

Human factors paradigms encompass a wide range of models concerning psychology of the individual, social psychology, organizational behaviour, sociology, ergonomics and training. Such paradigms are of particular interest to people engaged in human resource development (personnel, selection, manpower planning, training etc.), general management, risk management and product design.

Because human factors paradigms seek to encapsulate particular 'human factors', there are inherent difficulties. Many of the phenomena involved have no physical manifestations *per se* and can only be inferred from what people say or do. There are also difficulties of a human analyst having ontological and epistemological biases seeking to interpret behaviour of other humans, each with their own biases. In addition, the infinite variability of human behaviour means that prediction and control are very unreliable compared with engineering paradigms. Nevertheless, in the author's experience a typical functionalist view of human factors is restricted to ergonomics.

ERGONOMICS

Ergonomics concerns the study of relationships between people and work. In particular, ergonomics seeks to ensure by design a good 'fit' between an individual and a particular task. The emphasis is on fitting the task (equipment, procedures, software, physical environment etc.) to the user rather than expecting the user to adapt to the task. One example of where ergonomics would be a prime requirement is the human-machine interface (HMI) model which is exemplified in Fig. 5.6 (p. 111). Ergonomics failures occurred in the Three Mile Island LOCA case outlined earlier in this chapter.

STRESS

Stress is a phenomenon experienced by individuals when their mental and/or physical needs and capabilities are out of balance with their physical and/or social environment. For example, extremes of temperature (heat stress, cold stress), lack of oxygen (e.g. altitude sickness), time pressure, real or imagined threats, loss (e.g. divorce, redundancy, burglary), serious illness, and so on.

Pressures of various kinds are unavoidable throughout life. Most people cope with such pressures, and indeed some pressure is necessary for good functioning. Stress may be regarded therefore as excess pressure beyond what the individual can cope with satisfactorily. The effects of stress are various. Short-term stress often has no lasting effects. Long-term stress, however, may be damaging to health unless individuals develop coping strategies e.g. physical exercise to reduce excess adrenalin released by stress. Stress may also contribute to SYSTEM FAILURES through faulty decisions and actions if affected individuals are preoccupied, depressed or emotionally upset.

MOTIVATION

Motivation concerns the goals which people have and the mental processes involved in seeking to attain them. Motivation, therefore, is involved in human decision and action and could be instrumental in a particular SYSTEM FAILURE. There are many theories of motivation and none is sufficiently comprehensive to explain the phenomenon. Values, risk estimations, meanings of success and expectations of outcomes are generally considered to be important factors in motivation – see for example Locke (1984); Waring (1993).

ORGANIZATIONAL CULTURE

Culture has a number of meanings and a discussion of cultural dimensions is beyond the scope of this book (See references listed in Some Perspectives, p.5). However, it is generally accepted as a metaphor for the complexity of shared beliefs, values, attitudes, behaviours and artefacts which characterize a group of people. As discussed in Some Perspectives, ideational culture and world-view are closely linked, and for many purposes in systems work may be regarded as identical. The group could be an entire nation, a region, an organization or a sub-group within an organization. Culture reinforces identity and behaviour and so is difficult to change by purposeful intervention. Although it is sometimes said that an organization's culture is determined by the board and by strong leaders, this is a very narrow and unrealistic view of the phenomenon. For example, many organizations have diverse subcultures of which senior managers are only one group.

As discussed in chapter 4, the role of culture in either preventing or promoting failure in human activity SYSTEMS is now well recognized. For example, it has been said that the Barings Bank failure in 1995 was in part a result of the culture of the organization and of the sub-culture of futures trading. However, preventing failure through successful culture change is a lengthy process on a timescale which many managements find difficult to accept. Some idea of the complexities involved may be gained from Johnson's book *Strategic Change and the Management Process* (1987), *The Awakening Giant* (Pettigrew 1985) and *Shaping Strategic Change* by Pettigrew *et al.* (1992) – see References and Further Reading.

POWER RELATIONS

Analysis of an organization's culture focuses on shared characteristics of its members. Analysis of power relations focuses on differences of interest between and among groups and individuals and the political processes which ensue.

Power has a number of dimensions too complex for discussion in this book (See Some Perspectives). However, power and politics in organizations are generally recognized as concerning the control and distribution of valued resources and rewards, both material and symbolic (Bacharach and Lawler 1980; Pfeffer 1982). For example, competition for share of budgets and skilled personnel, promotion or transfer to an élite or favoured department, decisions about future expansion or redundancies. In common parlance, power and politics are about *who* decides and *how* it is decided, who gets what, when and how. However, regarding power in organizations as a 'structural commodity' (Checkland and Scholes 1990) is a narrow and rather functionalist view (see wider reading list in Some Perspectives p. 5).

Power and politics may well be involved in particular SYSTEM FAILURES. For example, one particular individual or group may claim the authority to decide the nature of a relevant 'problem' and its solution and overrule a more knowledgeable individual or group, for example the apparent failure of Barings Bank to heed the warnings of independent auditors in 1994 about its Singapore futures trading. It is axiomatic that organizations should seek to synthesize the most powerful arguments and not pander to the arguments of the most powerful (Waring 1992, 1994, 1996). The power to allocate or withhold resources to carry out a necessary activity may be used unwisely with the result that the SYSTEM fails, as in the Baring's Bank case where vast sums of money were transferred from the London headquarters to Singapore to support dubious trading activities, despite warnings from the Singapore authorities.

To a significant extent, risk perceptions, motivation, culture, and power are interwoven. Two books which address these issues are *Risk and Blame* by Douglas (1992) and the forthcoming book from Waring and Glendon, *Management, Risk and Change* – see References and Further Reading.

ANALYSING SYSTEMS FAILURES

From the preceding sections you should have at your disposal a large repertoire of paradigms and representational models for comparison with an apparent failure situation. However, such comparisons are unlikely to be effective or useful if carried out in a disorganized or undisciplined way. A SYSTEMS framework for studying apparent failures is required, into which paradigm comparisons can be fitted. By analogy, a surgeon needs to be able to establish which bodily systems and organs are showing signs of failure before deciding on the most appropriate instruments to use. A suitable framework for analysing apparent system failures is described in Chapter 10, with fully worked case studies in Chapter 11.

SUMMARY

The objectives of this chapter were to (a) introduce and discuss the concept of SYSTEM FAILURES thinking, (b) discuss the implications of SYSTEM FAILURES, (c) describe the 'formal system paradigm' and its applications, (d) describe various paradigms for control, communication, engineering reliability and human factors and their applications.

A 'failure' exists in the mind of someone whose expectations have not been met. Many people can agree that a failure has occurred, especially in cases of accidents and misfortunes which may be regarded as emergent properties of SYSTEMS which are perceived to have failed. Comparison of the failure situation with various paradigms, and especially with the 'formal system paradigm', can illuminate the causes of failure, and aid the prevention of future failure.

There are a large number of paradigms which can be used to analyse SYSTEMS FAILURES. Especially useful are the formal system paradigm, control, communication, engineering reliability, and human factors.

The control paradigm concerns the maintenance of a SYSTEM in a desired state. Control processes may be either adaptive or non-adaptive, either linear or non-linear, and either continuous or discrete. Managerial, organizational, procedural and behavioural controls differ significantly from engineering or technical control in terms of reliability and speed of response.

The communication paradigm includes human-human, human-machine, and machine-machine communications models. System 'noise' affecting encoding, communication channel and decoding is a common cause of apparent failure with all three types.

The engineering reliability paradigms concerns failure mechanisms and failure prevention in 'engineered systems' and their components. Particular paradigms include fault trees, cascades, common mode, and failure modes and effects.

Human factors paradigms derive from the broad range of applied psychology and social sciences. Examples include ergonomic models, stress, motivation, culture and power.

SUGGESTED ANSWERS TO EXERCISES

5.1 It was a success in the sense that no one was injured, radioactivity was contained, and the plant safety SYSTEMS operated as they were intended to. However, the massive disruption of surrounding communities, the chaotic management of the emergency and the consequent damage to public confidence would probably be described as failures by most people.

5.2 Employees lose their jobs, families experience stress, creditors and investors lose money, the local economy can be damaged because affected people spend less, and so on. The beneficiaries of a SYSTEM are likely to be those who suffer most when the system fails. Of course, competitors are likely to gain as a result (i.e. perceive success).

5.3 Attributing the cause of an accident solely to human error or to technical failure suggests an erroneous view of how accidents occur. First, it is well established that accidents have more than one cause, and usually many causes. Second, although human error and technical failure, may form part of a causal explanation, they are essentially *symptoms* of more fundamental causes rather than being *the* causes. In other words, human error and technical failure, along with the accident event, are emergent properties of a SYSTEM which has failed.

5.4 (a) *Continuous monitoring*: temperature control of car engines; temperature and pressure control in chemical plant; homeostatic (self-maintaining) control of body functions such as blood pressure, blood CO_2 etc.

(b) *Discrete monitoring*: some gas monitors sample only every 20 to 30 seconds in order to prolong sensor life; operators in plant control rooms may have to monitor series of dials in sequence; stock audits are carried out periodically.

5.5 (a) *Linear control*: a driver steering a vehicle; a driver using the footbrake to decrease speed.

(b) *Non-linear control*: a refrigerator pump switches on only when the temperature rises to a particular value; companies chase unpaid invoices when the credit period expires; companies chase bad debts once a pre-set figure is exceeded.

5.6 The reaction may remain stable for a long time. If it becomes unstable and a runaway occurs, the sampling frequency may be too low to identify a rapid and potentially dangerous rise in temperature and pressure. Even with continuous monitoring, communication between monitor and controller must operate at least as fast as conditions change. This did not happen at the Three Mile Island LOCA (see Exercise 5.1) where computer printouts of vital data on which control staff had to act issued more slowly than plant signals to the computer were changing.

5.7 Technical overshoot: turning a boat's rudder too sharply in one direction causes the boat to overshoot the intended new course; prediction of overshoot allows counter-control action (turning the rudder in the opposite direction) to reduce the overshoot.

5.8 Organizational control: large organizations, especially bureaucractic ones, often take a long time to institute changes owing to cultural characteristics, inertia in their administrative processes etc.

5.9 Communication noise: extraneous sounds, false assumptions of the originator about the knowledge of the receiver; poor expression of ideas by the originator; false expectations of the receiver about message content; receiver's visual or hearing difficulties.

5.10 A reliability of 0.4 is equivalent to only a 40% chance of success. Therefore, the overrun device is more likely to fail than to complete its mission successfully, i.e. to work effectively for the next six months.

5.11 The safety factor approach assumes that test data from a laboratory accurately reflect how the component would actually behave in a wide variety of service conditions. Service conditions may be far more rigorous than allowed for. The safety margin calculated in this way may be far wider than is warranted and so may create a false sense of safety.

5.12 Redundancy itself cannot overcome common mode faults. The effects of common mode faults can be limited by the technique of diversity, i.e. using a range of components and a modular design. For example, instead of using a common power supply which would make all sub-systems vulnerable to power failure, critical sub-systems could be powered by independent or back-up units such as standby generators and power packs.

PART TWO
THREE SYSTEMS
METHODOLOGIES

INTRODUCTION TO PART TWO

In Part 2, it is assumed that you are fully conversant with the ideas, principles and approaches described in Part 1. Part 2 describes hard systems methodology, basic soft systems methodology and systems failures methodology in more detail and provides fully worked case studies. Although a step-by-step approach is needed in order to describe what to do, you should always be wary of getting into the mental rut of 'recipe thinking'.

THE HARD SYSTEMS
METHODOLOGY

The objectives of this chapter are to:

- revisit the concept of HARD SYSTEM thinking introduced in Part 1;

- discuss further the nature of 'problems' and a HARD SYSTEMS view of problems;

- Demonstrate, with the aid of case examples, the HARD SYSTEMS methodology.

INTRODUCTION

Chapter 3 introduced the concept of HARD SYSTEMS thinking and gave a very brief introduction to the HARD SYSTEMS approach to problem solving. This chapter expands upon the HARD SYSTEMS methodology. First, however, HARD SYSTEMS thinking will be reviewed in relation to its potential role in decision support.

HARD SYSTEMS THINKING REVISITED

APPROACHES TO PROBLEMS

Some perceived problems may be solved satisfactorily by using past experience or practice as a guide. In fact, most day-to-day 'problems' fall into this category. If the car will not start, for example, a few obvious possible causes can be quickly checked. If lucky, you find the cause, deal with it and proceed on your journey. If you fail to find the cause, you can still solve the problem of a delayed journey by catching a taxi, bus, train or even by walking. A 'quick fix' is the appropriate response to the situation until you or the garage has time to find the fault and rectify it.

With perceived problems which involve higher stakes, i.e. the costs of failing to achieve goals are high, a more systemic (or at least systematic) approach to solving

---

NB SYSTEM, HARD SYSTEM, SOFT SYSTEM and SYSTEM FAILURE in small capitals refer to metaphorical and perceptual constructs.

them is appropriate. When such perceived problems are well understood and the range of possible solutions have been tried and tested over a long period, a 'quick fix' on a more elaborate scale may be quite satisfactory. Here, a formal problem-solving procedure should be considered, as outlined in Fig. 3.3 of Chapter 3. The nature of the 'problem' and the range of solutions are considered by the problem-solver to be self-evident; in principle, all that is required is a systematic appraisal and selection procedure. Fig. 2.12 in Chapter 2 gives an example of an application to the 'problem' of deciding what should go into a product promotional campaign. Formal problem-solving like this would probably be appropriate in a market that was mature and stable and one in which the product manufacturer had considerable experience. Nevertheless, *quality* of experience is not always related to *length* of experience and so cannot be relied upon implicitly.

COMPLEX PROBLEMS

Formal problem-solving is likely to be effective only in cases where uncertainty about the 'problem' and possible solutions (i.e. about cause and effect) is minimal, the problem setting is stable, and the level of complexity is low. In cases where these conditions do not apply but none the less the perceived problem appears to be well structured and quantifiable, a HARD SYSTEMS approach is likely to be more effective. The analyst must decide when formal problem-solving will suffice and when to use HARD SYSTEMS methodology.

The choice of an inadequate problem-solving tool will reveal itself only too well when the solution has been implemented. The solution may not work at all, or may work counter-intuitively and make the problem worse, or may produce unexpected new 'problems'.

Exercise 6.1
Bearing in mind the full 'definition' of a 'SYSTEM' from Chapter 1, what do these kinds of failure of solutions suggest about the problem-solver's understanding of the nature of the problem?

Complexity is often, but not always, a function of size and scale. Typical are problems relating to public transport. Railway companies in Britain, for example, have often been criticized for running overcrowded trains. In order to make travel more comfortable for commuters coming into London, one company increased the number of carriages on an early morning train which previously had been very overcrowded each day. Within a short time, however, the extended train also became very overcrowded each day. The new overcrowding arose because some commuters who had previously switched to an earlier train to avoid overcrowding switched back to their preferred train after it had been extended. The result of this solution was a continuation of overcrowding in the 'problem' train, and an earlier train now running half empty.

Problem-solving which only tinkers with the SYSTEM of which the problem is perceived as an emergent property often results in 'migration' of the problem. People who regularly experience traffic jams at particular places and times will recognize how attempts to solve queuing 'problems' at one location often simply shift the queue further up the road. For example, main arterial roads into London have undergone major alterations in order to prevent existing queuing problems at the many roundabouts. The massive investment of capital certainly reduced local queuing, but in many cases the net effect has been to shunt all the local queues into a number of single queues nearer London.

A similar 'problem' has been identified with road traffic accidents. When accident black spots (i.e. sites on the road traffic network which have a relatively high number of accidents) are treated to reduce accidents, for example they are provided with anti-skid surfacing, pedestrian refuges, increased lighting etc., the number of accidents at such locations goes down. However, the number of accidents at untreated locations in the vicinity shows a corresponding increase. The suggestion is that drivers show increased attention at treated blackspots and then relax their attention elsewhere. The accident 'problem' has migrated rather than been solved.

NEED FOR SYSTEMIC INTERVENTION

Problem-solving represents an intervention in relation to a perceived system. A further graphic example of problem-solving which was not sufficiently systemic in its approach is provided by the World Health Organization's intervention into a public health problem in Borneo. Traditionally, Borneo Dayaks live in communal long huts, often with several hundred inhabitants. Standards of health among such people were low and insect-borne diseases were identified as a prime cause. The WHO solution was to systematically spray all such dwellings with DDT. A dramatic improvement in the inhabitants' health followed, as intended and expected. However, a cascade of wholly unexpected 'problems' then followed, as indicated in Fig. 6.1.

The DDT entered the food chain of insects and mammals who were natural cohabitants in the huts. DDT-contaminated cockroaches were eaten by lizards which in turn were eaten by cats. At each successive stage in the food chain, the DDT dose became more concentrated, to the extent that the cats received fatal doses. Soon the villages were invaded by a plague of woodland rats which the cats previously had kept under control. These rats brought fleas and other parasites with them which were infected with sylvatic plague. Eventually, the RAF had to air-drop new cats into isolated villages to bring the rats under control again. If the sylvatic plague problem were not enough, the DDT had also killed off the natural predators of caterpillars which fed off, and caused minor damage to, the thatch roofs in the villages. Soon a plague of caterpillars was devouring the roofs and causing them to collapse (see C.S. Holling and M.A. Goldberg 1973).

The use of DDT in this case represented an obvious solution to an 'obvious' problem – a quick fix to what was *thought* to be a well-known and understood problem. However, as is clear from the above, the health problems of the long hut people were much more complex and would have been more usefully perceived as symptomatic of disruption of a finely-balanced natural system. The people could have been regarded as being part of an 'ecosystem' which the DDT blockbuster solution threw into disarray.

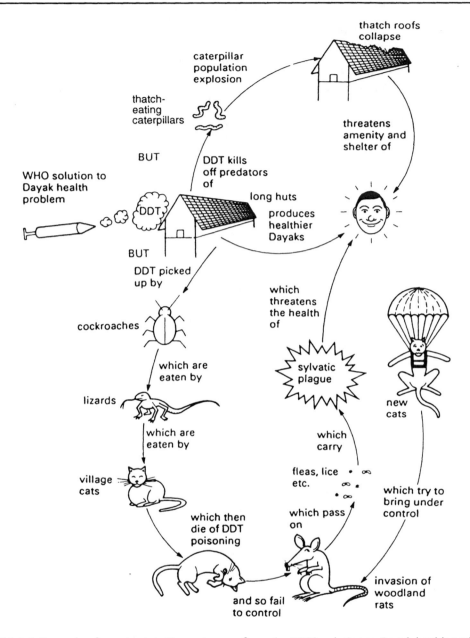

Fig. 6.1 Example of counter-intuitive outcomes from the WHO solution to Dayak health problem.

Another example is the disarray caused to a finely-tuned agricultural SYSTEM on the island of Bali. In 1983, Western aid agencies pressed Balinese farmers to adopt more 'efficient' methods of rice production and to aim for rice export as part of the 'green revolution' in SE Asia. The Balinese had developed over a thousand years an intricate system of waterways and irrigation channels feeding down from volcanic Lake Batur. Under the new scheme, new dams and canals were built, new cropping patterns were started and new 'miracle' rice varieties were introduced. The expected economic boom did not occur.

Wherever the miracle rice was introduced new 'miracle' pests arrived. Use of insecticides resulted in a decline in soil fertility. According to studies by Kremer and Lancing from the University of Southern California, the intervention failed because foreign experts had relied on Western assumptions about technological 'cures' and had not studied the social and ecological dimensions of the Balinese agricultural system. It became clear that pests were kept to a minimum by planting all the rice at the same time and cropping it at the same time. That required a lot of co-ordination, a fact which had gone unnoticed by the aid agencies. Water-sharing down the waterway network from Lake Batur had to be at an optimal level so that no farmer went short. The co-ordination needed for this also went unnoticed by aid workers. It transpired that what was holding all this co-operation and co-ordination together was a SYSTEM of elected farmer representatives who worked closely with priests at a series of strategically placed water temples on the waterway network. Water-sharing rituals were important to the farming culture and were symbolic of the social co-operation needed for successful rice growing, i.e. the hierarchy of dependence on upstream neighbours.

Systematic procedures such as formal problem-solving are inadequate for tackling real-world 'problems' where complex relationships exist and simplistic assumptions about them are unwarranted. The HARD SYSTEMS methodology tries to avoid the pitfalls of oversimplifying the problem by adopting a series of steps designed to develop a wider, systemic perspective and an awareness of all the significant aspects of the problem situation. The methodology is outlined in Chapter 3, and Fig. 3.5 summarizes the steps involved. The following sections run through the methodology step-by-step in some detail. Remember, however, to try to avoid seeing any systems methodology as if it were a simple recipe for success.

STEP 1 GROUNDWORK

The groundwork involves identifying and establishing a working relationship with the client-set, i.e. all those with whom the study seeks to gain credibility. This process may seem easier than it sometimes is in practice. An external consultant, for example, has to negotiate access to the client-set. The person who commissions the analyst to do the work (the effective client) is usually only one of a number of people in the organization who have an interest in the study and its outcome. Establishing what those various interests are (who 'owns' the SYSTEM concerned, who 'owns' the 'problem', who can give or withhold approval, what attitudes are prevalent, etc.) often takes time and skill. For example, while the analyst is trying to extract information from key people, *they* will be appraising the analyst and may well be guarded in their responses. Inexperienced analysts often fail to recognize that access to, and relationships with, the client-set have to be negotiated *continually* throughout the study, and not just at the beginning. Similarly, awareness of the client-set's world-view is important throughout. In addition to any written contract, there are bound to develop informal contracts between the analyst and individual members of the client-set. For example, the analyst may be able to furnish the name of a useful contact who may help one of the client-set with a problem quite unrelated to the one at issue. Building and maintaining trust and confidence is essential for the study to be effective.

Even if the analyst is an 'insider', perhaps within the department with the perceived problem or from another part of the organization, he or she will still have to negotiate and maintain access. Defining or explaining exactly what needs to be done is not easy. Since a SYSTEMS study is going to form the basis of the contract between the client-set and the analyst as problem-solving facilitator, it is clearly worth taking time to get it right. Even if the analyst is also the 'problem owner' and/or 'system owner', formally clarifying the nature of the problem and the problem-solving task is still necessary.

There are three practical ways to clarify these matters. The fairly obvious first step is to agree formally with the client-set what the project topic is and its likely scope. This will at least avoid a response to the first progress report which is either shocked silence or utterances such as 'typical consultants – never do what they're asked to do'. The analyst can also ascertain whether the client is in a position to act on recommendations or whether he or she is seeking a convincing argument to persuade colleagues that action is needed. In the latter case, the 'problem' may need restating.

The second practical action is to find out the client-set's world-view in relation to the task and whether there is general agreement about the nature of the current position. Is the topic regarded as a 'problem' or as an 'opportunity'? Is the client-set composed of risk-takers or risk-avoiders? The latter question is not only relevant to how possible solutions are presented but will also be a constraint on the avenues to be explored for potential solutions. What does the client-set, or organization as a whole, view as being acceptable action? Attitudes towards research and development, loyalty to employees, standing in the community, dealings with other organizations and so on will clearly be of major importance throughout the project.

Exercise 6.2

If you discovered apparently markedly different values among the client-set, clashes of opinion on major relevant issues, personality clashes or other signs of conflict, how ought you to proceed?

Third, find out as early as possible what the client-set would consider to be a successful outcome. Establishing clear and realistic expectations is a way both of refining the topic to be addressed and further cementing the contract between client-set and the analyst-consultant as problem-solver.

Very often, however, the client-set does not have a clear idea of what is required, and the project brief may be couched in very general terms. Equally, very large projects are rarely agreed upon without a well-structured project proposal from the consultant which could be on a competitive tender basis. In such cases the consultant would be briefed by the client and would have to marshal and assess all the relevant information right at the beginning of the groundwork stage in order to formulate a project proposal.

Once a clearer picture of the problem situation has been established, the analyst-consultant can define his or her own commitment to the project in terms of the 'problem', the consultant's role, the problem owner's main objectives and the consultant's main objectives.

STEP 2 AWARENESS AND UNDERSTANDING

This step may be implicit in other problem-solving approaches. The HARD SYSTEMS approach makes it explicit and, in particular, encourages the use of systems description. The discipline of examining the SYSTEM which is perceived to contain the problem and identifying components in systems terminology should enable the analyst to gain a clear perspective of where the perceived problem fits and what the possible effects of trying to solve the problem will be on the rest of the SYSTEM. The aim is to reduce the number of counter-intuitive outcomes of any change, or at least to anticipate those outcomes.

A structured approach to systems description at this pre-analysis stage is that outlined in Chapter 2. The diagramming techniques learned from Part 1 of this book can be used to advantage. No single diagram type is inherently better than any other at this stage, although one would normally expect to see at least a systems map to set the overall scene and a diagram showing processes within the notional system of interest. As a prelude to system mapping and drawing influence diagrams, spider graphs or spray diagrams can be very useful as they may reveal a number of relevant SYSTEMS. Teasing out several, perhaps overlapping, SYSTEMS may enable the 'problem' to be considered from different perspectives.

System description sets the scene and enables selection of a SYSTEM which seems to hold the key to a fruitful resolution of the 'problem'. Detailed analysis of what goes on in that SYSTEM must now be made. It is this detailed analysis which shows up what the knock-on effects of change are likely to be.

Influence diagrams and causal loop diagrams can be useful at this stage. The following case study serves to demonstrate how to establish patterns of influence and then progress to causal loops.

AIR TRAFFIC CONTROL – A CASE STUDY

For those whose holiday flights are delayed for many hours owing to 'air traffic control problems', the civilian air traffic SYSTEM may seem to exhibit aspects of failure (see further discussion in Chapter 10). The 'problem' is complex and the following presents only a limited view of it.

The International Air Transport Association (IATA) estimated that the number of civilian aircraft movements over Europe during the first six months of 1988 increased by between 10% and 14% compared with the same period in 1987. These increases were part of a trend which goes back several years and which still continues in the 1990s. For example, between 1986 and 1989 the number of civilian aircraft movements involving Europe's busiest 42 airports increased from over four million to nearly six million. A similar pattern has arisen in the United States. In the UK, delays in scheduled air flights averaged 22% per annum for the three years 1992–94 and with charter flights delays in the peak summer months averaging between 50% and 60%. The 'problems' of air traffic increases are not uniform and some holiday routes at weekends experience passenger increases of 20–30%.

Existing computer facilities in each of the European air traffic control centres are not integrated and many are outdated. When Mr Neil Kinnock was appointed a European Commissioner with responsibility for transport in 1995, he ordered an immediate investigation into the 'problem'. He is quoted as saying that air traffic controllers were operating from 52 centres using 22 computer systems, which has both efficiency and safety implications. At any one time large numbers of planes are likely to be 'stacked' and unable to land for considerable periods, a problem made worse by restacking caused by 'near-misses' and 'go-rounds' after missed slots. Although existing computers can pinpoint the present location of an aircraft, air traffic control staff still have to anticipate the aircraft's future positions. This makes it difficult to maintain air separations to avoid 'near-miss' accidents.

Maintaining safety is a vital consideration in air traffic control. Controlling the pattern of take-offs, stacking and landings is therefore essential. Better computer facilities are being introduced but in the short term aviation authorities continue to seek any available capacity gains. The air traffic 'system' is a victim of its own success. The more successful it is in increasing capacity, the more passengers are likely to use it. Competition among airlines and tour operators contributes to the 'problem' of too many passengers for the existing capacity. Current palliatives include: employing more controllers, increasing controller productivity, allowing more night flights, transferring military air space for use by civil aircraft, and stopping small aircraft from using major airports. In May 1995, the Civil Aviation Authority announced that it had approved a reduction in time intervals between take-offs at Heathrow from 120 seconds to 60 seconds.

Exercises

6.3 Draw an influence diagram of the air traffic control problem situation and then convert it to a causal diagram. Remember to start with a small number of components at low resolution, i.e. general topics rather than fine detail.

6.4 From the description above of the air traffic control 'problem', what would lead you to expect counter-intuitive outcomes from current solutions?

Most SYSTEMS, particularly those involving human activity, require relative stability in order to function effectively. Although not always destructive, the presence of destabilizing (positive) loops in causal diagrams should alert the analyst to what may be important aspects of the perceived problem. For example, instability in one area may greatly affect the defined problem. In consultation with the client-set, the unstable area may need to be addressed first as a precursor problem.

To complete the essential groundwork and development of understanding, the SYSTEM needs to be defined formally. This system should be given an accurate name ('a system to.....') and its 'owner' should be identified. Inputs, outputs and essential sub-systems need to be listed and a convenient reference for this is the formal system paradigm (FSP) as described in Chapter 5. Depending on the degree of urgency, one or more iterations should have been carried out in step 2. By this stage, it is likely that the problem-solving analyst will understand more about the SYSTEM and its functioning than do any of the client-set.

STEP 3 OBJECTIVES AND CONSTRAINTS

It would be tempting at this stage to start focusing on practical solutions. The client-set will probably be anxious for results and their perception of the task may be quite unrealistic. Once trust and confidence have been established, it is common for the client-set to regard the analyst as 'the expert' – someone with a magic wand who can produce a perfect solution like a rabbit out of a hat, and for whom no practical constraint is insurmountable.

In order to avoid disappointment for the client, it is essential to draw up clearly-defined objectives for the system project. In essence, agreed objectives represent another contract between the client-set and the analyst. Such an agreement is another test of the client-set's shared world-view and the likelihood of the project's success. Defining what success means to the client-set, what resource limits they have and what things they cannot entertain must be done before searching for solutions.

A goal is the overall target to be reached and may be expressed in more detail as a set of objectives or measurable results to be aimed for. Objectives and constraints will be a mixture of quantitative and qualitative 'things'. Objectives themselves need to be organized systematically rather than simply being jotted down as a random list or, worse, not recorded at all. They also need to be phrased unambiguously and with some clear, if broad, action in mind. In other words, each objective should have a verb in it such as 'plan', 'develop', 'implement', or 'attain'. An ideal way to make objectives manageable is to draw up an objectives hierarchy. This is an organization chart of objectives and assumes that some objectives are subordinate to others and that some must be reached before, logically at least, others can be. The following example demonstrates the principle.

INFORMATION TECHNOLOGY IN FURTHER EDUCATION – A CASE STUDY

In recent years, Colleges of Further Education in the United Kingdom have been forced increasingly to address pressures for change in their role, outlook and methods. For example, in the 1980s there was growing concern among politicians, employers and educationists about college attitudes towards local market conditions. The Education Reform Act of 1988 reinforced the trend towards FE colleges adopting a more businesslike approach to their activities.

Imagine you are the head of the information technology (IT) section in the business studies department of an FE college. Traditionally, your section has taught computing on day-release, evening class and full-time courses. Education reform, however, has negated many of the traditional assumptions. There are pressures to run more self-financing courses. There is competition from commercial training companies which local employers may prefer and this threatens your day-release market. At present, computing courses are over-subscribed and so you are not unduly worried about the short term. The danger to the viability and survival of your section lies in the longer-term (five to ten years hence) when competition could be stiff and your resources not assured.

The head of department and other key figures share your concern because unless the IT section is viable the future of the department is less certain. You have been allocated £100 000 to set up a custom-built IT suite which is intended to provide better facilities for students and act as an IT training resource for the College's own academic and administrative staff.

Acting as problem owner, client and analyst rolled into one, you have started a HARD SYSTEMS study of the problem. You have entitled the SYSTEM of interest 'the department of business studies system for IT education and training'. The long-term objective is to ensure viability and survival of the IT section, but the achievement of other objectives would be necessary to reach this long-term objective. Three parallel branches are identifiable, as in Fig. 6.2. In contrast to some objective trees, in this example all three branches would have to be pursued.

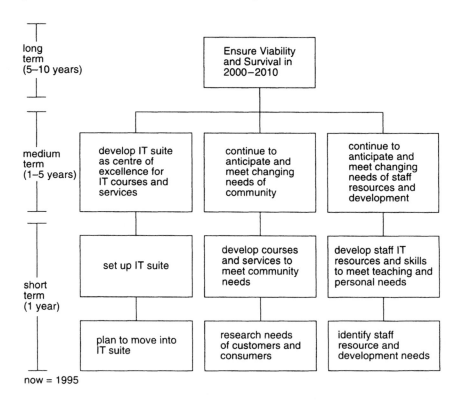

Fig. 6.2 Objectives hierarchy for the viability and survival of the IT section of the Business Studies Department in a local FE College.

Exercise 6.5
An obvious constraint to the viability of the IT section is the amount of money allocated to provide the IT suite. What other constraints could there be?

STEP 4 STRATEGIES

In some projects there may be only one realistic pathway to the primary objective. For example, if the objective is to reduce the number of grades of hourly-paid workers in a factory from 50 to 25, there is no real choice in the method to be used. A choice only presents itself in the technique or techniques adopted, e.g. merging grades. In many projects, however, distinctly different options are available. For example, if the project objective is to increase company profits, this could be achieved either by cutting costs or by increasing sales while maintaining prices. Both are potential options and although one may be preferred at the outset by the client-set a HARD SYSTEMS examination of these routes may cause them to alter their view.

In complex cases, the analyst has to take the initiative in a creative search for solutions. Creative searching comprises two phases, expansion or divergent thinking followed by contraction or convergent thinking. Expansion seeks to provide as many ideas and potential strategies as time and other resources permit. Contraction seeks to classify and refine the potential strategies into practical propositions. Brainstorming is one good method of creative search which seeks to encourage among a group of people (e.g. the client-set) creative and almost anarchic thinking, but set within a systematic framework. Even apparently ludicrous ideas are not discouraged. For example, one group faced with the agreed problem of how to gain access to windows on the outside of tall public buildings for cleaning and maintenance considered and rejected a whole stock of 'standard' solutions which would have been acceptable for lower buildings. Someone then suggested training a team of flying squirrels to do the job and someone else said 'What about sending in the SAS?' From this rather amusing diversion came a more fundamental question 'Why should any living thing, man or beast, be expected to do it?' The group proceeded to focus on automatic mechanical means for doing such work.

Obviously, brainstorming is not possible if the analyst is working alone and is his or her own client. Discussing ideas with friends and colleagues or just quiet contemplation may be helpful. In any event, creative search is an iterative process and may involve a number of different techniques.

In devising strategies, care needs to be taken to distinguish between project objectives and client objectives. Although the two are connected, the client's objectives are likely to encompass the project objectives and, in effect, to act as a constraint on them. For example, a long-established technical consultancy firm was seeking to secure its future by developing into allied areas of management consultancy. This was a long-term project requiring investment of time and effort by senior consultants in client development. Consultancy is by nature labour intensive and the more senior the level of work and the larger the consultancy job the longer the lead-times tend to be. However, once established in high level work, the rewards can be very high, and client decisions on awarding work tend to be quality-sensitive rather than price-sensitive. The consultancy's parent group sold out to a manufacturing group. The new owners had a higher-order objective, namely to raise profitability quickly and maintain it as a secure base for the future. However, their objective constrained the consultancy's project objective in terms of how it could be achieved, i.e. the strategic options. For example, short-term profits require high utilization of consultants on fee-earning work whereas the project required the best consultants to spend up to 40% of their time on non-fee earning client development. High-utilization is more easily achieved by winning long-term technical contracts at competitive rates. However, because technical contracts are price-sensitive, fee rates are typically half those obtainable for higher-level consultancy work of the kind the consultancy wished to develop. Thus, the parent group's higher objective seriously constrained the consultancy's project objective, which in fact was never achieved.

STEP 5 MEASURES TO ASSESS ACHIEVEMENT

Assessment measures are those which can be used to determine how well a strategy performs in meeting objectives. Such measures have to include quantitative ones because the HARD SYSTEMS methodology depends on them. Typical quantitative measures are: cost, return on capital employed, savings (time, materials, energy, labour), reduction in queue lengths, number of energy units produced per unit cost, miles per gallon etc.

Quantifiable measures need to be framed so that a clear target level or rate is specified and a time-factor built in. For example, an objective such as 'achieve a high return on capital' needs to be specified in terms of per cent (net or gross?) over so many years (yearly, on average, or in total?).

Qualitative measures stemming from the client-set's world-view include such factors as declared policies, senior management's current interpretation of those policies, current enthusiasm for a particular technology, and their criteria for what 'acceptable' means to the organization. Other qualitative measures relate to possible effects of implementing a solution, such as effects of potential workplace or job changes on workforce morale and attitudes or effects of a potential major building or transport programme on public opinion. Appropriate measures might include pressure group reaction, opportunities for staff development, corporate image projection, and so on.

Measures of assessment must be specified before proceeding to modelling and evaluation. Quantitative measures will feature prominently in these next two steps, whereas both quantitative and qualitative measures will also be important in step 8, 'making a choice'. As with other steps in the methodology, assessment measures should be specified in consultation with the client-set.

STEP 6 MODELLING

A model is a representation of either something in the real world or a concept, which shows either what it looks like or how it works. The representation may be either a replica or a reduced version which seeks to capture the essence of the thing or concept. In HARD SYSTEMS studies for decision support, models are mainly numerical. In systems engineering, physical or computer-generated models of designed technical systems might also be created.

Typically, mathematical models are selected or devised to simulate the relationship between independent (causal) variables, and the dependent variable, i.e. the measure of performance. For example, if cost is the assessment measure specified in step 5, this depends on a number of other variables and, in particular, fixed costs and variable costs. At a simple level, the relationship may be expressed as:

Total costs = Fixed costs + Variable costs

or expressed with symbols as:

TC = FC + VC

Fixed costs comprise items such as heating, lighting and local premises taxes, whereas variable costs include the wages bill, advertising, and so on. It is therefore possible to refine the simple model above to include all the ingredients which are perceived to contribute to TC. The result is a numerical model which simulates total cost, the assessment measure chosen in step 5 to test in step 7 each of the strategy options on the list from step 4. Another simple numerical model is C = A – L where C is capital, A is assets and L is liabilities.

'Return on investment' is a popular measure of assessment. A principal sum (P) at the start of the investment increases as each year the amount of annual interest, e.g. 10%, is added. The total amount of accumulated investment or performance (R) after (y) years of investment can be predicted from the following numerical model or formula:

$R = P \times (1 + i)^y$

where i is the annual interest rate expressed as a decimal. For example, if the interest rate is 10% then i is 0.1. Of course, this formula for the level of return assumes a fixed interest rate and ignores tax liability.

Although some models, especially financial models, are available off-the-shelf, others have to be devised and refined from such sources as causal loop diagrams from step 2. A well-established financial model for comparing the relative worth of several potential investment projects is the net present value (NPV). The basis of the NPV approach is to compare the return from investment in each project (e.g. launching a new product, buying in someone else's) with the return obtained by simply leaving the investment money in an interest-bearing bank account.

For example, if £100 000 is deposited in a bank at a fixed interest rate of 10% per annum, then in five years' time that investment will be worth £161 051. Investing £100 000 in each of the possible project strategies would also generate revenue in the future, for example from sales. However, without the NPV approach it is not clear whether any of the project options would perform significantly better than simply leaving the money in the bank.

NPV is a single value or index calculated by adding up the present values (PVs) for each year of the investment period. The PV represents the value at today's prices. In the example above, £161 051 in five years' time would be worth only £100 000, i.e. its present value. If the project cost was only £80 000 and achieved a return in five years' time of £161 051, then the return on the investment would be better than that of the bank.

The PV for each year is calculated from the formula

$$PV = I/(1 + i)^n$$

where I is the investment sum, i is the annual interest rate (expressed as a decimal), and n is the period of investment. However, project cash has a flow to it – either income is greater than expenditure (positive cash-flow) or is less than expenditure (negative cash-flow). The net result of adding total income (+ values) to total expenditure (- values) for each year is the net cash-flow and it is this figure which is used as I in the PV formula. Table 6.1 shows an example of how PV is calculated for each year of investment to give a discounted cash-flow.

The example in Table 6.1 has been greatly simplified, and in practice the main contributions to net income and net expenditure would be separately itemized. The effects of payments or rebates of corporation tax would also be included. Financial modelling techniques can be very useful. Even use of elementary computer software such as spreadsheets enables 'what if?' projections to be made. Knowledge-based computer programs also enable aspects of a particular perceived problem to be modelled in conceptual terms as an aid to definition.

The negative sign to an NPV is not encouraging, for it indicates that the investment will make a loss in real terms. However, five years is a relatively short period over which to judge performance, and extension of the cash flow table might well produce a healthy positive NPV.

It is worth noting that in calculating PVs many companies do not use the current minimum lending rate or business loan rates. Instead, they set a 'hurdle rate' which is several percentage points above business interest rates. The higher gearing is to

Table 6.1 Example of NPV calculation for an investment project

Item	Cash-Flow (£000) in year					
	0	1	2	3	4	5
a) Net income			45	250	432	335
b) Net expenditure	-133	-101	-380	-231	-100	-95
c) Net cash flow (a + b)	-133	-101	-335	+19	+332	+240
d) PV @ 10% (c as I in formula)	-133	-92	-277	+14	+227	+149
e) NPV @ 10% (sum of all PVs) = -£112 000						
f) Total income less total expenditure = 1062-1040 = +£22 000						

Note that although there is an apparent net profit of £22 000, the NPV is *negative*.

take account of the desired profit and is indicative of a particular management's world-view.

STEP 7 EVALUATION

Any model to be used for evaluating potential options must have been 'dry-run' tested in step 6 to ensure that it is sufficiently accurate for its purpose. Once confidence in the model is established, different sets of likely values for the independent variables can be used on a 'what if?' basis to calculate corresponding values of the performance measure. The result might be a set of NPV figures or some other set of data which enables the financial value of each strategy to be compared.

Both the analyst and the client-set need to be aware that such numerical evaluations do not represent certainty. They are rule-of-thumb indicators which suggest that one or two routes look more promising than others. The degree of uncertainty can be controlled by such techniques as decision analysis which involves estimates by the client-set of the probabilities that certain factors (e.g. market conditions) will prevail over the period concerned. For example, the NPV might be £10m at 10% growth rate and £25m at 18% growth rate, but the client-set reckon that the chances of 18% growth rate are 0.7. Combining these data (0.7 x 25) + (0.3 x 10) gives an expected monetary value (EMV) of £20.5m. The client-set could examine its other options in a similar manner so that the EMVs may be compared.

STEP 8 MAKING A CHOICE

Useful as quantitative modelling may be, it should only be regarded as a support for decision-making. The client-set and client organization will have qualitative objectives to consider, and there may well be hidden agendas of which the analyst is unaware. Quantitative evaluation suggests an optimum solution but qualitative evaluation by the client may result in a lower performance route being selected. Such a selection is based on what is considered to be the most satisfactory on all counts rather than the numerical best.

Various scales and weighting factors can overcome some of the incompatibility of quantitative and qualitative factors at selection stage. A formal presentation to the client-set supported by a detailed project report is a normal requirement at this stage.

STEP 9 IMPLEMENTATION

Many problem-solvers feel that their work has finished at the end of step 8. However, planning for implementation and the changes which may be involved should have been clearly in the minds of both analyst and client-set from the beginning of the study. This is especially important where major organizational or technological changes are likely. Where employees are going to be affected directly it is wise to keep them informed, or even involved, from an early stage. This will help avoid suspicion and worry about 'secret working-parties' planning the demise of this or that group in the name of cost-cutting and efficiency. Joint working-parties and steering committees, for example, can aid communication and dispel unsubstantiated rumours in addition to helping to plan the implementation phase.

SUMMARY

The objectives of this chapter were to (a) revisit the concept of HARD SYSTEM thinking introduced in Part 1 of the book, (b) discuss further the nature of 'problems' and a HARD SYSTEMS view of problems, and (c) demonstrate, with the aid of case examples, the HARD SYSTEMS methodology.

A HARD SYSTEMS approach to managerial problem-solving guarantees nothing. It is an aid to decision-making. Where there is general agreement about the nature of a quantifiable well-structured problem and the goal to be reached, it provides a rational tool for finding a range of solutions and aiding the selection of the most satisfactory one from the client's point of view. Chapter 7 provides two worked case studies using the HARD SYSTEMS methodology.

SUGGESTED ANSWERS TO EXERCISES

6.1   When solutions work counter-intuitively or produce unexpected new 'problems', it suggests that the problem-solver did not understand the systemic context of the perceived problem and/or that relevant information was not available. When introduced, the solution will affect other components in the SYSTEM and their interaction. If these components and their relationships are inadequately identified and understood, the solution is likely to be ineffective.

6.2   A HARD SYSTEM approach is unlikely to be successful if the client-set does not have a shared world-view or if there is conflict between key individuals or groups. If such tensions and mismatches surface and interfere with the problem-solving work, the analyst should consider switching temporarily to SSM so that issues can be confronted and dealt with. The art of switching methodologies is described in Chapter 12.

6.3   A causal diagram of the air traffic control 'problem' is shown in Fig. 6.3. Thick lines usually denote major influences or causal links. However, in this diagram, thick lines denote the simple initial diagram from which the larger diagram was developed.

6.4.   Counter-intuitive outcomes are to be expected because the highly complex SYSTEM and the nature of the 'problem' are inadequately understood. Short-term solutions ('palliatives') are being implemented as common-sense responses simply to keep the SYSTEM operating at all.

6.5.   Staff numbers and staff time are two obvious constraints. Teaching staff can only be in one place at a time. For example, if IT lecturers are teaching in a classroom they cannot be visiting local employers to carry out market research.

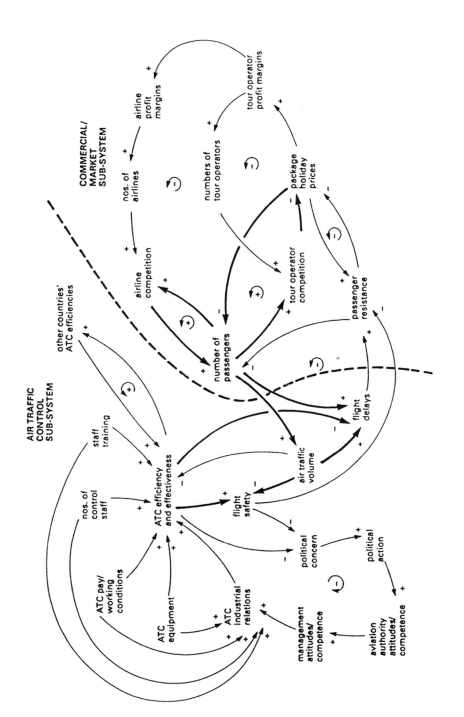

Fig. 6.3 Causal loop diagram of the air traffic control problem situation in relation to holiday traffic (second iteration). *Note*: thick lines denote initial diagram and *not* main causal links.

7 HARD SYSTEMS CASE STUDIES

The objective of this chapter is to demonstrate the application of the HARD SYSTEMS methodology through two case studies.

INTRODUCTION

Previous chapters (3 and 6) have provided a grounding in HARD SYSTEMS thinking and the HARD SYSTEMS methodology. In this chapter two case studies demonstrate rather different uses of the HARD SYSTEMS approach. The first case, Redwood Breweries, concerns decisions about business strategy in a changing market environment facing a small regional brewery. The second case, Drillcorp, concerns the establishment of effective management systems in a drilling contractor in the offshore oil and gas business. Whereas both cases concern decision support, the emphases are different.

REDWOOD BREWERIES – A STUDY OF STRATEGIC DECISION-MAKING IN A RAPIDLY CHANGING MARKET ENVIRONMENT

Redwood Breweries is a small, traditional brewing firm in the West Country. Over its 150-year history Redwood has enjoyed respect in the region for its beers. It currently runs two breweries, one at Bodmin and the other at Yeovil, which support Redwood's 390 pubs spread throughout Devon, Cornwall, Somerset, Dorset, Avon and Wiltshire. The West Country is a magnet for summer tourists and seasonal demand is evidenced by the fact that some 90% of Redwood's profits are generated in the summer.

As a traditional real ale brewer, Redwood still uses beechwood fermentation tanks for most of its production but even Redwood has had to recognize the change in drinking patterns since the early 1970s, especially among 18–24 year olds. Whereas

---

NB SYSTEM, HARD SYSTEM, SOFT SYSTEM and SYSTEM FAILURE in small capitals refer to metaphorical and perceptual constructs.

it used to brew only real ale bitters, milds and stouts, now 25% of production is lager brewed in stainless steel tanks. Anti drink-and-drive laws have seen a massive R&D initiative in the brewing industry to develop low-alcohol beers and Redwood has had to follow suit. However, its product mix is still dominated by real ale at 50% of total output. The small brewer/real ale market has become increasingly buoyant.

In the last financial year, Redwood produced 110 000 barrels divided roughly equally between Bodmin and Yeovil. The Yeovil site also has a bottling plant which handled 12 000 barrels. Both plants also bottled mineral water of which 1 600 000 litres in total were produced in 1994. In addition to distribution direct from the two breweries, Redwood also has distribution depots at Barnstaple and Chippenham. While Redwood is strong in the region, its assets, capacity and output are small when compared with major UK brewers.

Like most of the major brewers, Redwood has tried to develop into the hotel trade. This move was prompted by the growth in leisure spending and the opening up of the West Country by the M4 and M5 motorways. Tourists and short-break holiday makers from London and the Midlands can now be in the West Country in under two hours. Redwood set up a subsidiary company in 1980, initially to purchase two seafront hotels, the large Duchesne Hotel in Exeter and a smaller summer season hotel, The Vista, in Truro. After costly refurbishment, the hotels reopened during the recession of the late 1980s. Poor profits from the hotels have led to their recent sale.

Redwood's board of directors has seen several recent changes. David Redwood-Curry retired after twenty years as chairman and nearly 50 years as a director. The new chairman is John Hutchinson, whose former post as finance director is now held by Alan Walker previously group accountant with Coopers, a major UK brewer. Coopers own 25% of Redwood shares. Alan Walker is a very experienced accountant with an MBA from Warwick Business School and has a reputation for applying modern management techniques.

The arrival of Alan Walker was influenced by Coopers who last year were dismayed to learn that following a revaluation of Redwood's properties a surplus of £24m over the previous book value had been revealed. In essence, Redwoods had become 'asset rich' in terms of property values but 'profit poor' in terms of return on capital employed in its revenue operations. As a major shareholder, Coopers were bound to take action to protect their return on investment. The UK property boom in the 1980s had boosted the value of Redwood's property portfolio, even taking account of the subsequent recession. In addition however, Redwood's pubs tend to command premium locations in villages where residential property is in high demand from retired couples, families seeking second or holiday homes, and affluent professionals willing to commute by motorway to jobs in Bristol, London and the M4 high-tech corridor. Thus, the value of Redwood's pubs on the property market is well in excess of their commercial value to the company, a situation that is unlikely to change in the foreseeable future.

Last year, Redwood spent £1.9m as capital expenditure on refurbishing pubs, new vehicles, and minor upgrading of brewing capacity at its Yeovil brewery. This expenditure was financed by retained earnings and the sale of four pubs. Redwood has loans of only £0.5m against assets of more than £40m, a reflection of historically low borrowings.

In addition to the changing drinking habits of 18–24 year olds, Redwood's market is changing rapidly in a number of ways. Not only is the residential population of West Country villages changing but so too is the transient holiday population. Cheap package holidays in sunny countries have drawn away domestic holiday-makers. Whereas fifteen years ago holiday makers decided well in advance to spend two or three weeks annual holiday in the West Country, nowadays the trend is for holidays abroad with perhaps a short second holiday in the UK. *Ad hoc* weekend break holidays have come to the fore. Although demand for small hotel and guest house accommodation has remained steady, short camping and caravan breaks are on the increase. The unpredictability of the English weather has added to the uncertainties about the future of tourism in the West Country, the main plank of Redwood's markets.

In the face of market volatility, Alan Walker is keen to reduce Redwood's vulnerability and intends to embark on a rapid growth strategy. Such a strategy has been encouraged by the decision of the Monopolies and Mergers Commission to force the six major brewers to divest themselves of large numbers of their public houses so as not to stifle smaller competitors like Redwood. The board has agreed to an independent study by Axis Management Consultants of how rapid growth could best be achieved.

STEP 1 GROUNDWORK

The Axis analyst had an initial two hour meeting with Alan Walker to establish rapport and to obtain essential facts and figures about Redwood. Alan handed over a number of reports and files. The analyst also probed discreetly Alan's relationship with the rest of the board. Did he enjoy their full confidence or was he seen as a 'new broom' to be tolerated but not allowed full rein? What did Alan see as the chairman's attitude, bearing in mind that John Hutchinson previously held the finance director's position? Alan's responses indicated that there were no divisions within the board as to the need for rapid growth and a new strategy to achieve that goal.

The analyst outlined a programme for a study lasting three months and agreed with Alan when interim reports would be submitted to him and when a final presentation to the board would be made. Alan would personally authorize payment of staged invoices for the study. This convinced the analyst that Alan was both the problem owner and the client and, importantly, appeared to have influence over the board's ultimate decision. Nevertheless, the analyst needed to interview the remainder of the client-set to assure himself that there were no hidden world-views that would work against an eventual decision for concerted action. At this stage, the analyst considered the client set to comprise Redwood's board but he held in reserve the possibility of others with whom the study might have to be credible. For example, major shareholders, Redwood's bankers or other sources of finance might need to be convinced about recommendations for change in Redwood's market strategy.

The analyst interviewed each member of the board separately. It became clear that although there were 'old guard' and 'new guard' directors, there was no fundamental disagreement about the need for a new approach to the business. Although as an old family firm in a traditionally conservative industry there was a natural tendency to evolve slowly, the board were enlightened enough to recognize the need for change. Far from antagonism towards Alan Walker, he was described in warm terms and his enthusiasm, up-to-date business skills and experience in the industry were clearly valued. He was seen as an insider.

Before starting on systems analysis the analyst requested a brief meeting with the board to review the nature of the study and the overall goal (rapid growth with profitability) and to confirm that Redwood was seeking compatible rather than radical non-brewing solutions. Although he never used the term 'world-view', the analyst also sought confirmation that the client-set's world-view was essentially that they were the inheritors of an ancient social industry for providing alcoholic refreshment products and convivial meeting places where people could enjoy them. The client-set felt an obligation to maintain tradition but also recognized an obligation to change with the times and so continue to meet market needs and wants. They regarded their beers with pride but were not real ale campaigners. They would strive to achieve excellence in whatever refreshment products and related leisure services the public demanded. In short, although their attention had been drawn to an imbalance between assets and profits, the client-set saw this as a short-term problem whose resolution presented an opportunity to strengthen their position in the product market. While they were not risk-aversive, they were used to evolutionary change and were unlikely to agree to radical high-risk proposals. Diversifying into other leisure areas such as bingo halls and theme parks would not fit their own identity or the image they wanted to maintain. Brewing and pubs were central to their past, present and future.

STEP 2 AWARENESS AND UNDERSTANDING

The analyst summed up his impressions of the 'problem' to be solved as one of finding viable ways to improve Redwood's market position as a traditional, regional brewer in a rapidly changing leisure industry and market. Redwood's board were committed to fulfil opportunities for expansion that would also solve a temporary problem of low profitability and stabilize their position *vis-à-vis* a volatile market. The analyst's own commitment as a management consultant was to help the client-set achieve their overall objectives by presenting viable choices within an agreed three-month study period. The analyst drew a spray diagram of the situation as shown in Fig. 7.1.

Was the commitment of Redwood's board in the person of Alan Walker a systemic one? Would a 'hard systems' study be worthwhile, for example, or would a formal problem-solving exercise be adequate? Since Redwood was subject to a complex and volatile market situation with many variables operating, the analyst concluded that formal problem-solving would be inadequate. Was the exercise seeking some achievable, measurable goal? Was there some definite action in mind at the end of the study? Was Alan Walker a key figure in the decision process? On all counts, it was clear that the situation was systemic and that a HARD SYSTEMS methodology was warranted.

Using the spray diagram as reference, the analyst then separated out what seemed to be a key SYSTEM, namely Redwood's system for achieving a market mix to provide rapid growth with profitability in the brewing and leisure markets. Fig. 7.2 shows one iteration of component separation and an adjustment of resolution.

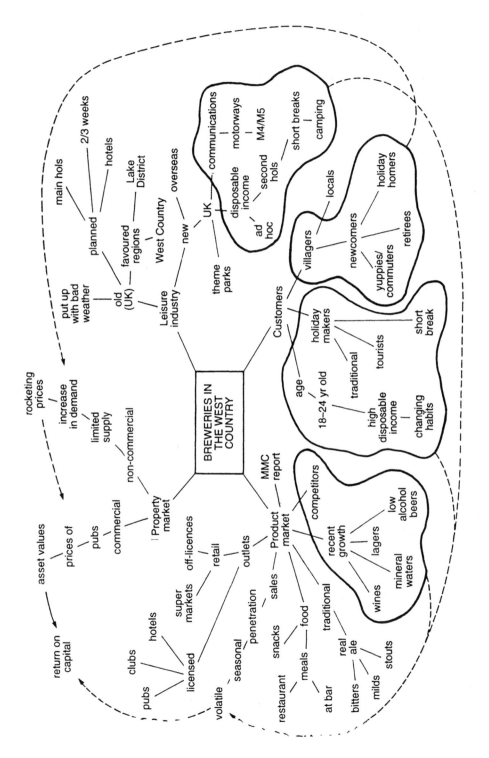

Fig. 7.1 Spray diagram of the Redwood Brewery situation (first iteration).

A fruitful area in Redwood's situation: market mix
A potential system: the Redwood system for achieving a market mix to provide rapid growth with profitability in the brewing and leisure markets.

(a) first iteration

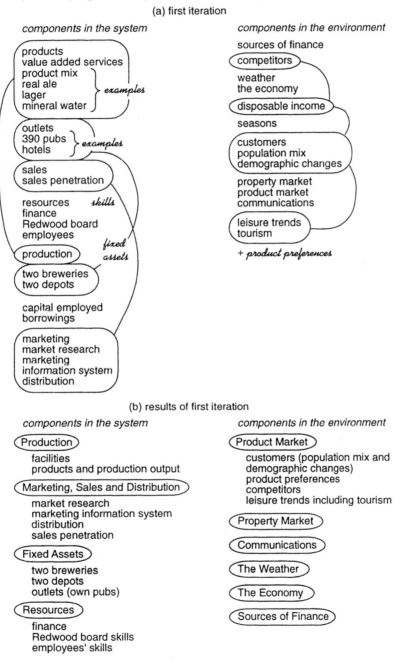

components in the system

products
value added services
product mix
real ale
lager   } *examples*
mineral water

outlets
390 pubs   } *examples*
hotels

sales
sales penetration

resources   *skills*
finance
Redwood board
employees
              fixed
production   *assets*

two breweries
two depots

capital employed
borrowings

marketing
market research
marketing
information system
distribution

components in the environment

sources of finance
competitors

weather
the economy
disposable income

seasons

customers
population mix
demographic changes

property market
product market
communications

leisure trends
tourism

+ *product preferences*

(b) results of first iteration

components in the system

Production
  facilities
  products and production output

Marketing, Sales and Distribution
  market research
  marketing information system
  distribution
  sales penetration

Fixed Assets
  two breweries
  two depots
  outlets (own pubs)

Resources
  finance
  Redwood board skills
  employees' skills

components in the environment

Product Market
  customers (population mix and
  demographic changes)
  product preferences
  competitors
  leisure trends including tourism

Property Market

Communications

The Weather

The Economy

Sources of Finance

Fig. 7.2 Separation of a system relevant to Redwood's problem.

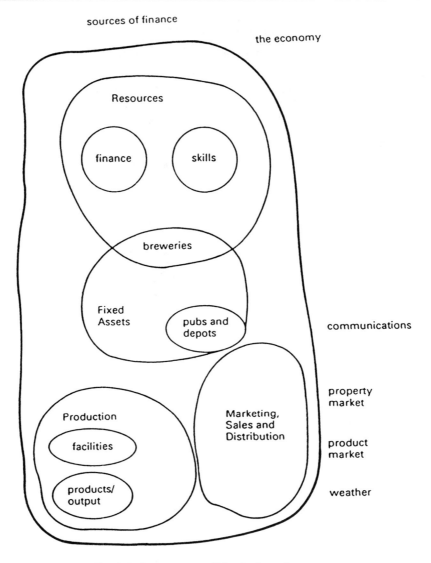

Fig. 7.3 System map of the Redwood system.

From this separation, it was possible to draw a system map as shown in Fig. 7.3. The client-set's overall objective of growth with profitability (i.e. an acceptable return on capital employed) is influenced by a number of factors under Redwood's control:

- finance;
- fixed assets (especially property);
- capital employed (on revenue operations);

- skill resources (especially at board level);

- production (production facilities, capacities etc.);

- sales (volumes, values, penetration etc.);

- marketing (market research, market information system, product positioning, product portfolio etc.);

- distribution (methods, capacities etc.)

Fig. 7.4 shows how these influences affect return on capital employed.

The Axis consultant began to view the growth 'problem' as one of how to ensure that Redwood used its capital investment to increase its share(s) of the market(s)

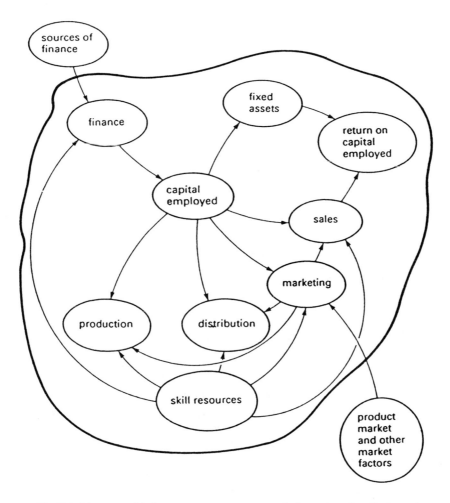

Fig 7.4 Diagram of influences on return on capital employed at Redwood.

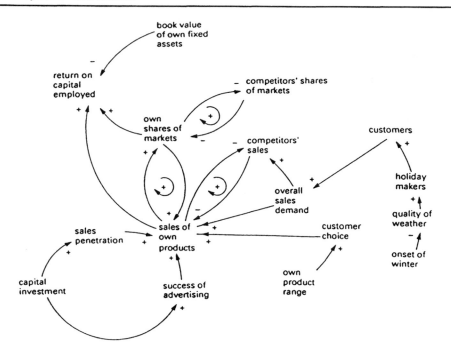

Fig. 7.5 Causal loop diagram of variables affecting return on capital employed at Redwood (first pass).

available to it. If its market shares were small and sales were sluggish, return on capital employed was bound to be poor. Fig. 7.5 shows his initial attempt to address the main dynamic variables; Fig. 7.6 shows an expanded version. These diagrams have no control loops on the supply side of the market and so by inference if Redwood failed to increase its own sales and market shares then competitors would almost certainly make their position stronger at its expense.

STEP 3 OBJECTIVES AND CONSTRAINTS

The twin threats of increasing competition and inconsistent but static overall demand in the West Country convinced the consultant that Redwood had to increase its total sales, whether at the expense of existing competitors or by the creation of new markets. The overall objective of growth with profitability was confirmed. Sub-objectives were to reduce Redwood's reliance on its traditional market and to achieve a healthier balance between profits and assets.

Time was an obvious constraint. Although Redwood was not at crisis point, the situation demanded fairly urgent action. The consultant's study alone would take three months, and implementing a decision could well take a further six to nine months.

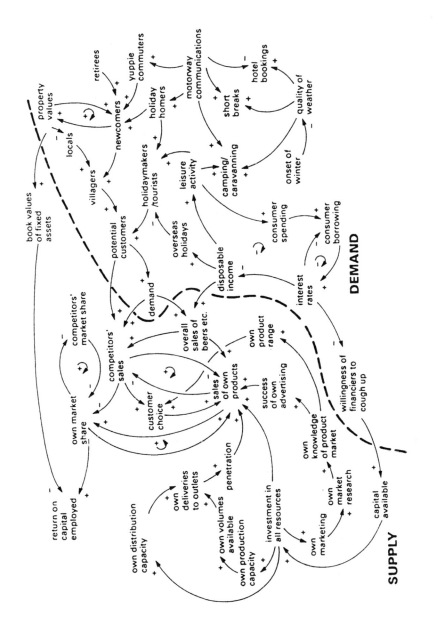

Fig. 7.6 Causal loop diagram of variables affecting return on capital employed at Redwood (third iteration).

The board had already signalled their reluctance to go for a non-brewing solution and so this limited the possible ways of reaching the objectives. A further possible constraint was the availability of capital to finance growth. Although Redwood had sold assets when it thought it necessary, it was not going to sell off large numbers of its pubs and other premises as these were an integral and necessary part of its sales operation. However, if it had to borrow money a rapid rise in interest rates could adversely affect cash flow and servicing of the loan. Redwood would therefore be considering very carefully how the growth strategy would be financed.

STEP 4 STRATEGIES TO MEET OBJECTIVES

The consultant identified four possible growth strategies on the basis of a 10-year plan:

(A) go for a larger share of their current West Country market;

(B) create new product market(s) allied to existing ones;

(C) enter/take similar markets outside the West Country;

(D) move into different product markets.

Strategy D was eliminated as it involved diversification by acquiring a non-brewing company, something that Redwood did not want to do.

STRATEGY A: ACQUIRE DARTSTONE TAVERNS

Strategy A involved the acquisition of a smaller brewer in Redwood's market area as a means of increasing Redwood's market penetration and therefore sales. The purchase of Dartstone Taverns and its fifty pubs would cost £9.0m. The consultant estimated that this acquisition would generate a cash-flow of £2.0m per annum growing at 10.0% per annum on the assumption that it was an even chance that the West Country holiday market would remain strong. A worst-case estimate if the holiday market was poor would be an annual cash-flow of £0.6m. In the latter case, a decision would have to be made after two years whether to retain or sell the Dartstone brewery. If sold, the Dartstone site would realize £1.5m and would produce operational savings of £0.4m per annum.

STRATEGY B: DEVELOP FAST-FOOD OUTLETS IN MAIN REDWOOD PUBS

This strategy involved developing fifty fast-food outlets at an estimated investment cost of £4.0m, including refurbishment. If successful (0.65 probability), this strategy would produce a cash-flow of £1.0m per annum growing at 10% per annum. Success would lead to a decision in three years' time either to invest in fifty more outlets or to retain the first fifty and invest in a different area of the business. If unsuccessful, the fast-food chain would generate an estimated cash-flow of £0.3m per annum. As an alternative, the chain could be sold after three years for £1.5m or, if market conditions were poor, for £1.0m (0.5 chance of either selling option).

STRATEGY C: ACQUIRE MIDLAND BREWERIES

Although this would be the simplest way to enter new markets, the takeover could either go smoothly or there could be a battle with competitive bids pushing up the price. The estimated cost of a smooth acquisition was £10m whereas with a competitive bid the cost could rise to £15m. The chance of either is 0.4. If the bid failed, there would still be a capital gain of £2m on Redwood shares.

In the event of a successful take-over of Midland, Redwood would have to decide about the future of its Bodmin brewery which would probably be uneconomic in the enlarged company. The Bodmin site would fetch £2.5m at the end of the first year. Closure would also yield a saving of £0.75m per annum. In any event, demand for Midland beers could be either high or low and the effects of both eventualities (at 0.5 probability) would have to be calculated.

STEP 5 ASSESSMENT MEASURES

The Axis consultant considered what the most appropriate measures would be to estimate how well each of the three proposed strategies would perform in relation to the defined objectives. The overall objective was growth with profitability. Therefore, quantitative measures would be needed to predict return on investment. The most appropriate measures would be present value (PV) and net present value (NPV) as outlined in Chapter 6. Once these values had been calculated, expected values (EVs) could be computed to provide financial indices for each strategy.

Quantitative measures are essential but alone they provide no indication of intangibles relevant to the all-important world-view of Redwood's board. Maintaining Redwood's identity as a traditional West Country brewer and its assumed image in the West Country as a solid, dependable employer would be important. Each strategy would have to be tested against these and other qualitative measures. For example, patterns in consumer taste, both regional and over time, need to be relatively stable. Qualitative measures from market research therefore would have to be taken into account.

STEP 6 MODELLING

Quantitative modelling involved the creation of discounted cash-flows for each option within each of the three strategies. Cash-flows were discounted at 15% at Alan Walker's insistence. Although commercial lending rates were at 8%, he was seeking a clear net return of 5% and so a 13% overall return would be needed. Lending rates had fallen consistently from 1991 to 1994 but had begun to rise again. Allowing for a further 2% rise in lending rates, he had specified a hurdle rate of 15% return.

The discounted cash flows in Table 7.1 summarize how the present values and NPVs were calculated. PVs for each year (right hand column) were calculated by multiplying the cash flow value for that year (second column) by a factor for 15% discount (third column) obtained from published tables. The PV of the 10-year investment was calculated by adding up the PVs. Subtracting the investment gives the NPV.

Table 7.1 Discounted cash flows for Strategy A: acquire Dartstone Taverns

Scenario 1: Strong holiday market and retain Dartstone brewery

year	cash flow (£m)	discount factor	present value (£m)
1	2.0000	0.8696	1.7392
2	2.1000	0.7561	1.5878
3	2.2050	0.6575	1.4498
4	2.3153	0.5718	1.3239
5	2.4310	0.4972	1.2087
6	2.5526	0.4323	1.1035
7	2.6802	0.3759	1.0075
8	2.8142	0.3269	0.9200
9	2.9549	0.2843	0.8401
10	3.1027	0.2472	0.7670

present value of 10-year investment: 11.9475
less investment: (9.0000)
net present value (£m):   2.9475

Scenario 2: Poor holiday market and retain Dartstone brewery

year	cash flow (£m)	discount factor	present value (£m)
1	0.6000	0.8696	0.5218
2	0.6000	0.7561	0.4537
3	0.6000	0.6575	0.3945
4	0.6000	0.5718	0.3431
5	0.6000	0.4972	0.2983
6	0.6000	0.4323	0.2594
7	0.6000	0.3759	0.2255
8	0.6000	0.3269	0.1961
9	0.6000	0.2843	0.1706
10	0.6000	0.2472	0.1483

present value of 10-year investment: 3.0113
less investment: (9.0000)
net present value (£m):   –5.9887

Scenario 3: Poor holiday market and sell Dartstone brewery after two years

year	*cash flow (£m)	discount factor	present value (£m)
1	0.0000	0.8696	0.0000
2	0.0000	0.7561	0.0000
3	0.4000	0.6575	0.2630
4	0.4000	0.5718	0.2287
5	0.4000	0.4972	0.1989
6	0.4000	0.4323	0.1729
7	0.4000	0.3759	0.1504
8	0.4000	0.3269	0.1308
9	0.4000	0.2843	0.1137
10	0.4000	0.2472	0.0989

present value of 10-year investment: 1.3573
less investment: 0.0000
net present value (£m):   1.3573
*Residual values have been ignored for simplicity

The sale of the Dartstone brewery after two years at £1.5m would be worth £1.5m x 0.7561 or £1.1341m (discounted at 15%). Therefore the present value of investment under poor market conditions and the sale of Dartstone brewery would be:

sale of brewery site (PV):	1.1341
operational savings (PV):	1.3573
poor-market cash flow (PV):	3.0113
present value of 10-year investment (£m):	5.5027

Taking the original investment of £9m into account, gives an NPV of -3.4973 £m. Thus, in a poor market, selling the Dartstone brewery would be better than keeping it even though it would merely be reducing the loss. The negative sign of the NPVs indicate that in poor market conditions the Dartstone option would be risky, but even in a strong market the NPV is only weakly positive.

Table 7.2 summarizes the discounted cash flows for strategy B: fast food outlets. If the outlets are not successful and they are sold after 3 years, they will have produced income of (0.2609 + 0.2268 + 0.1973) = 0.6850 £m. If market conditions are good, the sale price is estimated at £1.5m which has a present value of (1.5 x 0.6575) = 0.9863 £m. Under bad market conditions, the estimated sale price of £1m would have a present value of 0.6575 £m.

sale of outlets under good market conditions:

income over 3 years:	0.6850
selling price:	0.9863
present value (£m):	1.6713

sale of outlets under bad market conditions:

income over 3 years:	0.6850
selling price:	0.6575
present value (£m):	1.3425

The discounted cash flows for strategy C: acquire Midland Breweries are shown in Table 7.3. If the Bodmin brewery were sold at the end of year 1 for an estimated £2.5m, the present value of the sale would be (2.5 x 0.8696) = 2.1740 £m. This value together with operational savings of 3.1119 £m gives a PV of 5.2859 £m.

(a) high demand for Midland beers/retain Bodmin brewery:
present value: 8.9059 £m

(b) high demand for Midland beers/sell Bodmin brewery:
present value: (8.9059 + 5.2859)   14.1918 £m

(c) low demand for Midland beers/retain Bodmin brewery:
present value: 5.6464 £m

(d) low demand for Midland beers/sell Bodmin brewery:
present value: (5.6464 + 5.2859)   10.9323 £m

Table 7.2 Discounted cash flows for Strategy B: fast food outlets

Scenario 1: if successful and 50 outlets retained

year	cash flow (£m)	discount factor	present value (£m)
1	1.0000	0.8696	0.8696
2	1.1000	0.7561	0.8317
3	1.2100	0.6575	0.7956
4	1.3310	0.5718	0.7611
5	1.4641	0.4972	0.7280
6	1.6105	0.4323	0.6962
7	1.7716	0.3759	0.6659
8	1.9487	0.3269	0.6370
9	2.1436	0.2843	0.6094
10	2.3579	0.2472	0.5829

present value of 10-year investment: 7.1774
less investment: (4.0000)
net present value (£m):   3.1774

Scenario 2: if successful and extra 50 outlets installed

Year	1st 50 cash-flow (£m)	2nd 50 cash-flow (£m)	Σ* cash flow	discount factor	present value (£m)
1	1.0000	–	1.0000	0.8696	0.8696
2	1.1000	–	1.1000	0.7561	0.8317
3	1.2100	(3.0000)	(1.7900)	0.6575	(1.1769)
4	1.3310	1.0000	2.3310	0.5718	1.3329
5	1.4641	1.1000	2.5641	0.4972	1.2749
6	1.6105	1.2100	2.8205	0.4323	1.2193
7	1.7716	1.3310	3.1026	0.3759	1.1663
8	1.9487	1.4641	3.4128	0.3269	1.1156
9	2.1436	1.6105	3.7541	0.2843	1.0673
10	2.3579	1.7716	4.1295	0.2472	1.0208

present value of 10-year investment: 8.7215
less investment: (4.0000)
net present value (£m):   4.7215

*Income of £1.21m less purchase of 50 more outlets at £3m gives a cash flow of –£1.79m.

Thus, the larger NPV in the latter case indicates that if the first 50 fast food outlets are successful it would be better to install an extra 50 than simply to retain the initial ones.

Scenario 3: if the market is sluggish but the initial outlets are retained

year	cash flow (£m)	discount factor	present value (£m)
1	0.3000	0.8696	0.2609
2	0.3000	0.7561	0.2268
3	0.3000	0.6575	0.1973
4	0.3000	0.5718	0.1715
5	0.3000	0.4972	0.1492
6	0.3000	0.4323	0.1297
7	0.3000	0.3759	0.1128
8	0.3000	0.3269	0.0981
9	0.3000	0.2843	0.0853
10	0.3000	0.2472	0.0742

present value of 10-year investment: 1.5058
less investment: (4.0000)
net present value (£m):   –2.4942

Table 7.3 Discounted cash flows for Strategy C: acquire Midland Breweries

Scenario 1: if high demand for Midland beers and Bodmin brewery retained

year	cash flow (£m)	discount factor	present value (£m)
1	1.3000	0.8696	1.1305
2	1.5000	0.7561	1.1342
3	1.7000	0.6575	1.1178
4	1.8000	0.5718	1.0292
5	2.0000	0.4972	0.9944
6	2.1000	0.4323	0.9078
7	2.1000	0.3759	0.7894
8	2.1000	0.3269	0.6865
9	2.1000	0.2843	0.5970
10	2.1000	0.2472	0.5191

present value of 10-year investment:	8.9059
less investment:	(10.0000)
net present value (£m):	−1.0941

Scenario 2: if low demand for Midland beers

year	cash flow (£m)	discount factor	present value (£m)
1	0.5000	0.8696	0.4348
2	1.0000	0.7561	0.7561
3	1.1000	0.6575	0.7233
4	1.1000	0.5718	0.6290
5	1.3000	0.4972	0.6464
6	1.4000	0.4323	0.6052
7	1.5000	0.3759	0.5639
8	1.5000	0.3269	0.4904
9	1.5000	0.2843	0.4265
10	1.5000	0.2472	0.3708

present value of 10-year investment:	5.6464
less investment:	(10.0000)
net present value (£m):	−4.3536

Scenario 3: if Bodmin brewery sold

year	cash flow (£m)	discount factor	present value £m)
1	0.0000	0.8696	0.0000
2	0.7500	0.7561	0.5671
3	0.7500	0.6575	0.4931
4	0.7500	0.5718	0.4289
5	0.7500	0.4972	0.3729
6	0.7500	0.4323	0.3242
7	0.7500	0.3759	0.2819
8	0.7500	0.3269	0.2452
9	0.7500	0.2843	0.2132
10	0.7500	0.2472	0.1854

present value of 10-year investment:	3.1119
less investment:	0.0000
net present value (£m):	3.1119

STEP 7 EVALUATION

Evaluation seeks to draw meaning from the data emanating from the modelling stage. What the data mean relates to the client-set's world-view: what do Alan Walker and his colleagues on Redwood's board make of all the PV data for the three strategies and various options within them, taking uncertainty into account?

Estimates had already been made for the likelihood of certain outcomes occurring if a particular strategy were to be followed. In order to estimate the effects of such uncertainties on present values, the Axis consultant first constructed a decision analysis tree (as in Fig. 7.7) to clarify the relationship between the strategic options.

In Fig. 7.7, reading from the root on the left, each square represents the client's decision or choice of action in the options which follow on the right of the square. Each circle represents a point of uncertainty in the possibilities which follow to the right of the circle. For example, tracing the Dartstone option, the chances of a strong market are judged to be no better than 50/50. If the market is strong, Redwoods would almost certainly keep Dartstone's brewery (i.e. assume probability of 1.0). If the market is weak, Redwoods could either retain or sell Dartstone's brewery. Each path would produce different financial outcomes.

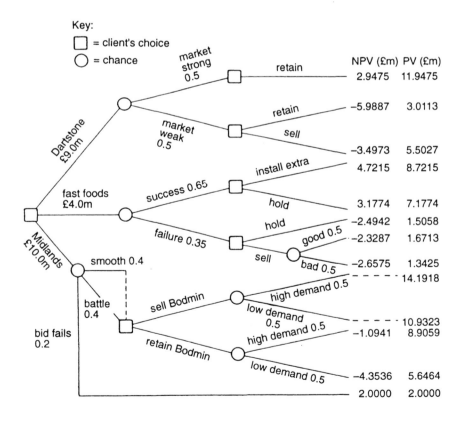

Fig. 7.7 Decision analysis tree for the Redwood strategy options.

The next step is to calculate the expected values (EVs) for each likely pathway or combination as follows:

EXPECTED VALUES FOR STRATEGY A: ACQUIRE DARTSTONE TAVERNS

The estimated chance of the holiday market remaining strong is 50%. Thus, the expected value of the Dartstone investment under strong market conditions would be 0.5 x the cash flow PV:

(a) expected value (strong market):
0.5 x 11.9475 = 5.9738 (£m)

(b) expected value (weak market/retain Dartstone brewery):
0.5 x 3.0113 = 1.5057 (£m)

(c) expected value (weak market/sell Dartstone brewery):
0.5 x 5.5027 = 2.7514 (£m)

Option 1: acquire Dartstone and retain its brewery

expected value (a + b):	7.4795
less investment cost:	(9.0000)
expected value of option (£m).	−1.5205

Option 2: acquire Dartstone and sell its brewery if necessary

expected value (a + c):	8.7252
less investment cost:	(9.0000)
expected value of option (£m):	−0.2748

Thus, the Dartstone acquisition appears to be a loss-making venture.

EXPECTED VALUES FOR STRATEGY B: FAST FOOD OUTLETS

If failure occurs, the expected value on selling is 0.5 x (1.6713 + 1.3425) = 1.5069 £m. This suggests that selling would be only marginally better than retaining the outlets (1.5058 £m).

Option 1: if successful install more outlets/if unsuccessful then sell

expected value: (8.7215 x 0.65) + (1.5069 x 0.35) =	6.1964
less investment cost:	4.0000
expected value of option (£m):	2.1964

Option 2: if successful hold position/if unsuccessful then sell

expected value: (7.1774 x 0.65) + (1.5069 x 0.35) = 5.1927
less investment cost: 4.0000

expected value of option (£m):   1.1927

EXPECTED VALUES FOR STRATEGY C: ACQUIRE MIDLAND BREWERIES

Option 1: sell Bodmin brewery

expected value: 0.5 (14.1918 + 10.9323) = 12.5620
operational savings + selling price: 5.2859

expected all-up value (£m):   17.8479

expected value (smooth takeover):
0.4 (17.8479 – 10) = 3.1392 £m

expected value (competitive takeover):
0.4 (17.8479 – 15) = 1.1392 £m

expected value of option 1: 3.1392 + 1.1392 = 4.2784 £m

Option 2: retain Bodmin brewery

expected value: 0.5 (8.9059 + 5.6464) = 7.2762 £m

expected value (smooth takeover):
0.4 (7.2762 – 10) = –1.0895 £m

expected value (competitive takeover):
0.4 (7.2762 – 15) = –3.0895 £m

expected value of option 2: –1.0895 – 3.0895 = –4.1790 £m

Thus, option 2 with its negative value is poor in comparison with option 1.

The probability of the bid failing is 1.0 – (0.4 + 0.4) = 0.2. In the event of such a failure, the expected value of the capital gain of £2m on Redwood shares is 0.2 x 2.0 = 0.4 £m.

Thus, the overall EV of the Midland bid strategy is:
(4.2784 + 0.4) = 4.6784 £m

The Axis analyst discussed these preliminary figures with Alan Walker and his colleagues to gauge their general reactions. He showed them the results of 'sensitivity analysis'. For example, all the previous computations had assumed a hurdle rate of 15%. What if interest rates rocketed? Using his computer spreadsheet, he showed the effects of various changes in basic assumptions in the model. He also wanted to get some rule-of-thumb indications of how they would rate the three strategies on qualitative aspects. He asked them to score the following from 1 to 10 (1 = bad; 10 = good):

- fit with consumer taste;

- pay-back period;

- fit with Redwood identity (borrowing history, brewing history, traditions, culture etc.);

- fit with Redwood's desired image (solid local employer, traditional but with dynamic edge, change to meet opportunities and not for its own sake);

- perceived risk (probability of damaging outcome, effects of rise in interest rates, consequences of poor return).

Table 7.4 summarizes the client-set's qualitative scores:

Table 7.4 Client-Set's qualitative scores for the three strategies

strategy	consumer demand	pay back	identity	image	perceived risk	total score
A: Dartstone	5	3	6	6	5	25
B: Fast food	7	7	3	5	4	26
C: Midland	6	3	5	8	4	26

For the final evaluation, the consultant drew up a table for comparing each option as follows (Table 7.5):

Table 7.5 Comparison of performance of each strategy

	Assessment measure	
Strategy	Quantitative (EV)	Qualitative (total score)
Buy Dartstone option 1: retain brewery	−1.5205	25
option 2: sell brewery	−0.2748	
Fast Foods option 1:	2.1964	26
option 2:	1.1927	
Buy Midland option 1: sell Bodmin	4.2784 ⎫ 4.6784	26
option 2: retain Bodmin	−4.1790 ⎭ combined	

STEP 8 MAKING A CHOICE

The Axis analyst reported back once again to Alan Walker and his colleagues with his findings and the summary assessment table. Although the overall qualitative score for the Dartstone option was roughly the same as for the other two, on financial grounds this acquisition would result in a loss even if Dartstone's brewery were sold. Strategy A was eliminated.

The fast-food strategy is a strong contender financially. The investment required is a lot less and the pay-back period shorter than for the Midland acquisition. However, such a move would take Redwood into unfamiliar territory with commercial hazards and risks they know little about. Fast-food represented an uncomfortable fit with Redwood's identity and desired image.

On purely financial grounds, the best bet appeared to be to buy Midland Breweries and then sell their own Bodmin brewery. Such a move would also be well in keeping with Redwood's world-view, traditions and expertise. It would take them from minor to middle league in the brewing industry. Once this venture had settled, Redwood could always reconsider a fast-food operation.

Thus, the choice was not made on a 'bottom line' basis alone, although clearly financial considerations are very important. In the event of, say, the fast-food strategy indicating better expected values than the Midland strategy, there would be nothing to stop the client-set still choosing Midland simply because it fits their world-view and instincts more closely.

STEP 9 IMPLEMENTATION

Once the Midland strategy had been decided, Alan Walker set about the task of raising finance to see the acquisition through. His task was greatly helped by the facts, figures and general understanding gained during the three months' Axis study.

DRILLCORP – ESTABLISHING EFFECTIVE MANAGEMENT SYSTEMS IN AN OFFSHORE DRILLING CONTRACTOR

BACKGROUND

The 1970s and 1980s saw unprecedented exploration and production activity in the North Sea for offshore oil and gas. In simple terms, oil and gas field operators such as BP, Shell and Agip hire drilling contractors to carry out test drills in likely locations seeking oil or gas in quantities large enough to warrant extraction. Successful wells are capped off until the operator decides to exploit the find, at which time the skeleton of a production installation is floated to the spot and constructed ready for production.

Most drilling installations are not fixed but are mobile offshore drilling units (MODUs), in the form of either jack-ups (whose feet rest on the sea bed) or semi-submersibles which float in anchored positions. MODUs are much smaller than production installations and typically have a crew of about thirty whereas a production rig may have several hundred.

The drilling business is very competitive and also cyclical. There are periods such as 1992–1994 when demand for drilling is low and contractors may have half or more of their rigs laid up. The drilling business is also hazardous, whether from gas kick-backs and sour gas (hydrogen sulphide – H_2S) release during drilling or from storms during towage. The Piper Alpha disaster in 1988 resulted in new regulations in the UK, Holland and Norway requiring all offshore operators and drilling contractors to have adequate 'safety management systems' and setting these up added considerably to contractors' overhead costs. 'Quality management systems' have also become more or less essential in the drilling market world-wide, not only to ensure improvement in management performance but also as a pre-qualification to obtain contracts from discerning operators. Effective 'management systems' have thus become a high priority for drilling contractors.

Drillcorp, like most offshore contractors, was a well-established company which ran 'lean-and-mean' with no over-manning. A paternalistic culture reigned and it was common to find managers and rig crews who had been with the company for many years. The company prided itself on the ability of a roughneck or roustabout to rise to the highest level. Formal qualifications outside the drilling industry were few although some newer recruits had degrees. Experience was highly valued and paperwork was anathema. There was a strong sense of camaraderie and very little evidence of 'them-and-us' divisions – indeed self-preservation in the dangerous setting of drilling work demanded strong cohesive teams.

Despite Drillcorp's good track record and respect in the industry, it had become clear to the directors that in order to thrive in an increasingly tough world market the company would have to become more formal and more professional in how it managed itself. A systems consultant was appointed to lead the development.

STEP 1 GROUNDWORK

The consultant undertook an initial study of Drillcorp which entailed structured interviews with directors and shore-based managers and with offshore installation managers (OIMs), rig masters, barge engineers, drilling managers and crews on a sample of drilling installations in the North Sea. The essential activities and processes of the drilling business were studied, both onshore and offshore. Drillcorp's existing management methods and assumptions were noted, as were the world-views of the various groups within the company.

STEP 2 AWARENESS AND UNDERSTANDING

The results of the groundwork showed that there was a generally shared world-view about the need continually to strive for improved performance and competitiveness and that this would inevitably require improved management. Drillcorp people were all team players. They were used to open discussions and debate at daily 'toolbox' meetings on the rigs or at weekly management meetings. Although reservations were

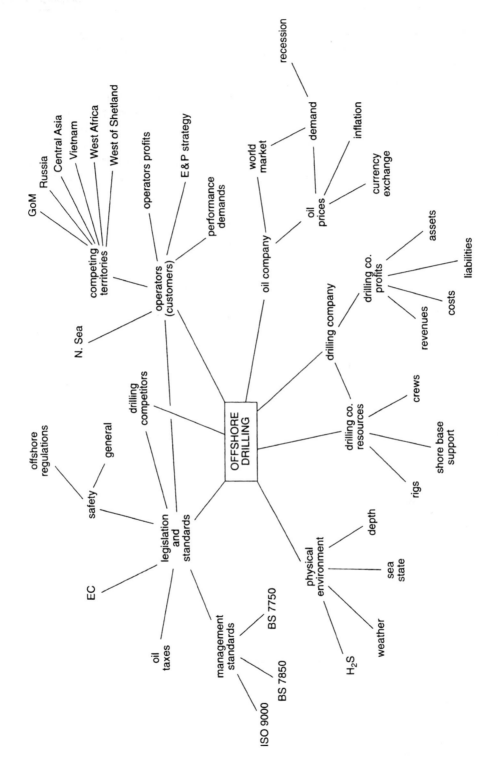

Fig 7.8 Spray diagram of offshore drilling.

expressed about whether the results of the consultant's study would mean 'more paperwork and less action', as hard-nosed pragmatists they accepted that changes were necessary. A number of recent instances of projects getting into a mess, inability to answer straightforward customer queries easily and stocks of vital equipment at shore-base running out at critical moments had convinced everyone of the need for better organization and procedures. Fig. 7.8 is a spray diagram of the offshore drilling situation.

The shared world-view was both a help and a hindrance. Although everyone agreed about the need for change, they found it much harder to accept that a new approach would also require changes in some long-held beliefs and attitudes. A new approach to management could not be expected to be effective without changes in two basic aspects of Drillcorp culture, namely a belief that experience was the best teacher and formal training was a necessary evil, and an acceptance that time pressures were not a good reason for managers not managing their time – or as one person commented 'We don't have time to manage our time!'

The consultant formed the view that although it was clear that a new approach to management was required and the board were committed to it, formal problem-solving would not be adequate. Too many variables were operating in a changing environment. New management arrangements would not only have to be functionally adequate but would also have to deal effectively with issues such as perceptions of time, the value of training, the adequacy of measures of performance etc.

Since the perceived problem and issues related to everything that Drillcorp was doing, the consultant decided that a 'company management system' was a particularly fruitful area to address. A potential system was derived entitled: 'the Drillcorp company management system to provide efficient and effective application of company resources so that:

- operating costs are reduced and the company remains competitive and profitable;
- the company meets performance demands of customers'.

At first iteration, the 'company management system' was separated as in Fig. 7.9.

From the separation in Fig. 7.9, it was possible to construct a system map as in Fig. 7.10.

The board's overall objective of efficient and effective management was influenced by a number of factors under their control:

- finances;
- skill resources and competent personnel;
- time made available;
- information;
- organizing and planning;
- standards and performance criteria.

Components in the SYSTEM	*Components in the environment*
Policy and strategy	Product market
board	customers
shore-based senior managers	drilling competitors
objectives	world E&P market
	oil prices
Resources	new E&P territories
	management standards
offshore personnel	
onshore personnel	Economy
experience	
skills	inflation
information	industrial demand
	currency values
Organizing and planning	
	Legislation
operating functions	
contract schedules	safety and environment
projects	oil revenue taxation
audit schedules	
	Physical environment
Operating functions	
	sour gas fields
Drilling operations	weather
Engineering/asset management	sea state
MODUs	sea depth
shore premises and facilities	
Marketing, sales and contracts	
Stores and logistics	
Finance	
Safety, quality, environment	
Administration	
Performance monitoring/control	
performance standards/criteria	
methods	
Audit and review	

Fig. 7.9 Separation of a Key SYSTEM Relevant to Drillcorp's Problem

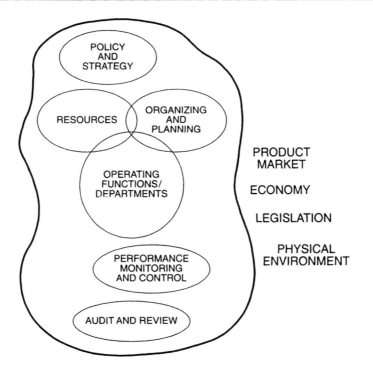

Fig. 7.10 System map of the Drillcorp management system.

Fig. 7.11 shows how these influences operate.

Reflecting on the analysis so far, the consultant took the view that the dynamic variables of costs and competitiveness were linked causally to that of management efficiency and effectiveness, as in Fig. 7.12. Absence of control (i.e. negative) loops indicates the necessity of ensuring management efficiency and effectiveness.

STEP 3 OBJECTIVES AND CONSTRAINTS

Although the ultimate objectives were to increase sales and profitability, the overall objectives of the company management system were to improve contract competitiveness and customer satisfaction through:

- reduced operating costs;
- competitive tender prices;
- improved work quality (reliability, accuracy, fewer operational problems etc.);
- reduced time to complete contracts.

The objectives hierarchy is expressed diagramatically in Fig. 7.13.

Constraints included resources available such as skilled and experienced manpower, time, managerial commitment and demand for drilling from oil and gas operators.

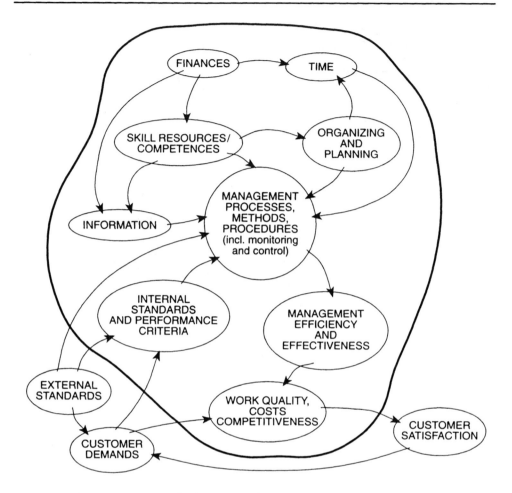

Fig. 7.11 Diagram of influences on Drillcorp's management objectives.

STEP 4 STRATEGIES TO MEET OBJECTIVES

The consultant identified three possible strategies for developing an efficient and effective company management SYSTEM:

(A): Develop the management SYSTEM and obtain certification to the relevant international standard, with periodic re-audits.

(B): Develop the management SYSTEM using relevant international standards as a guide, but without third-party certification.

(C): Develop the management SYSTEM from first principles using Drillcorp's own internal standards, with third-party certification as a reserve option.

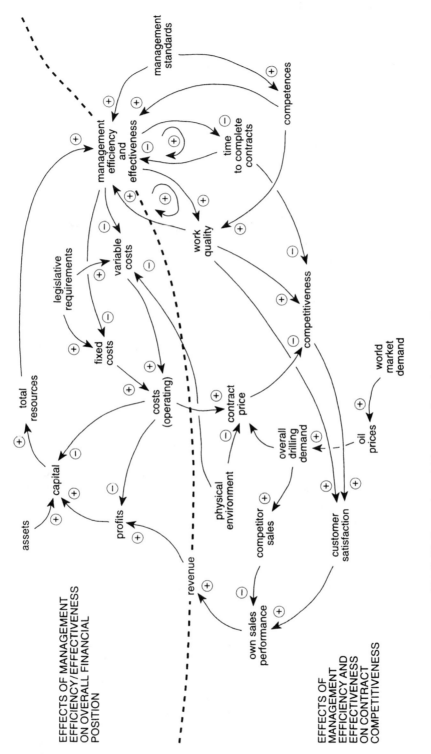

EFFECTS OF MANAGEMENT
EFFICIENCY/EFFECTIVENESS
ON OVERALL FINANCIAL
POSITION

EFFECTS OF
MANAGEMENT
EFFICIENCY AND
EFFECTIVENESS
ON CONTRACT
COMPETITIVENESS

Fig. 7.12 Dynamic variables operating relative to Drillcorp's management system.

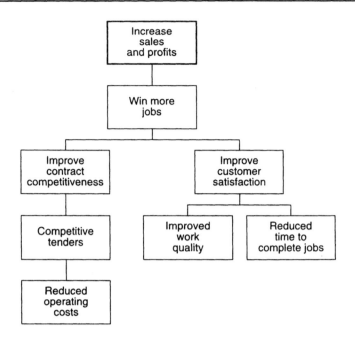

Fig. 7.13 Objectives hierarchy for Drillcorp's management system development.

STRATEGY A: ISO 9000 CERTIFICATION

This strategy would involve Drillcorp obtaining the services of an accredited third-party agency who would examine the company's management SYSTEM, providing consultancy advice and assistance to develop the management system, and finally conducting an audit. The results of the audit would decide whether Drillcorp would be granted an ISO 9000 certificate which would indicate whether the company was deemed to have in place a 'quality management system'.

STRATEGY B: UNCERTIFIED SYSTEM TO ISO 9000 AND BS 7850

Strategy B would involve Drillcorp developing its management SYSTEM using as guides the ISO 9000 standard and British Standard BS 7850: 1992 Total Quality Management. Consultancy assistance might be required.

STRATEGY C: UNCERTIFIED SYSTEM FROM FIRST PRINCIPLES

This strategy would involve Drillcorp in developing its management SYSTEM from first principles and not taking for granted the paradigms built into external standards such a ISO 9000 and BS 7850. Consultancy assistance would almost certainly be required. In the event of subsequent irresistable market demands for evidence of certification, Drillcorp could always apply for certification.

STEP 5 ASSESSMENT MEASURES

In relation to the defined objectives, how well would each of these three strategies perform? What measures could be used to assess performance?

It was judged that quantitative measures should include basic outcome measures of efficiency such as contract tender price (incorporating operating costs, time to complete contracts, and manpower efficiency) in relation to development and maintenance costs of the three strategies. Quantitative measures of effectiveness would include profit margins and quality assurance measures such as equipment reliability, drilling accuracy, damage and accident rates.

Qualitative measures would include the relative realism of the management SYSTEM paradigms implicit or explicit in the three strategies i.e. how well the paradigms represent the real world of organizations and the actual SYSTEM in place. This would be an important measure since some models of management SYSTEMS are more complete in real-world terms than are others. Other measures were: fit with customer worldviews, and fit with Drillcorp world-view. For example, customers' perceptions of what constitutes a good management SYSTEM would be important as would Drillcorp's priorities of operating in a 'no frills' lean-and-mean market.

STEP 6 MODELLING

Three typical contract specifications were used from recent jobs – one in a sour gas field, one in an H_2S-free field and one in deep water west of Shetland. Modelling of present values and NPVs was judged to be inappropriate to these cost-efficiency data. A relatively simple financial model based on costs and savings was used to generate comparative data as summarised in Table 7.6.

By dividing the costs by the contract savings for each, the following pay-back data were obtained as in Table 7.7.

Table 7.6 Costs and savings data for Strategies A, B and C

Financial element	Strategy		
	A	B	C
Development costs (2 years)			
staff costs	£75,000	£50,000	£75,000
consultants	£100,000	£35,000	£50,000
	£175,000	£85,000	£125,000
Maintenance costs (5 years)	£150,000	£75,000	£75,000
Overall costs	£325,000	£160,000	£200,000
Estimated savings on contract price	5%	6%	7.5%
Sour gas, savings on £2m	£100,000	£120,000	£150,000
No H_2S, savings on £1.5m	£75,000	£90,000	£112,500
Deep water, savings on £2.2m	£110,000	£132,000	£150,000

Table 7.7 Pay-back ratios (numbers of contracts to pay for strategy costs)

| | Strategy | | |
Contract Type	A	B	C
Sour gas	3.25	1.33	1.33
No H$_2$S	4.33	1.78	1.78
Deep water	2.95	1.21	1.33
Average number of contracts before payback	3.51	1.44	1.48

From these data, it can be seen that all three strategies offer a fairly quick return, although strategies B and C are more favourable. B and C would have paid for themselves on the first two contracts whereas A would take 3–5 contracts depending on the type of contract.

STEP 7 EVALUATION

The costs and savings summary was then discussed with the Drillcorp client-set. At first glance, it would appear that strategy A provides a weaker financial return but many factors are involved. The assumption that greater savings on contract price would be achieved in B and C was based on the fact that certified schemes represent a less complete model of a human activity SYSTEM and hence fewer variables are accounted for. Actual quality assurance is likely to be better with a management SYSTEM developed from first principles by the company to meet its precise needs, as in strategy C. This statement may seem at odds with the titles of the relevant standards which refer to 'quality management' or 'total quality management'. The fact remains, however, that these standards are non-holistic and, based on a simple input-process-output-feedback model, refer to only some important parts of management systems. They do not cover important factors such as world-views, power relations in the organization, or the many factors in the organization's environment – any one of which may be pivotal to success.

Nevertheless, Drillcorp recognized that strategy A would be helpful in winning contracts from those operators whose world-view incorporated a belief in ISO 9000 as a mark of supplier quality. However, many operators were divided internally about the real value of such certification. Some departments had very bad experiences with certificated suppliers whose actual quality on the contract turned out to be very poor (see comments above) whereas others, publicly at least, were committed.

By nature, Drillcorp was very independent and preferred to be in control of itself. The idea of 'cook-book consultants' and third-party auditors 'crawling all over us' as in strategy A did not fit the Drillcorp world-view. If consultants were to be used, Drillcorp wanted to feel comfortable about the consultants' allegiances. Would they be truly independent management consultants working in Drillcorp's best interests or would they be motivated by easy pickings from offering a prescriptive formula which might suit the consultants but not meet the company's needs?

The client-set was asked to score the following factors from 1 to 10 (1 = bad, 10 = good):

• estimated contract savings;

• pay back period (based on numbers of contracts);

• actual quality assurance provided (equipment reliability and availability, drilling accuracy, safety and loss prevention);

• realism and completeness of management SYSTEM model;

• fit with customer world-views;

• fit with Drillcorp world-view.

The client-set's qualitative scores are summarised in Table 7.8.

Table 7.9 summarizes the comparison of the three strategies for the final evaluation.

STEP 8 MAKING A CHOICE

From Table 7.9, the client-set decided that strategy A was too unfavourable on both financial and qualitative grounds to warrant further consideration. Strategy B was slightly more favourable than C on pay-back but slightly less favourable on the overall qualitative score. Although comparable, the client-set felt that strategy B would put them in a kind of limbo – following the prescription of the standards but not gaining recognition for it. It would also leave them not feeling confident that the management system was adequate despite having followed 'the formula'.

Table 7.8 Drillcorp client-set's scoring of indicators

Strategy	Savings	Pay-Back	QA	Management system model	Customer world-views	Drillcorp world-view	Total score
A: ISO 9000	7	5	5	4	8	5	34
B: Non-cert	8	8	6	4	7	7	40
C: First Principles	8	8	7	7	6	7	43

Table 7.9 Overall comparison of drillcorp's potential strategies

Strategy	Assessment measure	
	Quantitative (pay-back ratio)	Qualitative total score
ISO 9000 certification	3.51	34
ISO 9000/BS 7850 non-certification	1.44	40
Own system, first principles	1.48	43

On balance, it was decided to adopt strategy C which would develop a management SYSTEM which they all 'owned' and which they felt would be more complete and realistic than external standards required. There would always be the option to apply for ISO 9000 certification at a later date if a commercial advantage could be gained from so doing.

STEP 9 IMPLEMENTATION

Once the strategy had been decided, the client-set began the task of organizing, planning and resourcing its implementation.

SUMMARY

The two cases studied in this chapter have shown how markedly different kinds of perceived problem may be tackled using a HARD SYSTEMS methodology. In the Redwood Breweries case, the application was in the realms of strategic planning and decision-making covering a range of uncertainties about current and future markets, business trends and strategic choices. Here, a HARD SYSTEMS approach enabled uncertainties to be rationalized and options to be clarified by quantification i.e. a fog-clearing exercise. In the Drillcorp case, HARD SYSTEMS methodology helped decisionmaking about the best strategy for developing an efficient and effective management SYSTEM, again using quantification but more explicitly tempered by qualitative judgements. The three Drillcorp strategies were not markedly different in their character but were likely to have different impacts on the intended results.

SOFT SYSTEMS METHODOLOGY

The objectives of this chapter are to:

- Revisit the concept of SOFT SYSTEMS thinking introduced in Part 1 of the book.
- Discuss further a SOFT SYSTEMS view of problem situations in notional human activity systems
- Demonstrate, with the aid of case examples, the basic SOFT SYSTEMS methodology (SSM).

INTRODUCTION

Chapter 4 introduced the basic seven-stage form of the SOFT SYSTEMS methodology (SSM), pioneered by Checkland (1981) in the 1970s and 1980s and from which a more advanced methodology has now arisen (Checkland and Scholes 1990). In this chapter, the basic methodology is reviewed and some of its trickier aspects, in particular the CATWOE test and conceptual modelling, are examined in more detail. Refer back to Fig. 4.4 in Chapter 4 for an overview of the basic SSM steps. Refer to Checkland and Scholes (1990) for an authoritative exposition of the developed form of SSM.

STEP 1 DATA COLLECTION

Collecting information about the 'mess' follows the same kind of approach as data collection in the 'hard systems' and 'systems failures' methodologies. Interviewing key figures is usually a necessary part of the process but particular attention should be paid to expressions of dissatisfaction and concern. Equally, watch out for signs that a key figure is apparently satisfied or unconcerned whereas other key figures are not. Often apparent lack of concern about a problem situation may be contributing

---

NB SYSTEM, HARD SYSTEM, SOFT SYSTEM and SYSTEM FAILURE in small capitals refer to metaphorical and perceptual constructs.

to a 'mess' or system of problems which defies solution simply by tackling each one separately.

There are no hard and fast rules for deciding who are key figures. Typically, the client or 'problem owner' will provide background information, and may offer an opinion as to what is wrong. Certain individuals may be cited as being involved and these can be assumed to be key figures. However, as the interview programme develops, further key figures may be identified. How many are interviewed depends on the analyst's resources and time constraints.

Interviews should be non-directive. Ask open-ended questions which start with phrases such as 'Tell me about...', 'Why...?', 'What...?' and so on. Avoid leading questions, which presume what the answers will be. Interviewees often expect some kind of instant diagnosis, and commentary on the situation should be kept as little and as neutral as possible. The analyst's views should only be revealed at steps 5 and 6 of the methodology. All interviews, and the analyst's notes on them, must remain confidential; this is a basic tenet of all consultancy and research.

Documentary information may also be useful. Typical examples are minutes of meetings, reports, memoranda and correspondence. To a large extent the analyst has to rely on what key figures consider to be important information. Sometimes documents that would be invaluable to the task are considered too sensitive to be revealed. The analyst just has to accept this inconvenience unless the client considers that all relevant documents are to be made available. This would be one of the negotiating points when agreeing to do a study using SSM.

At the end of data collection, the analyst should have available sufficient information about the unstructured problem situation to enable analysis to proceed.

Exercise 8.1
What clues to the existence of a 'problem' amenable to SSM would you look for in the collected information?

STEP 2 ANALYSIS

Analysis begins by drawing a rich picture of the messy situation. A rich picture is the analyst's own interpretive 'snapshot' of the 'mess'. Remember, a rich picture is not a system diagram. Although loose boundaries may be drawn around parts of the picture for ease of understanding, such boundaries should not attempt to represent SYSTEMS or SUB-SYSTEMS (see p. 82).

The technique of constructing a rich picture is described in 'building up a rich picture' in Chapter 4. There are several examples of rich pictures in Chapters 2, 4, 9 and 11.

From the rich picture, the analyst should be able to identify a number of issues, and perhaps one or two primary task areas, which seem important to the situation. Clues about these are to be seen in symbols and expressions of clashes, pressure and uncertainty.

PROBLEMS IN THE HEALTH SERVICE – A CASE STUDY

Several attempts to reorganize the National Health Service (NHS) in the United Kingdom have been made in recent years. From 1974 to 1989, a three-tier organization of regional, area and district health bodies operated. The Griffiths Report in the 1980s sought to introduce general management so that clinicians were more accountable for their efficiency and management of resources. Accountability and resource management were also high on the agenda of the 1990 restructuring of the NHS whereby the previous large district health authorities became small 'purchasing authorities' for clinical services, which were required to bid for contracts in competition with other providers elsewhere. Hospital managements now have much greater local autonomy than before.

Despite the competitive climate in hospitals, multi-disciplinary teams are supposed to function so as to achieve cohesion and a unity of purpose both in principle and in practice. This intention has not always been met. At district and hospital levels, for example, it is not uncommon today to find numerous value clashes: nurses versus doctors, clinical staff versus admin. staff, consultants versus everybody, everybody versus the Department of Health. Although health care is the assumed, and often stated, common purpose of all these factions, it is apparent that they often pursue different and conflicting objectives. In any event, health officials at almost every level complain about poor performance. A particularly graphic example is the account of the Normansfield Hospital Crisis in 1976 given by Victor Bignell and Joyce Fortune in *Understanding Systems Failures* (1984). The crisis in question was a strike by nursing staff that was 'unprecedented in the history of the National Health Service.' The account reveals a classic 'soft systems' problem situation with an escalatory spiral of conflicting values, objectives, clashes and communications problems which led ultimately to organizational failure – a strike. More recently, examples have been cited of particular health authorities in which 'health service officials are resigning and swarming to leave' and managers are 'broken and suffering from battle fatigue'. Clinical staff have also felt badly treated in terms of pay and conditions. For example, it was not until 1995 that the government agreed to institute a maximum 80-hour week for junior hospital doctors.

From a rich picture of the above situation, the following issues and 'problems' related to the primary task of providing patient-care might be derived:

issues	*primary task-related areas*
leadership	hospital administration
decision-making processes	clinical support
morale and motivation	ancillary services
authority and power	
managerial competence	
industrial relations	
coping with change	

STEP 3 RELEVANT SYSTEMS AND ROOT DEFINITIONS

As outlined in Chapter 4, steps 1 and 2 deal with what the analyst perceives to be happening in the real world – 'what is'. Step 3 requires a complete shift of thinking to the consideration of hypothetical or notional systems.

The first task in this step is to dream up relevant SYSTEMS for the list of issues and primary task areas. In the previous Health Service example, there are probably too many issues and primary task areas to carry. For example, as some issues are clearly related, the analyst could choose to coalesce some of them. Aim for three or four issues and one or two primary task areas.

Who decides what is relevant? Ultimately it will be the actors when the analyst debates with them in step 6. However, in step 3 the analyst must use his or her own judgement. As noted in Chapter 4, subtlety is required in naming the relevant SYSTEMS. In particular, focusing on 'obvious' input-process-output ideas should be avoided as these are likely to fix the analyst's thoughts back in the real world. To quote the Lucrative case from Chapter 4, 'a system for taking editorial copy plus advertisements and converting them into marketable yearbooks' is so real-world and unimaginative that its value in stimulating insights is virtually nil.

In the Lucrative case in Chapter 4, two relevant SYSTEMS were identified which can now be called RS1 and RS2. RS1 started as 'an editorial and advertising reconciling system'. Such a title is a short-hand description and it needs to be defined so that it makes a bit more sense. The author's first attempt at the Root Definition (RD1) of RS1 was 'a system to ensure that editorial decisions reflect the best interests of the publishing house'.

A root definition needs to be adequate, otherwise difficulty may be encountered with later steps in the methodology. There are two complementary ways of testing whether a root definition is adequate. The first is to assess it critically by examining it for ambiguities, woolliness and implicit assumptions which may be questionable. The result of this first iteration of RD1 was 'a system to be operated by Lucrative's managing director to ensure that editorial decisions reflect the objectives of the publishing house in terms of financial viability and profitability and in terms of reputation in the marketplace among purchasers and advertisers'. RS1 was also modified to 'a system for making cost-effective editorial decisions'.

The second test is more structured – the CATWOE test. CATWOE stands for:

- customers;

- actors;

- transformation;

- *weltanschauung(en)*;

- owner(s);

- environment.

Exercise 8.2
Define the terms which make up the CATWOE mnemonic.

If the CATWOE elements in the root definition can be identified clearly and unambiguously, then it has passed the test with flying colours. However, do not worry if you do not achieve this paragon. What is important is that you check and probe the root definition and, if necessary, justify to yourself why a CATWOE element is absent.

Applying the CATWOE test to the Lucrative RD1 (first iteration):

- Customers: purchasers and advertisers explicit; editorial staff, MD implicit.

- Actors: managing director explicit, although would he really be operating such a system?; other staff implicit.

- Transformation: editorial decision-making (see Fig. 4.5 in Chapter 4); the process is *not* 'converting editorial copy plus advertisements into marketable yearbooks'.

- *Weltanschauungen*: there is really only one world-view that is relevant here – the view that editorial decisions have to take account of economic circumstances and generally satisfy the legitimate interests of the system's customers.

- Owner: the managing director is both 'system owner' and owner in title.

- Environment: RD1 does not explicitly state constraints, but some obvious ones are sources of finance, competitors, bank lending rates, attitudes and changing tastes of purchasers, advertiser behaviour.

The second relevant system (RS2) in the Lucrative case was 'a system to satisfy the needs of customers'. After iteration, this was modified to 'a system to satisfy the needs of yearbook purchasers' with a root definition (RD2) thus: 'a system owned by Lucrative which aims to satisfy the needs of purchasers of its range of books coupled with a return on investment commensurate with at least maintaining its share of the yearbook/handbook market'.

Exercise 8.3
Critically assess RD2 and apply the CATWOE test to it.

As a result of critical examination, it is now possible to revise RD2 thus: 'a system owned by the managing director and operated by all Lucrative's staff which seeks to satisfy cost-effectively defined needs of purchasers of its range of books, and so at least maintain its defined share of the yearbook/handbook market and thereby secure for Lucrative a defined adequate return on investment, taking into account economic, product, market and labour-market constraints'. RD2 is improving but doubtless it needs further iterative development. The title of RS2 can now be revised to 'a system to satisfy cost-effectively the needs of yearbook purchasers'.

STEP 4 CONCEPTUAL MODELLING

A conceptual model for RD1 was developed in Chapter 4 (see Figs 4.5 and 4.6). Remember that a conceptual model depicts only what the SYSTEM *logically* would have to comprise in order for it to function.

Fig. 8.1 shows a first attempt at constructing a conceptual model of RD2. Note the level of abstraction in the main activities. There is no mention of real-world practical things such as 'set up sales order system on computer' or 'print yearbooks by web-offset litho' or 'send mail shot letters to potential purchasers'. Note also that the number of main activity verbs has been limited to seven deemed to be essential in this case.

TESTING CONCEPTUAL MODELS

Conceptual models have to be tested to see whether they are adequate from a SYSTEMS point of view. Tests are usually based on the formal system paradigm (see Chapter 5)

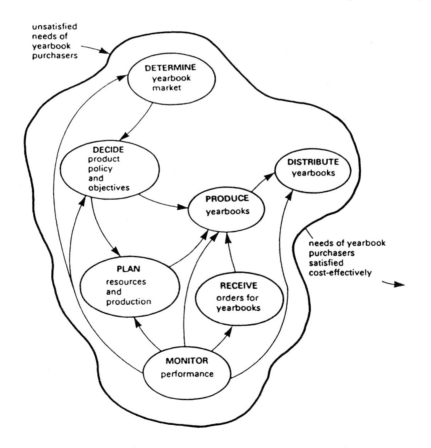

Fig 8.1 A conceptual model of a notional system for satisfying cost-effectively the needs of yearbook purchasers (first iteration).

or the 'formal system model' (Checkland 1981) which may be considered to be closely related to the formal system paradigm. Key questions include the following which are here applied to RD1 and Fig. 4.6 as per the comments in brackets:

a)   Does the model and its root definition suggest a continuous and relevant mission? (Cost-effective editorial decisions are obviously needed as a permanent feature of a publishing house.)

b)   Can performance be measured? (The model includes the establishment of criteria and monitoring activities.)

c)   Is a decision-making activity present? (Yes).

d)   Do any of the main activities comprise sub-systems of back-up activities? (Fairly obviously, they do. For example, in order to 'determine market needs and wants', one would have to: identify markets, research markets, and assess research data.

e)   Do the system components interact?

f)   Does the system interact with an environment? (Assume, for example, cash limits, market size, trade unions, legislation, page space limits etc.)

g)   Does the system have a boundary? (The wider system here is the managing director. Although he owns the system and may be involved in editorial decisions from time to time, the system is essentially operated by other actors, e.g. editorial, advertising, finance staff.)

h)   Can the wider system provide resources? (Assume that the managing director can appoint competent and sufficient staff and provide working accommodation, equipment, stationery etc.)

i)   Can the system be sustained? (The managing director as system owner (and actual owner of the company) is a sufficient power figure to ensure continuity of the system if he so wishes.)

Activity
Carry out the test on the conceptual model of RD2 (Fig. 8.1) and modify it iteratively as appropriate.

Note in test (d) the reference to back-up activities. Identifying these is an important part of expanding a conceptual model. Expansion, testing and modifying is continued until, in the analyst's judgement, the functional content of the notional system has been clarified sufficiently. Fig. 8.2 depicts an expanded version of the conceptual model RD1.

Activity
Expand your conceptual model of RD2 so that it incorporates back-up activities and then test it using the nine point check-list (a to i).

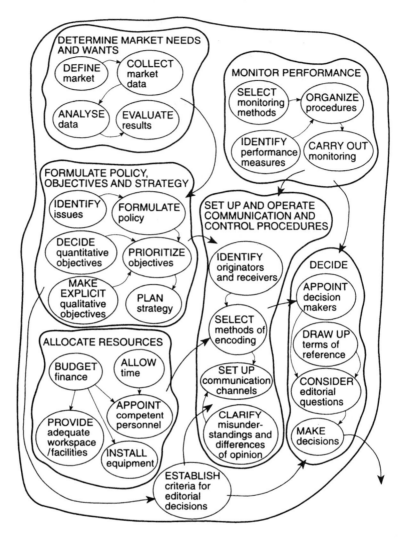

Fig. 8.2 Expanded conceptual model of a notional system for making cost-effective editorial decisions (first iteration) (see Fig. 4.6).

STEP 5 COMPARISONS TO PROVIDE DEBATING AGENDA

As indicated in Fig. 4.4, step 5 in the methodology returns to real-world thinking, but the analyst needs to avoid thinking or expressing him- or herself in terms of real-world practical *solutions*. The aim of the comparison step is to illuminate the problem situation analysed in step 2, for both the analyst and the actors, and not to state or suggest that the analyst now knows what must be done.

In step 5, 'what might be' (conceptual model) is compared with 'what is' (real-world situation from step 2 analysis). There is no single best way of carrying out the comparison. Each analyst develops his or her own approach, and some are more formal than others. One way is to use the conceptual model as a reference and check whether each activity occurs in the real-world situation. If it does, why does it? Who carries it out? Has it always been done? Why is it done like this? Similarly, if it does not occur, why is this so? This approach tends to illuminate activities whose existence or absence in the real-world setting is taken for granted, and therefore whose potential contribution to the problem situation may not be recognized. This approach may be especially useful for issue-based problems.

A second approach is to imagine the conceptual model in operation in the real world and note all the practical implications. Then consider how the same task is actually carried out in the real world. Mismatches and discrepancies should raise important questions. This approach is well suited to 'problems' embedded in primary tasks.

A third approach uses a template method. A conceptual model of what actually happens in the real world is constructed from the rich picture. The activities are derived to follow as closely as possible those of the conceptual model from step 4. By overlaying one model on the other, it should highlight matches and mismatches which can be tabulated for ease of reference.

Whichever approach is adopted, the result should be an agenda for debate with the actors. This agenda is a list of topics covering mismatches, omissions etc. together with 'what?' and 'why?' questions to stimulate the actors' thinking. This agenda still needs to avoid real-world prescriptive solutions.

It may also be useful to show the actors a rich picture of the current situation which is perplexing them. However, if your rich pictures tend to be on the rich side, it would be wise to draw a 'sanitized' version for this purpose. This is a good general rule for rich pictures since there is no value in causing offence to actors who might appear in the rich picture in an unfavourable or ridiculous light. Whether or not you show any rich picture at all is a matter of judgement. Will they be offended? Will they regard rich pictures as expensive 'doodling'? Will you go up or down in their esteem? If in doubt, keep rich pictures to yourself.

STEP 6 DISCUSSING THE AGENDA WITH THE ACTORS

For even experienced analysts, this stage can be the most anxious. The discussion takes the form of a debate with those in key roles, such as client, problem owner and actors identified in the CATWOE test. The important words here are 'discussion' and 'debate'. Analysts who are used to acting as conventional management consultants tend to act out the role of solution provider. In such a role, the analyst possesses 'expert power' grounded in the shared belief that the expert's task is to provide a prescriptive solution to the 'problem'. In SSM, however, the analyst's role is more that of a *therapist*; he or she may well possess considerable expertise and be capable of recommending solutions, but such temptation should be resisted. A debate does not consist of the analyst speaking all the words of wisdom and supine actors soaking it all up.

Nevertheless, actors on the client side may attempt to seduce the analyst into giving his or her solution. This is likely to happen in organizations in which collective rather than individual responsibility is the tradition, or in which 'fighting one's corner and watching one's back' makes buck-passing an endemic disease. Individual actors may feel very uncomfortable with having to address issues on the analyst's agenda for debate, and may prefer to transfer the mental effort back to the analyst. The analyst should be prepared for manoeuvring and attempts to impose control such as: 'Well, *you're* the expert. What's *your* answer?' The analyst is not there to provide practical solutions but to get the actors to examine critically the analyst's conceptual model of a possible future SYSTEM i.e. to work towards agreeing a change from 'what is' to 'what might be'.

The agenda should be organized and expressed in such a way that the analyst's ideas for possible change (stemming from rich picture, root definition, conceptual model and comparison) are not only desirable in system terms but are also compatible with the organization's culture. System desirability is relatively easy to address since much of the work on root definition and modelling, including testing, will have focused on the logical requirements of a notional system. The debate needs to consider among other things whether the analyst's suggestions are deficient or contain logical errors.

Aspects of cultural feasibility have been raised in previous paragraphs in so far as they affect the course of the debate itself. Chapter 4 discussed some of the difficulties surrounding the cultural aspects of proposed changes. Culture as a 'thing' is an easy label to apply but, as a complex and dynamic property of human activity SYSTEMS, it is a rather nebulous and difficult phenomenon to deal with. Although organizational culture can be referred to as if it were a uniform feature of all the people in the organization, sub- and micro-cultures are also usually discernible. Different departments, functions and specialisms have their own tribal interests, values, loyalties, terminology, coded language, attitudes, idiosyncracies etc. which characterize them. The Health Service case study earlier in this chapter provides an example. The analyst needs to recognize cultural diversity within the organization, which may well be represented among the actors in the debate. Cultures serve to protect their members' identities and interests and tend to be slow to change – evolutionary rather than rapid. Quick-fix culture change prescriptions offered by some management consultants are often based on ignorance of the phenomenon.

The analyst should anticipate that, even if actors agree with the systemic desirability of the proposed changes, they might oppose some or all of them for a variety of personal and cultural reasons. If and when this occurs, it is advisable for the analyst to accept the actors' verdict. Organizational culture is not a disease to be cured. By analogy, a therapist's task is not to 'cure the patient' but to help the patient face up to what may be ailing him or her, and to choose whether or not to work towards a better state. If the proposed changes involve changes in cultural aspects, the analyst's task is to sow the seeds in the actors' minds and bring to their attention the slow nature of such changes.

As outlined in Chapter 4, agreed changes will typically fall under the headings of structural, process, policy and cultural changes. If none of the proposed changes relating to a root definition are accepted, for whatever reason, the analyst can proceed with one or more of the other root definitions. If necessary, the analyst can return to the rich picture to identify other relevant systems to work up and debate with the actors.

STEP 7 ACTION FOR CHANGE

By this stage the actors should possess a list of agreed changes, expressed in terms of 'whats' rather than 'hows'. Converting 'whats' into 'hows' could involve formal problem-solving if the options are clear, or could suggest a HARD SYSTEMS approach for more complex matters. In principle, the analyst's task could be complete at the end of step 6, but in practice continuing or follow-up support should be offered. Even if the actors agree to a number of proposed changes and appear to accept their cultural feasibility, hidden agendas may surface after agreement which serve to thwart implementation of the changes. Alternatively, the actors may simply not know how to proceed with practical implementation. Checkland and Scholes (1990) suggest that SSM in its developed form often entails a collaborative relationship between the analyst and actors.

SUMMARY

The objectives of this chapter were to (a) revisit the concept of SOFT SYSTEMS thinking introduced in Part 1 of the book, (b) discuss further a SOFT SYSTEMS view of problem situations in notional human activity systems, and (c) demonstrate, with the aid of case examples, basic SOFT SYSTEMS methodology (SSM).

SSM offers a rational tool for tackling problem situations relating to perceived human activity which is wicked, messy, chaotic or seemingly intractable. Rather than attempting to define 'the problem' and then solving it, SSM identifies issues and primary task areas from which notional systems and conceptual models may be derived. Comparison of these logically defensible systems with the real-world situation provides the basis of debate with the actors, which in essence is a learning process for them. Chapter 9 provides two case studies of the basic methodology.

SUGGESTED ANSWERS TO EXERCISES

8.1 Evidence of a 'problem' amenable to SSM would include: references to 'a mess', 'shambles', 'worry', 'concern', dissatisfaction', 'dispute' etc. and signs of anger, resentment, mistrust and seemingly inexplicable poor performance.

8.2 Customers are those affected by the notional system and are not to be confused with people who buy goods and services (although sometimes they may be).

Actors are the social actors who operate the notional system, i.e. have roles to play in it. Mostly they are role categories and groups, but may include individuals.

Transformation represents the notional system's essential process and is usually quite different from real-world practical processes.

Weltanschauungen are the world-views of actors. Usually this is taken to mean a shared world-view which would be relevant to the notional system.

Owners are power figures who control the notional system and allow its very existence. They are not necessarily owners of the organization or its property.

Environment represents external constraints and influences.

8.3   The main problem with RD2 as it stands is that it has three aims: satisfying purchasers, securing return on investment, and maintaining market share. Each of these objectives is open to various interpretations. For example, what does 'satisfying purchasers' mean exactly? Getting books to them on time? Reducing complaints to a minimum? Responding to readers' suggestions for editorial improvement? It is likely that return on investment will depend on market share.

Applying the CATWOE test to RD2:

Customers: Purchasers explicit, but also Lucrative as a whole

Actors: Explicitly all Lucrative's staff

Transformation: Taking unsatisfied needs of purchasers and satisfying them cost-effectively

Weltanschauung: The view that purchasers' needs have to be met, but within the bounds of economic prudence.

Owners: Explicitly Lucrative's managing director

Environment: Financial resources, interest rates, competitors, labour market (experienced, competent staff may be hard to recruit), advertiser behaviour.

SSM CASE STUDIES

The objectives of this chapter are to demonstrate the application of basic SOFT SYSTEMS methodology through two case studies.

INTRODUCTION

Chapters 4 and 8 laid the groundwork for understanding and using the basic form of SSM. In this chapter, two case studies are presented which demonstrate the practical application of basic SSM. The first case is that of a publishing project that got into a crisis involving finance, staff relations and project management. The second case concerns development of a railway line in which engineering design and operational planning groups in the railway company expressed unease and uncertainty about aspects of the primary task.

NORTHWOOD TRAINING MATERIALS UNIT – A STUDY OF A PROJECT IN CRISIS

STEP 1 DATA COLLECTION

The following is a summary of data collected by the external systems consultant from interviews with staff at the training materials unit, minutes of progress meetings and other relevant documentation.

The year 1983 saw the start of a major training initiative by the Manpower Services Commission (MSC), a government department charged in part with addressing skill shortages in industry and commerce. The MSC and commercial sponsors together set aside multi-million pound 'pump priming' funds to help redress the skill shortage via open learning. Open learning entails the use of courses and learning materials which are made available with very few restrictions in the entry requirements. Typically, open learning materials comprise course workbooks, videos, audiotapes, and assessments. This systems book, for example, is written very much in open learning style.

A large part of the sponsored fund was available for bids by production and/or 'delivery' projects. Many such projects sprang up within existing bona fide educational

NB SYSTEM, HARD SYSTEM, SOFT SYSTEM and SYSTEM FAILURE in small capitals refer to metaphorical and perceptual constructs.

or training organizations. The training materials unit at Northwood College was such an example.

Northwood's training materials project soon found itself in possession of £600 000 'pump priming' money to cover an initial three-year period, at the end of which the project would have to be self-financing.

Northwood College is by tradition dominated by engineering and technology faculties. Malcolm was an ambitious senior lecturer in the engineering faculty and the advent of the open learning initiative provided him with an opportunity to advance his career ambitions. The College's directorate were dyed-in-the-wool traditionalists when it came to education, and did not know the first thing about open learning. Nevertheless, they appreciated the possibility of gaining kudos and 'Brownie points' in the increasingly competitive world of further and higher education; if the sponsors were happy to pay for the experiment, what had the College to lose? Malcolm was allowed to make his bid which was successful but like all grants there were strings attached. The money could only be used for specified purposes and had to be accounted for. Crucially, the money was intended only to fund the initial development and production phase, the assumption being that sales of the materials would then make the project self-financing within three years.

Malcolm had two great strengths. First, he was a visionary who foresaw the potential of open learning in meeting the needs of employers and employees during the rapid structural changes of employment and jobs that were gathering momentum. Second, he was good at promoting; he was able to convince College and sponsor officials, at least in the first two years of the project, that everything was going quite smoothly. He was similarly able to convince recruits to the project that they had a golden future ahead of them.

However, Malcolm also had a number of weaknesses. At a practical level, he had no experience of managing large sums of money or business projects with deadlines attached. Lack of management experience began to show itself all too clearly as production deadlines came and went without sign of real progress. To be sure, Malcolm held a 'progress meeting' with the project team once a week but as month after month went by it became clear that what was being monitored was 'slippage' rather than progress. As one of the project team cynically noted, 'We ought to call these lack-of-progress meetings'. Malcolm's personality became an added dimension when it became clear to members of the project team that things were going wrong.

The recruitment plan was to hire a mixture of academics (i.e. college lecturers) and 'outsiders' who had experience of writing or publishing academic materials. As it turned out, the three outsiders Joan, Jim and Don also had adult teaching experience which was an advantage.

Joan had substantial publishing experience as an editor and was ideally suited to manage the production side. However, she was appointed on an administrative grade whereas the other team members, whose main task was materials design and authoring, were appointed as academic staff members. This distinction was to have unfortunate consequences.

Although Jim had teaching experience in higher education, he was more commercially minded than most of the team. Early in the project he was concerned at the lack of market research and wondered whether Malcolm's assumptions about who would buy the course materials, and in what quantities, were warranted. Nevertheless, like Joan and Don, he was persuaded for the first year that Malcolm, the College and the sponsors must know what they were doing.

Don was the most experienced in writing open learning materials. Like Jim, he was returning to the academic world but he was much more of a purist. Whereas Joan and Jim wanted to temper academic excellence with economic prudence, Don was more interested in getting things right. Nevertheless, Joan and Jim were somewhat in awe of Don's expertise and he often won his case for an extension to his deadlines.

Avril, Bob and Susan had no previous experience of either professional writing or open learning. However, they had solid teaching experience in further education and it was planned that they would 'learn the ropes' under the watchful eyes of Joan, Jim and Don. In the first year, however, Avril and co. took much longer to plan and start to write their learning materials than expected. Allowances were made for inexperience and Don encouraged them to put accuracy and polish before meeting deadlines.

By mid-1985, storm clouds were gathering. Joan and Jim were losing patience with Malcolm for failing to inject a sense of urgency into Avril, Bob and Susan. Even Don was beginning to share their concern. Jim's appeals to Malcolm at progress meetings to 'do something about marketing before it's too late' met with underwhelming enthusiasm from many in the team. Jim no longer attended the weekly progress meetings, preferring instead to work on his own materials. Over a pint in the pub after work, Joan would refer to Malcolm as 'a wasted space' while Jim would mutter that 'he couldn't manage his way out of a paper bag'.

Joan tried valiantly to twist Malcolm's arm, appealing at once to his vanity and to his common sense: 'We're going to have to exercise much stricter control over authoring and production if we're ever going to generate enough income before the sponsorship runs out. Why don't you give me the authority to manage authoring and production while you concentrate on marketing and sales?' Malcolm's response was to hedge. 'Well, we're not sure which way the College is going to jump; whether they see us as a self-financing unit producing and selling course materials, or whether we're regarded as an integral part of the academic structure which recruits bona fide students.'

Until this moment, Joan, Jim and Don had understood the project to be definitely in the business of producing and selling course materials; now there was some doubt. Malcolm revealed that discussions were under way with the College's academic board to redesignate the project as providing bona fide courses partly through open learning materials. As if to underline the difference, whereas team members had become used to thinking and talking in terms of 'customers', a flurry of memoranda from the College's finance and administration department told Malcolm that the project team were not 'publishers' and under no circumstances was the team to describe purchasers of its materials as 'customers'; they were 'students'. The project's cash-flow was also quite unlike the normal year-on-year balancing of books within the College; the prospect of a deficit in the third year of a project (not unusual in businesses) could not be countenanced by the finance people; was it not set down in tablets of stone that no department can end the financial year with a deficit?

All this news was joy to the ears of Avril, Bob and Susan. They had been increasingly resistant to Joan's attempts to impose some discipline on their way of working and to extract some adherence to deadlines. Their argument was that they were academics and as such could not be answerable to an 'administrator'. As subject experts, they considered that they alone could decide whether or not they had injected sufficient thought, care and attention to the material. They also argued that as academics they had no role to play in the sales and marketing of the materials. It became clear to Joan and Jim that they were operating a kind of 'work to contract'.

Avril and co. were, in effect, thumbing their noses at Joan, Jim and Don. The difference in values between the two groups could not have been more marked. Whatever the shared values that had brought them together in one project, they had merely overlain a fundamental gulf in beliefs about personal responsibilities and employer–employee relations, and in perceptions of the project's purpose.

Malcolm chose to sit on the fence in the growing dispute between the two factions. Instead, he spoke about the project's 'glorious future' and acted as if there was nothing to worry about. While Joan, Jim and Don soldiered on with their own work and started to publish materials, progress from Avril, Bob and Susan was still minimal. Marketing and sales activity was non-existent. By Spring of 1986, the project was out of control. The sponsors notified both Malcolm and the College of their concern about an impending financial crisis. Systems consultants were called in to sort out the mess. After an initial reading of the situation, they advised against a 'quick fix' and embarked upon a soft systems study.

STEP 2 ANALYSIS

A RICH PICTURE

Fig. 9.1 captures the unstructured problem situation in rich picture form.

ISSUES AND PRIMARY TASK AREAS

The primary task of the unit was to publish training materials. The following appear to be issues and poorly-fulfilled primary task areas in the problem situation:

Issues	*Primary task areas*
staff competencies	production control
motivations, attitudes and values	marketing
	financial control
nature of project	strategic planning
– teaching?	business plan
– business?	
– publishing?	
roles	
leadership	
lack of clear objectives	
poor communications	

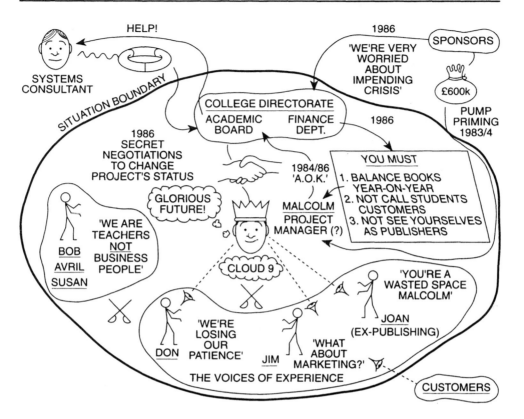

Fig. 9.1 A rich picture of the problem situation at Northwood College Training Materials Unit.

STEP 3 RELEVANT SYSTEMS AND ROOT DEFINITIONS

A number of the issues listed above are related. For example, differences clearly exist in motivations, attitudes, values and staff competencies. Lack of leadership and poor communications allow these differences to fester. A 'quick fix' would be to replace Malcolm with a more competent manager but this would only deal with a prominent symptom. What is clearly lacking in the project is any adequate sense of team-work. The project team is a team in name only. So one relevant system would be 'a system for team building'. Addressing the particular issue of staff competencies, another relevant system might be 'a system to harmonize staff skills'. On the issue of poor comunications, a further system could be 'a system to develop team member assertiveness'. Different understandings of what the project is about mean that different factions are motivated differently and work differently. A 'system to rationalize the project's identity' would be relevant.

Among primary task areas, the lack of a business plan and a marketing plan appear significant as does 'open loop' production control. Thus, the list of relevant systems is now:

ISSUE-BASED

RS1: a system for team building;

RS2: a system to harmonize staff skills;

RS3: a system to develop team member assertiveness;

RS4: a system to rationalize the project's identity.

PRIMARY-TASK-BASED

RS5: a system for business planning;

RS6: a system for marketing;

RS7: a production management system;

Owing to lack of space, only root definitions for two of the candidate systems – RS1 and RS4 – will be developed.

RD1 (FIRST PASS)

A system owned by the project manager for improving the work of the project team whereby team members develop an agreed set of team values, roles, goals and ways of working which make the best use of their individual competencies.

INSPECTION TEST – RD1

- What does 'improving the work of' mean? Tighten up wording.

- 'Ways of working' is a bit woolly.

- How will members know that agreement has been reached? Will it have to be written down for future reference/development?

- Is 'best use of' too qualitative?

- Will individual competencies need to be specified and agreed?

- Can the project manager's leadership be assumed?

RD1 (FIRST ITERATION)

A system owned and operated by the project manager for improving the work of both the individual members and the project team as a whole (as measured by performance criteria) whereby team members develop and record an agreed set of team values, roles, goals and work methods and procedures that make the most effective and efficient use of their individual competencies and needs.

CATWOE TEST – RD1

Customers: project manager and other team members are implicit beneficiaries; Northwood College, the sponsors and paying customers would also stand to benefit indirectly from improved teamwork.

Actors: project manager and team members (explicit);

Transformation: uncoordinated and misdirected individuals converted into a coherent, unified working team;

Weltanschauung: it is implicit that team work is desirable and that team building is a legitimate process;

Owners: the project manager explicitly owns and operates the system, even though by definition the other team members own a stake in it; it is assumed that without a formal leader the team cannot function;

Environment: constraints include the College's directorate, trade unions (e.g. NATFHE), the sponsors, customer demands, and time.

RD4 (FIRST PASS)

A system owned by Northwood College and operated by the project manager and project team for making explicit differing views of the project's identity, evaluating their relative merits, proposing viable identities, and selecting an identity acceptable to all those with a legitimate interest.

INSPECTION TEST – RD4

- Northwood College is too vague; perhaps the directorate or even the director;
- evaluating merits according to what and whose criteria?;
- viable according to what or whose criteria?;
- do the criteria for 'acceptable' need specifying?;
- define 'all those with a legitimate interest'.

RD4 (FIRST ITERATION)

A system owned by Northwood College's directorate and operated by the project manager and project team for making explicit differing views of the project's identity, evaluating their relative merits according to objective criteria agreed with the team, proposing identities that meet those objective criteria, and selecting an identity acceptable to all those with a legitimate interest at project level, at directorate level and at sponsor level.

CATWOE TEST – RD4

Customers: project Manager, team members, the directorate and the sponsors are explicit beneficiaries.

Actors: the project manager operates the system with the active participation of team members; others with a legitimate interest at directorate level also have a role to play.

Transformation: the essential process is the forging of a single agreed identity for the project from a variety of differing and possibly conflicting perceptions of the project's identity.

Weltanschauung: the assumption is that all actors will value the benefits of a single agreed identity for the project in preference to a variety of different and possibly conflicting identities.

Owners: Northwood College's directorate are the explicit owners as they legitimize the existence of, and have ultimate authority over, the project; they seek to ensure that the project's identity is compatible with the College's identity, constitution and goals.

Environment: constraints include the sponsors, paying customers who respond to the project's image which is influenced by its identity, and time.

STEP 4 CONCEPTUAL MODELLING

In view of space limitations, only RD1 has been developed. In order for RD1 to function, such a notional system would have to include the following main processes or verbs:

- identify: individual skills and needs;
- draw up: a list of team objectives;
- compare: team needs with individual inputs;
- specify: key team roles and tasks;
- allocate: individuals to roles and task responsibilities;
- agree: set of team values, goals, work methods and procedures;
- plan: a schedule of team work;
- carry out: the teamwork schedule;
- monitor: progress towards team objectives;

Fig. 9.2 shows a conceptual model of RD1.

INSPECTION TEST

a) Do the model and RD1 suggest a continuous and relevant mission? (A: Yes, team building and team work are obviously needed as a permanent feature of such a project.)

b) Can performance be measured? (A: Yes, establishment of criteria, and monitoring and control procedures are included.)

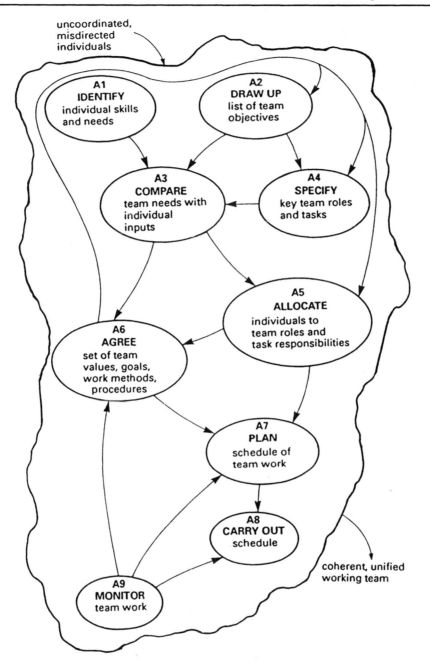

Fig. 9.2 Conceptual model of the notional team building system for Northwood College's Training Materials Unit (second iteration).

c)   Is a decision-making activity present? (A: Yes.)

d)   Do any of the main activities comprise sub-systems of back-up activities? (A: Yes.)

e)   Do the system components interact? (A: Yes.)

f)   Does the system interact with an environment? (A: Yes, NATFHE, the sponsors, paying customers.)

g)   Does the system have a boundary? (A: Yes, the wider system is the college directorate.)

h)   Can the wider system provide resources? (A: Yes.)

i)   Can the system be sustained? (A: Yes, the project manager has formal authority to sustain the notional system if he or she desires.)

EXPANDED CONCEPTUAL MODEL

Each main activity was examined in turn to identify back-up activities that logically would be required for the main activities to function. These were listed prior to drawing an expanded conceptual model, as in Fig. 9.3. The expanded model was tested with the nine point schedule and it was decided that no further expansion was needed.

STEP 5 COMPARISON

The following table compares the expanded conceptual model with the real-world problem situation (see Fig 9.4):

From the comparison table, an agenda of issues was drawn up as follows:

a)   Reconciling individual skills and needs with what would be needed to meet team objectives.

b)   Matching what team members can do, and want to do, with team roles and task responsibilities.

c)   Agreeing a set of team values, goals, work methods and procedures among a set of single-minded individuals.

d)   Planning a schedule of team work that everyone will adhere to for the good of the team.

STEP 6 DEBATE

A sanitized version of the rich picture (Fig. 9.1) was not presented to Malcolm and the team as the situation was judged to be too sensitive. The agenda was first discussed with Malcolm on his own to gauge his reaction and to see whether in principle the agenda had his support. Testing the water like this is an important part of confidence building. It demonstrated that the analyst was trying to be constructively critical and allowed Malcom time to prepare for the forthcoming wider debate with the other

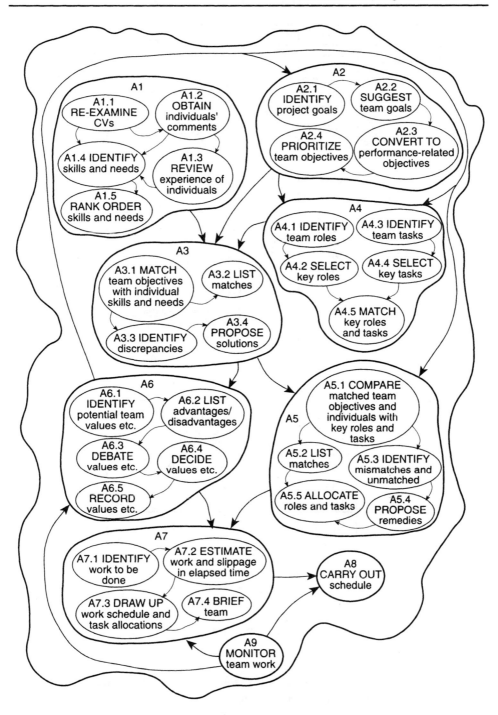

Fig. 9.3 Expanded conceptual model of the notional team building system for Northwood's Training Materials Unit.

Conceptual	Model	Real-world	Observation who? how? when? etc.	Add to agenda? Y/N
Main activity	Back-up activity	Activity present		
A1	A1.1	No	Only done on hiring	Y
	A1.2	No?	No purposeful interviews by Malcolm	Y
	A1.3	No	Progress meetings not suitable for this	Y
	A1.4	No?	Not in meaningful sense	Y
	A1.5	No	Amorphous at present	Y
A2	A2.1	No	Inside Malcolm's head?	Y
	A2.2	No	Do not exist	Y
	A2.3	No	. . .	Y
	A2.4	No	. . .	Y
A3	A3.1	No	Skill matching rests on original hiring process	Y
	A3.2	No	. . . .	Y
	A3.3	No	. . . .	Y
	A3.4	No	. . . .	Y
A4	A4.1	No	Only by guesswork and emergence	Y
	A4.2	No	Only be gravitation	Y
	A4.3	No	Guesswork and assumptions	Y
	A4.4	No	. . . .	Y
	A4.5	No	Malcolm's whim	Y
A5	A5.1	etc.		

Fig. 9.4 Table comparing expanded conceptual model of the notional team building system with the real-world situation at Northwood's Training Materials Unit.

actors. The second stage involved a joint meeting between the analyst, Malcolm and representatives of the College directorate to apprise them of the agenda and allow a free discussion. Again, the aim was to test support for the 'whats' of the agenda. The final stage was a debate involving the analyst, Malcolm and the staff of the unit using the conceptual models to steer the debate. The following changes were agreed:

a) Using the conceptual models as a guide, Malcolm would set up formal mechanisms to reconcile individual versus team conflicts, to set team objectives, and as far as possible to match team members' attributes with the requirements of meeting team objectives.

b) Although it was recognized that team values needed forging, it was felt that this would emerge from the formal mechanisms rather than requiring a special formal process of its own.

c) Malcolm agreed that Joan should take over the scheduling and with full authority for progress chasing; Avril, Bob and Susan agreed to this, although somewhat reluctantly.

STEP 7 ACTION

One of the outcomes of the debate was a general recognition that all team members needed to adopt a much more disciplined way of working. A series of team meetings were set up by Malcolm each with a clearly defined agenda dealing with only one topic at a time. Team members were told that each meeting had to secure a list of agreements. Proper minutes were kept with an action column. A 'team objectives' statement was agreed and at the beginning of each meeting members were reminded of its message. When new jobs or problems arose, Malcolm arranged 'team briefing' sessions to discuss and agree a plan of action. Each member was given agreed performance targets and progress was monitored both by Joan's Gantt chart and at team performance meetings.

The effects of team building soon became apparent in improved output and quality of work and a better atmosphere among the team. Malcolm concentrated his efforts on managing the project and temporarily foresook his fantasies about the future. However, it remained a tense and uneasy time for those involved and time and effort would be required to establish a firm foundation for the future.

DEVELOPING THE NEWTOWN LINE – A STUDY OF UNEASE AND UNCERTAINTY ABOUT PRIMARY TASKS IN A RAILWAY COMPANY

STEP 1 DATA COLLECTION

In recent years, the Newtown area of the UK has undergone various changes in its demography and industrial activity. Major employers moved into the area to benefit from lower overheads, many new companies set up in industrial estates and business parks and new housing estates have been developed. The population was increasing as their employees moved into the area. However, the existing railway line in Newtown did not extend across the region and the lack of adequate alternative passenger transport services was failing to meet public demand in the area. The railway company obtained government approval to expand the Newtown network.

Following the Kings Cross and Clapham Common railway disasters in the late 1980s and the proposed privatization of the railways, the Government brought in the Railways (Safety Case) Regulations 1994 requiring the railway industry to examine its actual and proposed activities to ensure that they were safe and that risks were 'as low as reasonably practicable' – the ALARP principle. The 'safety case' is a set of reports which seek to justify on safety grounds why the organization, or defined parts of it, should be allowed to start or continue to operate. A safety case is intended to demonstrate that the management:

- understand the inherent hazards, their causes and consequences;

- have provided sufficient and robust defences to avoid the hazards and mitigate the consequences;

- have reduced the risk to a level in accordance with ALARP.

In essence, managers must show that they understand what must be done to maintain a required level of safety in practical terms, for example key maintenance activities, decision criteria, and appropriate combinations of control measures. For the Newtown expansion project, its safety case would have to be submitted for acceptance by the Health & Safety Executive.

The Newtown expansion work comprised two main aspects. The first was the expansion project itself run by the engineering design team to design, plan and build the extension, and the second was the establishment of the systems to operate the extended line once handed over, including staffing, training, maintenance etc. During the project phase and prior to operation, the planning of the operational aspects was looked after by a team of experienced railway staff drawn from the existing Newtown line who worked closely with the engineering design team. A small specialist group within the engineering design team was set up to draw up the safety case for submission to the HSE so that approval to open and operate the new line could be obtained.

The safety case group comprised highly qualified safety engineers with knowledge of HARD SYSTEMS and SYSTEMS FAILURES techniques. Part of the safety case included a hazard identification analysis of the railway operation under both normal and abnormal/ emergency conditions. Although discrete electrical and mechanical (E&M) systems such as signalling and rolling stock underwent detailed analyses, these were only part of the overall railway. The safety case group therefore felt it was necessary to complement these analyses with a higher-level, integrated systems view in the form of a railway business model which could itself be subject to hazard analysis. The analysis would be based on hazard and operability studies (HAZOPS) to examine the causes and consequences of deviations from design intent *vis-à-vis* flows of assets, people and information. Railways may be seen as human activity SYSTEMS, and this needed to be fully appreciated. The safety case group was also aware that the design itself would include new technologies and so rules, procedures and work methods developed over many years through custom, practice and experience would need to be re-evaluated to show that they were (a) still valid, and (b) complete.

Two problems arose. First, the HAZOP would need a system diagram or system description of the railway business system, and this did not exist. An SSM approach could help to fill this gap by:

* establishing primary tasks;

* identifying issues for further systems analysis;

* Producing a cascade of conceptual models of the railway system which might be suitable for HAZOP if supplemented with notes about real-world implementation.

Such an approach involving participative 'talk-throughs' would also aid the design process by developing consensus about design requirements and operation.

The second problem was the unease felt by the safety case manager about a number of aspects of their work. Large engineering projects require a vast amount of technical expertise and close attention to technical detail. It is not always easy for those directly engaged in the work to stand back and see the whole 'system', either as it is during the project phase or as it will be once operational. Different disciplines and interests are likely to be involved not only within the project team but also between the project and client teams. Different groups such as train drivers, line controllers, station staff, electrical and mechanical system designers, safety personnel etc. may all have different beliefs about, and perceptions of what constitutes, the extended Newtown railway system. If the analyses or the system diagrams were developed in an unstructured way they could easily be contaminated by particular group biases, with the result that they would not be recognizable to the system owners when used in the HAZOP studies.

The safety case manager and the project director were sensitive to the fact that all these different groups would inevitably be making assumptions about 'what is' and 'what will be' and about what other people were doing and thinking. They were concerned that assumptions which were inaccurate could carry through into the operational phase and result in poor system performance as well as the safety case being invalidated if hazard identification and risk analyses failed to match the actual line operating conditions. The level of uncertainty about this issue was such that an SSM study was commissioned with the objectives of (a) identifying different understandings and conflicts about the nature of the extended railway system and approaches to the project task, (b) helping to resolve differences, and (c) providing the basis for proceeding confidently with the main system analysis and HAZOP programme by developing a jointly agreed set of primary tasks and notional system diagram(s). The systems consultant interviewed a range of people from both the engineering design and operational planning teams.

STEP 2 ANALYSIS

A RICH PICTURE

Fig. 9.5 is a rich picture of the problem situation.

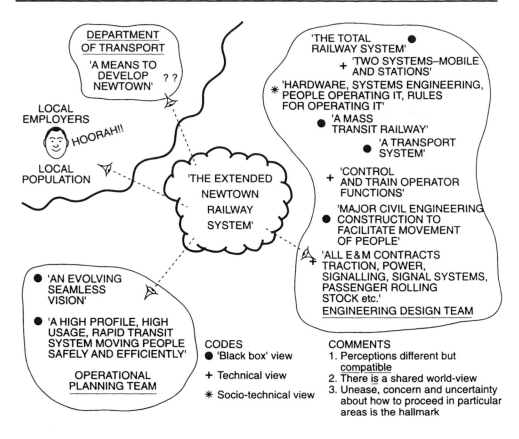

Fig. 9.5 A rich picture of the situation concerning the Newtown Railway Extension Project.

ISSUES AND PRIMARY TASK AREAS

Although the interviewees' perceptions of the railway 'SYSTEM' were often expressed differently, they were compatible. Concerns about who should do what at what stage were joint concerns rather than disagreements. In short, conflict resolution did not appear to be a major system requirement although how to deal with conflicts or system issues which *might* arise was an issue. Unease, concern and uncertainty were hallmarks of the problem situation. Most topics raised related to the primary task, i.e. what is the railway SYSTEM's primary purpose and function? Valuable information was gained on the influences on, and context of, the identified primary tasks. The following summarizes the concerns:

Primary-task-based	*Issue-based*
The overall system	Means to examine big issues
Maintenance and servicing	Noticing and adapting to changes
Skills, training and human resources	Passenger behaviour

Capturing experience of existing staff and
  maintaining these experiences

Decision support

Crippled trains and evacuation

Procedures

Testing system integration and interfaces
  with existing Newtown line

Driver boredom and driver needs

Car design and passenger needs

Line control centre

Performance standards, measures and
  measuring

STEP 3 RELEVANT SYSTEMS AND ROOT DEFINITIONS

The consultant and safety case team agreed that the most relevant system was 'the
overall system' which should be addressed first in logical terms. Rather than identifying relevant systems from the remainder of the primary task list, sub-systems of
back-up activities at Levels 1, 2 etc. would be developed from the overall system at
Level 0. Primary task concerns identified by the actors would then be located within
these developed (sub)systems. This would have the advantage of an economic use of
the consultant's and team's time and enable 'missing' elements to be identified –
especially important in later discussions with engineering design and operational
planning teams.

The following systems relevant to the Extended Newtown Line (ENL) were examined:

RS0: The overall notional system (Level 0) comprising the following Level 1 sub-
  systems:

RS1: A system for embarking and disembarking passengers;

RS2: A system to move passengers from train embarcation point to a chosen Newtown
  destination;

RS3: A system to provide an adequate pool of qualified staff and to allocate them to
  tasks and shifts;

RS4: A system to regulate the service on the line;

RS5: A system to maintain the railway (including inspections, cleaning and preventive
  maintenance);

RS6: A system to control emergencies.

Owing to space considerations, only RS0 will be fully developed. The root definition
and testing of RS5 is included as an example to show how RS1 to RS6 were developed. The root definition of RS0 was expressed as:

RDO (THIRD ITERATION)

'A system operated and maintained by the extended Newtown line (ENL) manager, facilitated by staff and contractors, to transport passengers from a chosen ENL embarcation point along the ENL route to an ENL destination of their choice, rapidly, reliably, safely and in comfort, within operating and cost criteria agreed with the Government and regulatory authorities, for the benefit of the public and the Newtown Railway Company.'

INSPECTION TEST – RDO

- Cost criteria of the railway company are included. Is there a need to mention tariffs which are acceptable to passengers?

CATWOE TEST – RDO

Customers:	passengers;
Actors:	staff and contractors;
Transformation:	passengers with travel requirements converted into satisfied, transported passengers;
Weltanschauung:	shared values of providing Newtown with a mass rapid transport system to support social and economic needs (implicit);
Owner(s):	extended Newtown line manager;
Environment:	constraints of time, budget, legislation, public opinion, regulatory authorities, etc. (implicit).

RD5 (FIRST ITERATION)

'A system owned by the ENL manager and operated by the ENL engineering manager, maintenance staff and contractors and monitored by the engineering department to maintain the ENL railway and including preventive maintenance, maintenance inspections, cleaning, and breakdown recoveries, so as to sustain a specified level of safety, reliability and availability of electrical and mechanical equipment, civil engineering infrastructure and configuration data for the benefit of passengers and staff.'

INSPECTION TEST – RD5

- Is it clear what 'infrastructure' means?
- Is it clear what 'configuration data' means?

CATWOE TEST – RD5

Customers:	Passengers and staff;

Actors: ENL engineering manager, maintenance staff and contractors, monitored by engineering department;

Transformation: safety, reliability and availability of hardware and infrastructure of the ENL railway sustained;

Weltanschauung: belief that inadequate maintenance contributes to service down-time and safety problems, with associated higher operating costs, higher overheads and decreased revenue (implicit);

Owner(s):   ENL manager

Environment: constraints of time, budgets, legislation, data available, public opinion, insurance requirements, statutory and company safety requirements (implicit).

STEP 4 CONCEPTUAL MODELLING

The logical verbs or main processes of RD0 were perceived to be:

* provide embarcation/disembarcation;

* move passengers from train embarcation to chosen destination;

* supply adequate pool of qualified staff, allocated to tasks and shifts;

* regulate the service on the line;

* maintain the railway.

In addition, the integrity of the whole notional system must be assured throughout its lifetime. Although integrity assurance is partly addressed by various monitoring and internal auditing activities subsumed within RS1 to RS6, it is essential that an independent audit and review function validates the whole system. Such a requirement relates in particular to Regulation 4 of the Management of Health and Safety at Work Regulations 1992 and Schedule 1 to the Railways (Safety Case) Regulations 1994. An independent audit and review activity is therefore located outside the system. Fig. 9.6 shows a conceptual model of RD0.

INSPECTION TEST

a)   Do the model and its root definition suggest a continuous and relevant mission? (A: Yes.)

b)   Can performance be measured? (A: Regulate and maintain both imply performance monitoring.)

c)   Is a decision-making activity present? (A: Each element implies a decision-making function within it.)

d)   Do any of the main activities comprise sub-systems of lower-order activities? (A: Yes, already identified as key sub-systems RS1 to RS6.)

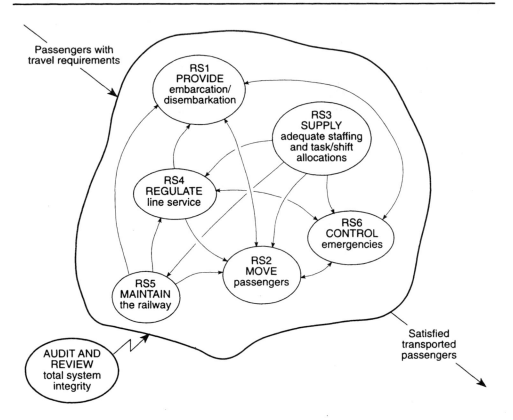

Fig. 9.6 Conceptual model of the overall notional Newtown railway system as defined by RD0.

e)   Do the system components interact? (A: Yes.)

f)   Does the system interact with an environment? (A: Yes, there are implicit constraints identified in the CATWOE test and an audit and review function acts on the whole.)

g)   Does the system have a boundary? (A: Yes.)

h)   Can the wider system provide resources? (A: It is assumed that the Newtown company will do so.)

i)   Can the system be sustained? (A: Yes, provided the system owner (ENL manager) continues to receive authority, policy and resources from the wider system.)

EXPANDED CONCEPTUAL MODEL

Fig. 9.7 shows the expanded conceptual model of RD0 which includes the sub-system elements of RS1 to RS6.

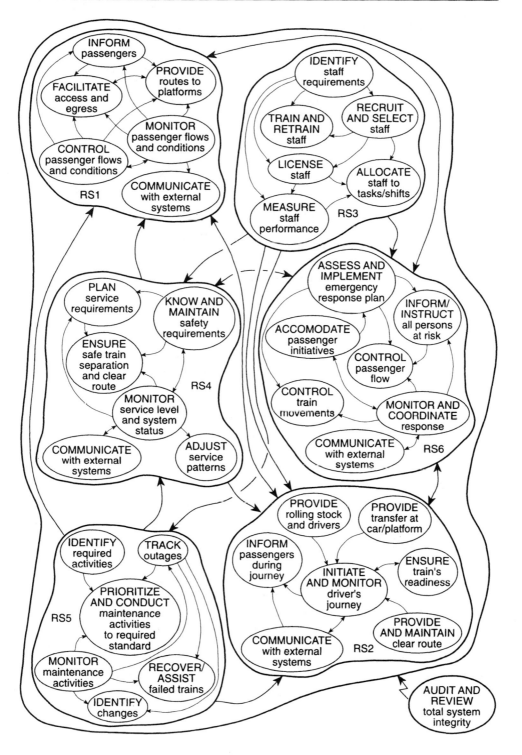

Fig. 9.7 Expanded conceptual model of the notional Newtown railway system.

STEP 5 COMPARISON

A tabulated comparison (too lengthy to detail here, but an essential part of SSM) revealed many matches between the cascade of conceptual models and the real-world setting. However, a number of mismatches and omissions were identified, particularly in relation to the railway system as it would be operated and matters that would have to be set in motion early in the design phase in order to meet the operational requirements. For example, arrangements for RS3, RS5 and RS6 would require much greater attention than had been recognized so far.

STEP 6 DEBATE

The safety case team had been kept fully informed of the SOFT SYSTEM study's progress and were able to ensure that the consultant's findings were drawn up in a form which the engineering design and operational planning teams would readily appreciate. Having studied the draft report, they were in an informed position to discuss the root definitions and conceptual models, how they compared with the real-world activity and what the implications were.

STEP 7 ACTION

The safety case team was able to proceed with the main systems analysis and HAZOP studies with renewed confidence that both the engineering design and operational planning teams shared a common understanding of the extended Newtown railway system requirements during development and when operational. The conceptual system diagram for RD0 was developed further and notes made for each sub-system about real-world implementation were drawn up into a full system description. These provided the basic inputs to the HAZOP study as well as providing a contextual understanding of the sub-system functions and the influences and constraints on them. This information could also be related to the organizational structure and processes.

SUMMARY

The two case studies have shown how SOFT SYSTEMS methodology can be used in rather different circumstances. In the first case, SSM was used to navigate a path through what at first sight seemed to be almost intractible problems involving factional disagreements, personality clashes and defensive behaviour. The second case involved unease, concern and uncertainty rather than world-view clashes. Whereas a HARD SYSTEMS approach would try to deliver a solution based on an assumption that 'the problem' was independent of the client set, SSM assumes that the actors are both creators and resolvers of the problem situation. Resolution is a learning process.

SYSTEMS FAILURES METHODOLOGY

The objectives of this chapter are to:

- revisit the concept of 'system failures' introduced in Part 1 of the book;
- describe the SYSTEMS FAILURES methodology;
- illustrate the stages of the methodology with the aid of a case study;
- introduce comparison techniques used in SYSTEM FAILURES methodology.

INTRODUCTION

Chapter 5 in Part 1 introduced the concept of SYSTEM FAILURE and showed how to use various paradigms to examine aspects of SYSTEM FAILURE. However, simply making comparisons with paradigms in a haphazard way does not represent a systems approach. The SYSTEMS FAILURES methodology (Open University T301 1984, 1993; Fortune and Peters 1995) provides a disciplined way of examining FAILURES which often reside in quite complex, messy situations. This methodology enables the analyst to gain understanding of situations which exhibit apparent failures and to draw lessons for preventing similar failures. The degree of understanding gained is determined largely by the number of iterations carried out, which in turn depends on the analyst's resources – especially time. However, even a single pass through the methodology can often be quite illuminating.

SYSTEMS FAILURES METHODOLOGY

The essence of SYSTEMS FAILURES methodology is comparison between the apparent failure situation and a range of paradigms. Some paradigms, such as control and

---

NB SYSTEM, HARD SYSTEM, SOFT SYSTEM and SYSTEM FAILURE in small capitals refer to metaphorical and perceptual constructs.

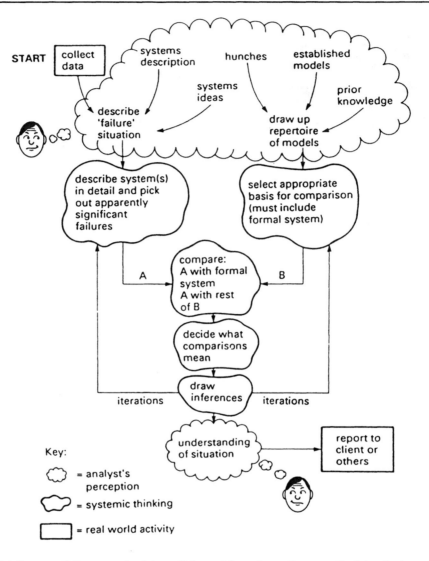

Fig. 10.1 Systems failures methodology (Adapted from Joyce Fortune, *Studying Systems Failures*, Open University T301 Course Material 1984 revised 1993).

communication, are desirable in the real world whereas others, such as fault trees and cascades, are undesirable. If elements of desirable paradigms are missing from, or elements of undesirable paradigms are present in,the situation it suggests possible contributions to the apparent failure from which lessons may be learned.

Fig 10.1 depicts the stages of the methodology. The starting point is to describe the failure situation. However, prior to this the analyst's objectives need to be outlined even though they may be vague. The point of this is to make the analyst (a) think about what he or she is doing, and (b) pay attention to his or her resources. Once you begin to describe the failure situation, you may well find that you will have to limit the scope of your study and revise your objectives. An objectives hierarchy is a good way of focussing the plan of work.

STAGE 1 DESCRIBING THE FAILURE SITUATION

The situation being studied may be quite local and self-contained but could easily be very complex, widespread and have many ramifications. Whatever the case, the analyst will be searching for evidence that someone at least is dissatisfied with the performance of something that seems relevant to the task. The analyst's own world-view and those of actors in the situation are obviously pertinent to the perception of failure and what is deemed relevant.

Searching for data involves obtaining documents, interviewing relevant people and perhaps visiting places where relevant failures are said to have occurred. Both at this stage and when reporting, or during later iterations, the analyst needs to avoid using the term 'failure' when communicating with relevant people. The fact that failures are apparent does not necessarily mean that everyone shares that perception and it is likely that 'failure' will be taken as a sign of criticism. Euphemisms such as 'difficulties' and 'problems' may be more appropriate.

Having gathered what the analyst thinks is enough information, a rich picture could be drawn to cover as much of the failure situation as possible. A spray diagram can be just as useful. This pre-analysis sketching should suggest particular areas to focus on, from which the analyst can begin to tease out specific SYSTEMS to study.

AIR TRAFFIC CONTROL – A CASE STUDY

The rest of this chapter requires the reader to do most of the work. If you get stuck at any point, refer to the comparable parts of the worked case studies in Chapter 11.

Chapter 6 referred to the seemingly intractable problems of air travel and air traffic control which still exist in the mid-1990s. In the summer of 1988, European flights to the Mediterranean were delayed on an unprecedented scale. Media interest was substantial and just one front-page newspaper article with the banner headline 'CAA Heads Must Roll' may be cited to convey the extent of failure (*The Observer,* Sunday 17 July 1988). The article suggested that a political row was threatening to break over the Civil Aviation Authority as government ministers blamed it for causing massive airport delays 'which could become routine for at least the next seven years'. Phrases such as 'mistaken forecasts', 'capitulation to chaos', 'the débâcle', 'failed to prepare for the surge in flights', 'crisis', 'hell of a mess of things', and 'past failings' are all indicative of apparent failures.

Gather a range of data about the air traffic control situation from newspaper articles, official reports, airport visits or whatever sources you have readily accessible. Construct a rich picture and/or spray diagram of the unstructured situation. Then carry out the steps of the methodology as described below.

The next step in describing the situation is to see if there are any SYSTEMS in relation to it which are worth studying. Here you need to use systems description as outlined in Chapter 2. Find a topic area in your rich picture or spray diagram which looks relevant to the failure situation; you may find several. An example might be air traffic control *per se*. Another might be flight safety. As you are using this case for study purposes rather than as a consultant working for a client, pick out a range of likely problem owners and construct a commitment statement for each.

Now test each commitment statement to see whether it is goal-orientated, whether analysis is more important than action, whether analysis is need-driven rather than curiosity-driven, and whether the problem owner's task is relevant to the failure situation. In other words, are any of the problem owners dealing with 'problems' that are systemic or system-borne and therefore would benefit from failures analysis? Examples of how to carry out the test are given in Chapter 2.

Having found at least one key problem owner, focus on two or three areas that your key problem owner would be interested in.

Exercise 10.1
Suggest three of four areas that the director of air traffic services at the CAA would almost certainly be interested in.

Now focus on one of the areas and separate from it at least one SYSTEM which exhibits apparent failures. For example, if you chose the operation of air traffic control centres, then one SYSTEM which exhibits apparent failures is the centre at West Drayton which covers most of the air traffic in and around southern England. All systems need a title which reflects ownership and purpose and so a title might be 'the CAA system for operating the air traffic control centre at West Drayton'.

From your collected data on the air traffic control centre at West Drayton, draw another spray diagram or rich picture of the situation. Then list some likely system components and divide them with a trial boundary between 'within the system' and 'in the environment'. Repeat the process of system separation, rich picture construction, and trial boundary for the other areas of interest.

You should now have several potential SYSTEMS to examine but are any of them crucial to understanding why failures occur in air traffic control? Check back against the commitment statement you constructed for your key problem owner, i.e. the director of air traffic services. Then peruse your data to see if there are any apparent failures which relate to this problem owner's task and which suggest paradigms for comparison. For example, evidence of lack of monitoring and control are key indicators of failure. Accidents and structural failures are usually prima-facie evidence. However, it should be noted that although there have been a number of 'near misses' there has never been a major air accident in the UK involving an ATC failure. The formal system, control, and fault tree paradigms would illuminate in these examples particular aspects of the failure situation of each key system.

DETAILED SYSTEMS DESCRIPTION

By now, you will have completed a first quick pass through the methodology and know whether or not you have identified a key 'system' which seems to relate to failures of significance to your problem owner's task. The next stage is to take a key SYSTEM and describe it in detail.

COMPONENTS

Examine the components listed when you separated the system. Are any important components missing? Do any need to be switched from system to environment or vice-versa? Are all the components at the same level of resolution? Fig. 10.2 depicts one iterative adjustment and shows that part (b) is more structured and easier to understand. Aim to keep the number of components to about ten.

Summarize the relationship between components in the form of a system map. Several iterations may be needed before you are satisfied with its development. What was once a foggy impression of the system should be starting to look clearer.

INPUTS

What ingredients enter this SYSTEM in order for it to function?. List them and adjust the resolution as necessary.

OUTPUTS

What are the system outputs? There are obvious outputs such as the majority of aircraft reaching their destinations safely, and some of them on schedule. Equally obvious is the unwanted output of flight delays.

Exercise 10.2
List other outputs from the West Drayton air traffic control centre.

ENVIRONMENT

What are the components outside the SYSTEM which affect it? Government, the media, air passenger volumes and other ATC centres are obvious components. The Civil Aviation Authority senior management are also outside the SYSTEM and represent its wider system.

STRUCTURE

What are the major sub-systems which make up the SYSTEM? Look for decision-making, monitoring, control, and operational sub-systems and list them. Your system map will help, but you may need to collect more data.

VARIABLES

The variables are those components whose contributions to the SYSTEM's properties and behaviour may vary. For example, in the West Drayton ATC centre system, job

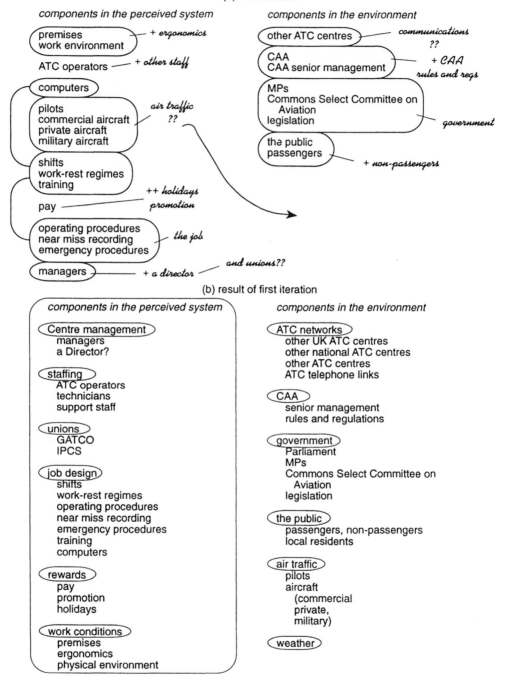

Fig 10.2 Iterative adjustment of component resolution of the notional CAA system for operating the air traffic control centre at West Drayton.

design will vary because sub-components such as training, work–rest regimes and operating procedures may vary. List the variables and adjust the resolution as appropriate.

RELATIONSHIPS BETWEEN VARIABLES

All that is needed here is an influence diagram which shows how variables affect each other, and an indication of where the boundary lies.

APPARENTLY SIGNIFICANT FAILURES

There are a number of ways in which this step could be tackled systematically. One is to consider apparent failures which occurred during different phases of a SYSTEM's life. Another is to categorize apparent failures according to the functions or sub-systems to which they relate. The case studies in Chapter 11 include both kinds of comparison. Categorization makes a large number of apparently sigificant failures more manageable. Examples of categories are resource provision, implementation, monitoring, equipment failures, and so on.

APPROPRIATE PARADIGMS

With organizations, the formal system paradigm (see Fig. 5.2 in Chapter 5) is a necessary 'model' to select for comparison. In addition, other appropriate paradigms should be selected for each failure aspect of each failure category identified. For example, a particular aspect of equipment failure may suggest the fault tree and/or cascade paradigms. Particular monitoring failures may suggest the control paradigm.

STAGE 2 COMPARISON WITH PARADIGMS

Select a number of apparently significant failures and corresponding paradigms for comparison. Which ones and how many you select are a matter of judgement and the time available. Comparison takes the form of a template exercise whereby the failure situation or particular failure is superimposed on the appropriate diagrammatic representations of the paradigms, as shown in Chapter 11.

STAGE 3 WHAT DO COMPARISONS MEAN?

In this stage the comparisons from stage 3 are interpreted. The formal system paradigm should always be compared first because it incorporates fundamental elements of control, monitoring and communication. Typically, deficiencies in sub-system structure or processes are highlighted, e.g. monitoring sub-system is absent or ineffective. Monitoring and control defects shown up by this comparison then need to be checked again by comparison with the control paradigm.

A simple 2x2 table is useful for aiding interpretation. Bear in mind that some paradigms are desirable and others undesirable and so, in principle, there are four possible combinations of desirable/undesirable and match/mismatch, as depicted in Fig. 10.3. Combinations in quadrants 1 and 4 may represent an 'acceptable' situation, depending on whether any discrepancies are significant.

Exercise 10.3
Place the following comparisons in the most appropriate of the four quadrants numbered in Fig. 10.3: (a) control paradigm shows absence of performance monitoring, (b) control paradigm shows maintenance sub-system not to be functioning, (c) FSP shows executive committee did not meet for many years, (d) fault tree paradigm shows hierarchy of events leading to component failure.

Sometimes it is not possible to allocate an interpretation clearly to one quadrant. This is often the case with communication failures where, on the one hand there is evidence that a message was received and apparently understood and, on the other hand the message was not acted upon as expected. In such cases, the allocation mark X has to float between quadrants 1 and 3 until further clarification is obtained. A communication failure of this kind, where behaviour of the receiver is inconsistent with having received and understood the message, suggests one or more human factors paradigms to consider in further iterations.

STAGE 4 LEARNING

The purpose of this stage is to summarize what has been learned so far from the FAILURES study. For example, the understanding gained about the behaviour of particular SYSTEMS may enable preventive action or treatments to be suggested. The understanding may point to the need for other kinds of study, e.g. using HARD SYSTEMS methodology and/or SSM.

The analyst then has to decide whether the investigation needs to be continued and whether resources, especially time, are available for this. Further iterations can include internal checks on, and refinements of, the analysis of key SYSTEMS as well as identification and analysis of new key SYSTEMS.

	Paradigm	
	Desirable	Undesirable
No/few discrepancies	1	2
Many discrepancies	3	4

Fig 10.3 Contingency table for interpreting paradigm comparisons

SUMMARY

The objectives of this chapter were to (a) revisit the concept of SYSTEM FAILURES introduced in Part 1 of the book, (b) describe the SYSTEMS FAILURES methodology, (c) illustrate the stages of the methodology with the aid of a case study, and (d) introduce comparison techniques used in SYSTEM FAILURES methodology.

SYSTEM FAILURES methodology enables the analyst to gain understanding about complex situations which exhibit apparent failures which enables the analyst or others to identify possible preventive or curative action. The methodology provides a disciplined approach to comparing key SYSTEMS deemed by the analyst to be relevant to the apparent failure with a repertoire of paradigms, both desirable and undesirable. Chapter 11 provides two case studies of the SYSTEM FAILURES methodology.

SUGGESTED ANSWERS TO EXERCISES

10.1 The director of air traffic services would probably be interested in at least the following:

A: maintaining flight safety;

B: the operation of air traffic control centres;

C: the use of computers in air traffic control;

D: industrial relations in air traffic control;

E: weather prediction;

F: predicted air traffic volumes;

G: new technology applications.

10.2 Other outputs are: industrial relations 'problems', possible increased stress on controllers, and computer breakdowns. Knock-on consequences of system outputs include: raised public anxiety about air safety, public anger at delays, anger among politicians.

10.3 Comparisons (a), (b) and (c) are all discrepancies with desirable paradigms, and so the allocation mark x would go in quadrant 3. Comparison (d) is a direct match with an undesirable paradigm and so the mark would be entered in quadrant 2.

SYSTEMS FAILURES CASE STUDIES

The objectives of this chapter are to demonstrate the application of SYSTEM FAILURES methodology through two case studies.

INTRODUCTION

Both the case studies in this chapter have something to do with the construction and building industries. This selection is coincidental and is not intended to suggest that these industries are failure-ridden or suffer more failures than any other industry. There is certainly evidence to suggest that these industries have got a considerable safety problem (as in the Littlebrook D case) but this is a reflection of general weaknesses of safety management throughout employment as much as it is of any special circumstances of construction work. The lessons to be learned from these cases should be of interest to all industries and all managers. Both cases actually occurred. In the Daleside case, names have been altered to avoid offence to those involved in what was a highly controversial case. Littlebrook D, however, was the subject of an official enquiry and court cases and is a matter of public record.

DALESIDE DEVELOPMENT GROUP – A STUDY OF FAILURE OF SYSTEM-BUILT HOUSING PROJECTS

During the 1950s and 1960s demand for public housing (council housing) increased dramatically. In order to reduce the time and costs of construction, 'systems building' methods were introduced by many local authorities. These methods are perhaps better described as 'kit building', for the so-called systems were little more than buildings assembled from pre-fabricated components. In the short-term, systems building methods achieved the aims of cutting costs and reducing the time before dwellings could be occupied. However, many serious counter-intuitive outcomes arose

---

NB SYSTEM, HARD SYSTEM, SOFT SYSTEM and SYSTEM FAILURE in small capitals refer to metaphorical and perceptual constructs.

between the late 1960s and the mid-1980s to the extent that system-built public housing was widely condemned as a failure.

A large number of different systems building methods using steel frame construction and prefabricated reinforced concrete were used in the 1960s. The number of houses involved were at least 170 000 plus hundreds of tower blocks i.e. those with at least ten storeys. By the mid-1980s, such dwellings had deteriorated to such an extent that many were considered irretrievable. Evidence suggested that many tenants had suffered ill-health and general loss of amenity. Pressure from tenants' action groups which had been building up over a fifteen-year period had, by the mid-1980s, forced local authorities to address the problem. However, by then the scale of the failure and the costs of remedying it were enormous. Local authorities were caught between two costly options: remedial treatment or destruction and replacement. Some estimates put the cost of dealing with the tower blocks alone at between £3bn and £5bn. In 1985 Manchester City Council hosted the Hulme Conference which was intended to bring together the main interest groups and outline an action plan. Following the Hulme Conference, over 100 local authorities formed the National Systems Built and Tower Block Housing Project in order to offer a more consistent approach to the failure. Many authorities have since decided to demolish tower blocks as the cheaper of two very expensive options.

The analyst's client was a local authority director of housing. You need to appreciate that the analyst's own world-view will affect his or her perception of the situation. The analyst who actually carried out this study was a former local government officer and his view of the housing situation was affected by that experience. Whereas housing problems clearly involve and affect large numbers of people in diverse groups, the analyst took the view that major day-to-day problems of exercising responsible action in public housing rests with local authority housing departments. A system map of such a department is given in Fig. 2.3 in Chapter 2. Fig. 11.1 shows the organization of a typical local authority housing department.

This case study concerns system building methods used in the 1960s. According to Marsh (1985), the methods as understood then were quite different from modern system building methods. Foster (1983) describes those earlier system methods as 'closed' in view of incompatibility between component designs across different methods. Current industrialized building methods use components which are interchangeable and are thus 'open'. The case study findings relating to poor engineering reliability of components refer to closed methods of the 1960s and should not necessarily be extended to system building methods in general.

CASE STUDY OBJECTIVES

The following hierarchy (Fig. 11.2) summarizes the initial objectives of the study. However, try to avoid setting initial objectives in metaphorical concrete. Be prepared to modify objectives after a first pass or first iteration once you have had time to reflect on what you have learned. Typically, a first pass through the methodology highlights objectives which are far too ambitious for the time and other resources at the analyst's disposal.

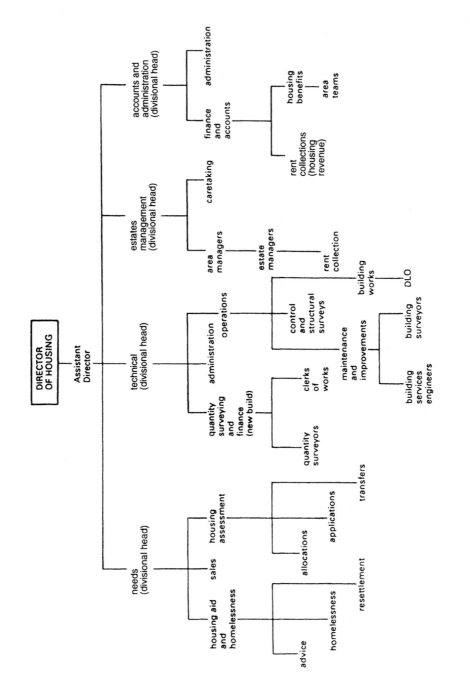

Fig 11.1 Organization chart of a typical local authority housing department.

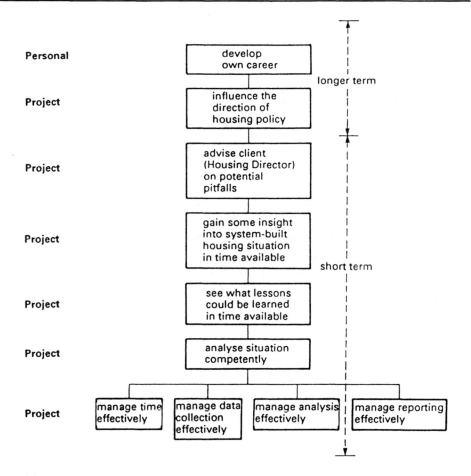

Fig 11.2 Objectives hierarchy for examination of the system-built housing situation.

DATA COLLECTION

The introduction above summarizes the data that were gleaned from a variety of sources. Data collection methods included:

- personal observation of system-built dwellings;

- personal interviews of relevant people in the situation;

- literature search (relevant reports and documents, reference books, press cuttings etc.);

- correspondence and telephone enquiries;

- TV reports.

ANALYSIS

The analysis follows the sequence described in Chapter 10.

STAGE 1 SYSTEMS DESCRIPTION AND PARADIGM SELECTION

Systems description as described in Chapters 2 and 10 is used to assemble key SYSTEMS to work on, as follows.

AWARENESS

As the introduction above indicates, public housing has experienced considerable difficulties. Problem areas giving cause for concern include the durability of council housing, and system-built properties in particular. However, there are considerable pressures on housing departments of local authorities to provide large numbers of dwellings cheaply. For example, council waiting lists remain long and obligations exist to house the growing number of homeless people. At the same time, housing subsidies from central government have been cut.

COMMITMENTS

The following commitment statement was summarized for the client, a director of housing, a problem owner in the situation:

'I am responsible for assessing the needs of people who want housing from public resources. My customers include a wide range of people such as the homeless and many people on housing benefit. Once needs are assessed, households are allocated accommodation as soon as available. Of course, it does not end there because flats and houses need maintaining and repairing – tenants soon let us know the problems. With increasing demand, the housing stock has to be replenished as properties are sold off to sitting tenants or get beyond economic repair. So I have to brief the council's Architects Department as to the functional requirements of 'new build' housing, the design of which is a joint responsibility more or less. I need to understand the situation to ensure that the council effectively discharges its statutory obligations in all these respects. I am aiming for success not failure.'

TESTING

- Is the client's purpose relevant to the failure situation? (Y)
- Is the commitment (of client and analyst) goal-orientated? (Y)
- Is analysis more important than action at present? (Y)
- Is analysis needed prior to action? (Y)
- Is analysis need-driven rather than just to satisfy curiosity?(Y)

The test results indicate that systems analysis is warranted.

SEPARATION OF SYSTEMS

The task of a housing director appears to be an ideal case systemically. As a problem owner, a housing director might be interested in the following potentially fruitful areas:

A: new build (including briefing, design and construction);

B: maintenance and improvement (e.g. tower blocks, refurbishment with *in situ* tenants);

C: housing the homeless.

A focusing topic for area A is system building and the particular system separated for this study was entitled the Daleside Development Group Project System for 'System Building', in which the client had an interest. The Daleside Development Group (DDG) was a consortium formed in the early 1960s by four city councils in the north of England. Some 4 000 DDG dwellings were system-built before the Group disbanded in 1968. The chairmen of the four councils' housing committees comprised the DDG senior management but from 1968 to 1982 they did not meet on DDG business. Over that fourteen-year period, water seepage, dampness, mould and fungus were constant problems for tenants. Local GPs stated categorically that living under these conditions had adversely affected the physical and mental health of many tenants. Tenants had been unable to get DDG to remedy the problem and some tenants had been driven to attempt suicide. By the early 1980s DDG dwellings, which had had an expected useful life of 60 years, were in an advanced state of decay. In one block of flats a three-ton parapet slab broke loose and emergency action had to be taken to prevent it falling through the roofs of adjacent dwellings. The national media were now focusing public attention on the DDG scandal.

    Apart from the DDG senior management, a key figure was their designer Richard Stevenson who was responsible both for design and selecting the building contractors. It appears that DDG management simply left the designer to choose a system-building method from the 90 or so available. Swallow Construction put in a very low bid and were accepted, although Stevenson claimed that before acceptance he asked them whether they were happy with meeting the specification and whether they were sure they put everything in. He later blamed Swallow for underestimating the difficulties involved in building to his complex design. He also blamed the factories where the prefabricated panels were made, as well as poor workmanship on site. Although a spray diagram could have been used, the analyst chose to summarize his perception of the DDG situation in the form of a rich picture (Fig. 11.3).

    Likely components in the DDG Project System (system A) are:

within the system	*in the environment*
four chairmen of housing committees	tenants
R. Stevenson, designer	Swallow Construction
briefing for designer	factory making pre-cast components

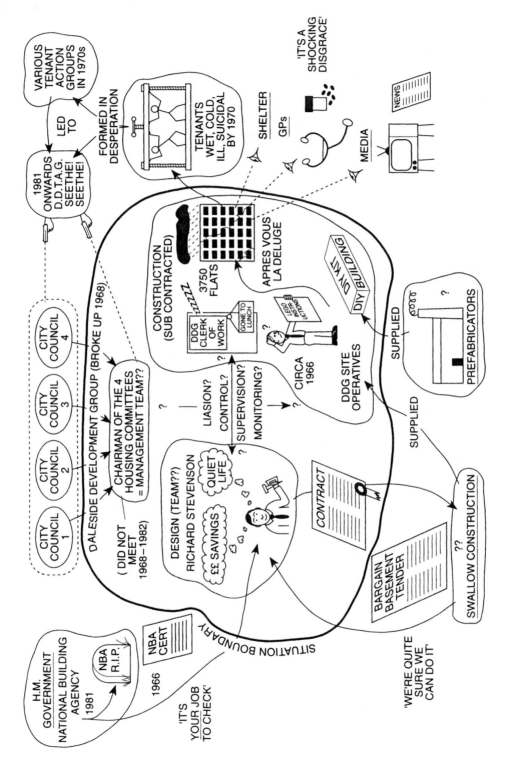

Fig. 11.3 A rich picture of the Daleside Development Group situation regarding 'system built' housing (second iteration).

design	factory quality control
tendering	GPs
construction	Shelter/Crisis
workmanship on site	NBA
repair/maintenance	tenant groups
checks on materials	Dept of Environment
fire precautions	government finance
	press/media reports

At this point, the analyst needs to consider whether the relevant system is a key or crucial system. In other words, is it essential to understanding why such apparent failures occur, and will it help the housing director carry out his task? As far as system A is concerned, there appear to be costly public housing failures associated with the design and construction of 'closed' system building projects. There is also the potential for apparent failures to be repeated if it becomes expedient to use unproven closed system building methods again. The housing director should be helped by gaining understanding of such methods and how they have failed. An examination of the DDG Project System, being typical of such projects in the 1960s, should provide understanding of system building failures and perhaps also failures to build durable habitation in general. On all these counts, system A is a key system.

SELECTION

A quick pass through the methodology showed that system A exhibited apparently significant failures, and is thus relevant to the housing director's task.

DETAILED DESCRIPTION OF SYSTEM A

(A) COMPONENTS

The resolution of the trial components listed above was adjusted and summarized as a system map. This map was developed through several iterations from Fig. 11.4 to the state shown in Fig. 11.5.

(B) INPUTS

- wider system policies;
- management skills;
- resources;
- design skills;
- repertoire of building methods;

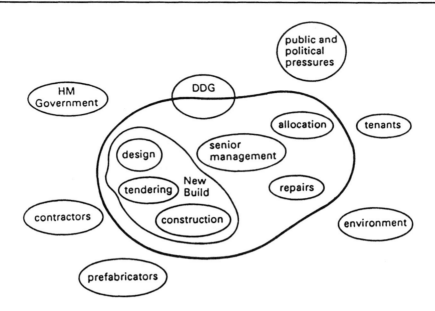

Fig. 11.4 A system map of the Daleside Development Group system.

- prefabrication skills;
- materials;
- tenants.

(C) OUTPUTS

- system-built estates (largely unserviceable);
- sitting tenants (largely dissatisfied);
- complaints from tenants to GPs, DDTAG, the press.

(D) ENVIRONMENT

- HM Government;
- physical environment;
- public and political pressures;
- Swallow Construction;
- prefabricators
- DDTAG (the tenants' action group).

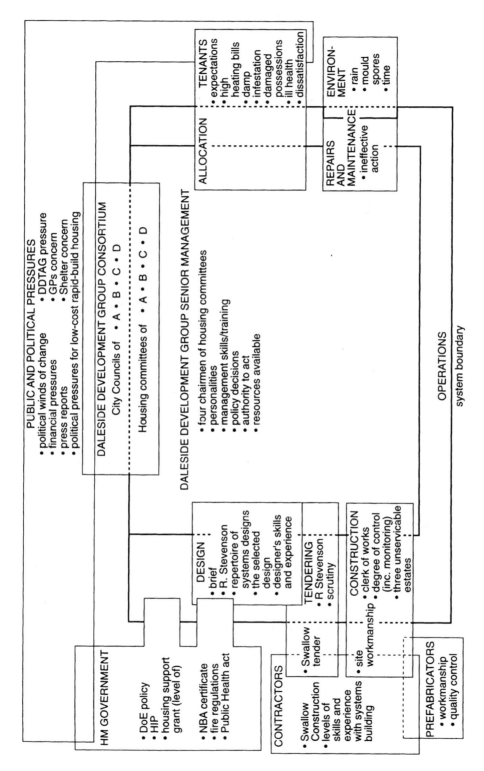

Fig. 11.5 A system map of the Daleside Development Group system from 1966 to 1982 (fourth iteration).

(E) STRUCTURE

The appointed decision-making sub-system within DDG was that comprising the four chairmen of the housing committees of the city councils in the consortium. It should be noted that unlike new build arrangements in a conventional local authority, DDG did not apparently use the architects departments of any of its four councils. Instead, it employed its own designer. The analyst tried to confirm the structure with the four councils concerned, but confirmation had not been received by the time the case study had been completed. This highlights the importance of two practical issues in this kind of study: (a) data collection is not a process carried out only at the start of the study – it continues throughout the project as circumstances dictate, (b) when new information is received it feeds further iterations. On the basis of the data available, the apparent DDG sub-systems were:

- design;

- tendering;

- construction;

- allocation;

- repairs and maintenance.

(F) VARIABLES

The variables identified in the first pass are those listed in the left-hand column of Table 11.1. However, the level of detail was too fine and iteration allowed the resolution to be adjusted to a more manageable level, as shown in the right-hand column.

(G) RELATIONSHIP BETWEEN VARIABLES

In the first pass, a relationship diagram between the variables in the left-hand column of Table 11.1 was drawn. On iteration, the diagram was adjusted, as shown in Fig. 11.6.

(H) APPARENTLY SIGNIFICANT FAILURES

Four failure categories over time are discernible:

category 1: pre-construction

The evidence suggests that the four chairmen gave the designer too much latitude in his work. There was no checking of the NBA certificate to ensure that it was appropriate to the task. Scrutiny of tenders was lax and the difficulty of the design was not fully conveyed to the builders.

Table 11.1 Adjustment of the resolution of variables

First pass	Iterative adjustment
councils in DDG housing committees	DDG consortium/sponsors
chairmen of four housing committees DDG management and administration	DDG senior management
briefing of designer designing tendering	preconstruction
job scheduling assembly erection monitoring of work	construction
monitoring for deterioration maintenance repair	post-construction
tenants' health tenants' expectations tenants' satisfaction level of tenants' complaints	tenants

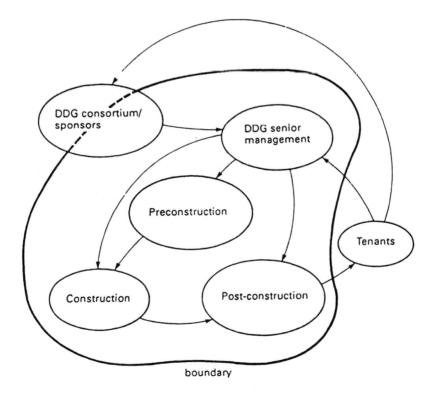

Fig. 11.6 Interaction of variables in the DDG project system.

category 2: construction

The quality of pre-cast panels and units supplied by prefabricators was not monitored and neither was the quality of workmanship on site. If indeed DDG supplied a clerk of works, his or her monitoring was unsatisfactory.

category 3: structural failures after completion

The most obvious FAILURE relates to the structural failure of pre-cast panels in the post-construction phase. Many concrete panels did not fit together properly and the resulting gaps could not be made watertight. Rubber seals protecting concrete joints linking the panels were sometimes poorly fitted or simply missing, which left joints open to rain penetration. Careless packing of mortar between walls and floors allowed water to pour into rooms below thus encouraging mould growth. Patches of cold concrete inside rooms arose from faulty insulation and caused condensation which was aggravated by poor heating and ventilation. Misshapen panels ensured that some window frames fitted badly so that rain seeped in. Some concrete links suffered load cracks which exposed steel reinforcement and this rusted due to water penetration.

category 4: management failures after completion

The four chairmen met only once in fourteen years, and effectively abandoned DDG tenants. After DDG disbanded in 1968, the four city councils involved took over the management of DDG properties in their respective areas. When tenants and tenants groups such as DDTAG complained over many years, they received little or no redress.

(I) APPROPRIATE PARADIGMS

In addition to the formal system paradigm, apparently relevant models from the repertoire are as follows in Table 11.2:

Table 11.2 Paradigms apparently relevant to the DDG failure

Failure category	Suggested paradigm	Justification
1	control	lack of control action
		lack of monitoring
	communication	builder's failure to perceive difficulties
2	control	lack of monitoring
3	fault tree	structural failure
	cascade	chain of events
	common mode	similar problems
4	control	controllers absent
	communication	misunderstandings
	stress	GPs' diagnosis
	group behaviour	concerted action by tenants

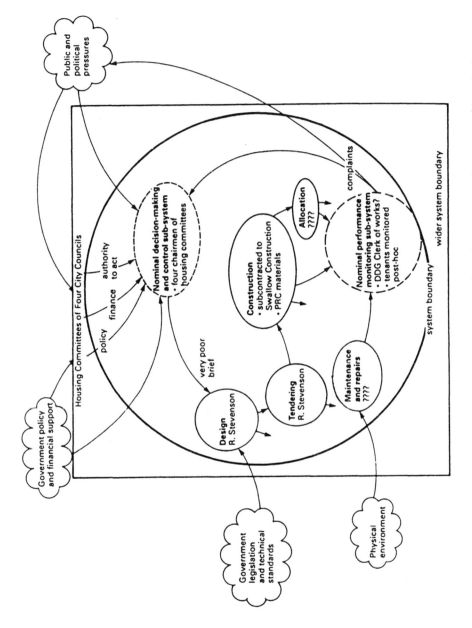

Fig 11.7 The DDG project system superimposed on the formal system paradigm (second iteration).

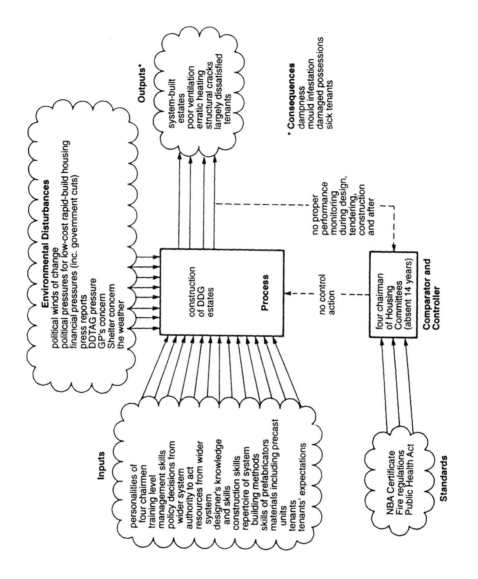

Environmental Disturbances

political winds of change
political pressures for low-cost rapid-build housing
financial pressures (inc. government cuts)
press reports
DDTAG pressure
GP's concern
Shelter concern
the weather

Inputs

personalities of
four chairmen
training level
management skills
policy decisions from
wider system
authority to act
resources from wider
system
designer's knowledge
and skills
construction skills
repertoire of system
building methods
skills of prefabricators
materials including precast
units
tenants
tenants' expectations

construction
of DDG
estates

Process

Outputs*

system-built
estates
poor ventilation
erratic heating
structural cracks
largely dissatisfied
tenants

* Consequences

dampness
mould infestation
damaged possessions
sick tenants

no proper
performance
monitoring
during design,
tendering,
construction
and after

no control
action

four chairman
of Housing
Committees
(absent 14 years)

**Comparator and
Controller**

NBA Certificate
Fire regulations
Public Health Act

Standards

Fig. 11.8 The DDG project system superimposed on the control paradigm (second iteration).

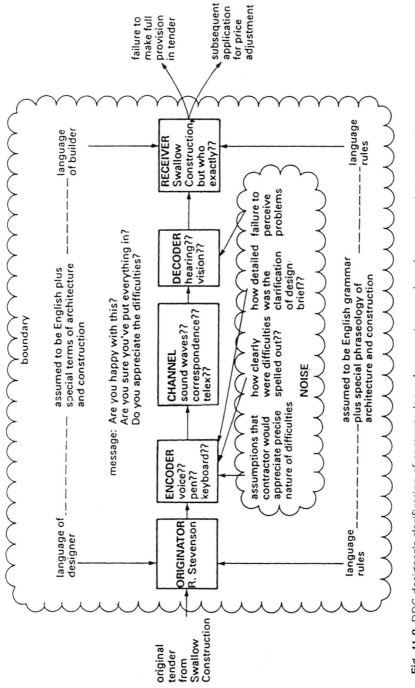

Fig. 11.9 DDG designer's clarification of contractor's tender superimposed on the communication paradigm (second iteration).

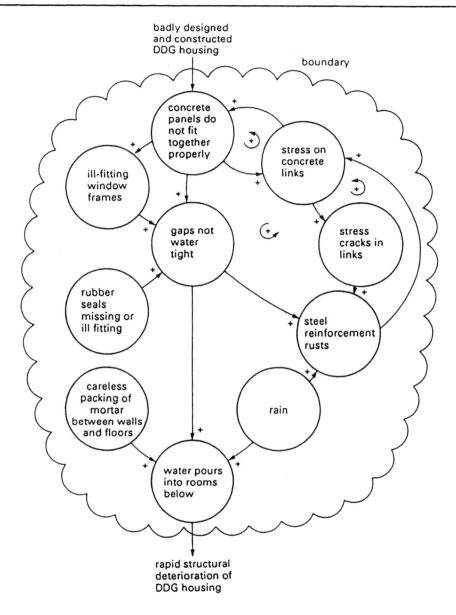

Fig.11.10 Structural failure of DDG system-built units superimposed on the cascade paradigm (second iteration).

STAGE 2 COMPARISON

Five comparisons were made between the systems description and the selected paradigms. These comparisons were made as described in Chapter 10, i.e. superimposing aspects of the systems description on the paradigms as shown in Figs 11.7 to 11.11.

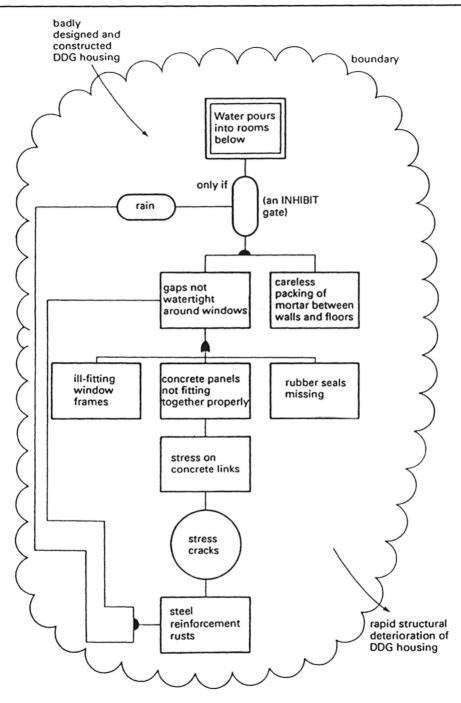

badly
designed and
constructed
DDG housing

boundary

Water pours
into rooms
below

only if

rain

(an INHIBIT
gate)

gaps not
watertight
around windows

careless
packing of
mortar between
walls and floors

ill-fitting
window
frames

concrete panels
not fitting
together properly

rubber seals
missing

stress on
concrete links

stress
cracks

steel
reinforcement
rusts

rapid structural
deterioration of
DDG housing

Fig. 11.11 Structural failure of DDG system-built housing superimposed on the fault tree paradigm (second iteration).

STAGE 3 MEANING OF COMPARISONS

Formal system paradigm versus the DDG project system

	paradigm	
	desirable	undesirable
no/few discrepancies		
many discrepancies	X	

There were considerable discrepancies between the DDG Project System and the FSP. For example, the fact that the four chairmen met only once in 14 years suggests that the control sub-system was nominal rather than actual. Their instructions and guidance to operational sub-systems seemed to be *laissez-faire* and there is no evidence of control beyond a perfunctory briefing of the designer. There also seemed to be no formal performance monitoring sub-system in operation throughout the entire DDG history. Monitoring only arose in an informal way *post hoc* in the form of tenants' observations and complaints.

Control paradigm versus the DDG project system

	paradigm	
	desirable	undesirable
no/few discrepancies		
many discrepancies	X	

Two major mismatches were (a) no proper monitoring during design, tendering and construction; (b) no control action during design, tendering, construction and the post-construction phase until tenants' complaints became irrepressible. These mismatches are consistent with the FSP interpretation.

Communication paradigm versus designer's checking of Swallow's tender

	paradigm	
	desirable	undesirable
no/few discrepancies		
many discrepancies	X	

The data are insufficient to confirm a mismatch. There appears to be a match because the designer asked questions of Swallow Construction and got answers. What is unclear is:

- what was the communication channel?;
- the originator's assumptions;

- precision and detail of originator's encoding;
- how detailed the clarification of the brief was;
- who the receiver at Swallow was;
- why the receiver failed to perceive difficulties.

Further iteration involving data collection would be needed to pursue this apparent failure.

Cascade paradigm versus structural failure of panels culminating in water pouring into rooms

paradigm

	desirable	undesirable
no/few discrepancies		X
many discrepancies		

There is a direct match between the system of apparent failures present in the structural deterioration of the DDG units and the cascade paradigm. The particular cascade is more than a simple serial or domino chain in view of the evidence of postive feed-back loops, i.e. the more the concrete panels fail to fit together properly the greater the stress on the concrete links; the greater the stress on the concrete links the more the panels do not fit together properly, and so on.

Fault tree versus structural failure of panels culminating in water pouring into rooms

paradigm

	desirable	undesirable
no/few discrepancies		X
many discrepancies		

As expected from the cascade comparison, there is a direct match. From the fault tree comparison it is harder to appreciate the self-sustaining nature of the failure process. However, the logic of the fault tree does highlight the original, underlying faults and so suggests which ones should be tackled first.

STAGE 4: LESSONS

The apparent failures of the DDG project system offer the following lessons:

a) Any large-scale project of this type ought to be under proper management, i.e. competent direction and control. There should be effective monitoring of every phase and aspect of the project.

b)   Communications between designers and building contractors should be seen to be on a formal written basis where important items are concerned. The designer should be obliged to detail explicitly the foreseeable potential construction difficulties for contractors prior to their tender.

c)   There should be strict quality control checks on prefabricated units received from factories and strict on-site monitoring of the standard of construction.

There is evidence that management, communications and engineering reliability failures were widespread throughout system building projects of the 1960s and 1970s. Although apparently more reliable open system methods are used nowadays, there will always be potential for new build failures unless projects are under sound management with effective communications and engineering reliability procedures.

POTENTIAL FOR CONTINUATION OF CASE STUDY

At this stage, the analyst called a halt owing to time constraints. Limited understanding had been gained of public sector 'new build' housing failures which would be of interest to the housing director. Further iterations involving further data collection would enable more careful examination of the DDG project system, if the client required it.

Beyond a FAILURES approach, the HARD SYSTEMS methodology could be used to examine and suggest improvements to engineering reliability of structural components. One aspect of new build failures which became apparent in the wider examination of public housing was the uncertainty about who has actual control over such building projects. Usually, the housing department is the client of the architects department (see Fig. 2.4, Chapter 2) but the analyst had the feeling that the Architects made most of the decisions. However, the Hulme Conference Report suggests that the public perceive housing departments and housing committees as being responsible for housing design failures. An SSM study would be most appropriate for examining organizational relationships, political processes and power relations between housing and architects and how these could be better harnessed to improve outcomes.

SELECTED REFERENCES

Deck Access Disaster (1985), Report of the Hulme Conference 22 February 1985, City of Manchester Council, May 1985

Foster J.S. (1983), *Mitchells Structure and Fabric Part 1*, Batsford Academic and Educational Ltd, London

Marsh P. (1985), Building systems and portable buildings, in *Specifications: Building Methods and Products Vol 1*, Technical and Product Information, 259–262, ed. D. Martin, The Architectural Press, London.

THE LITTLEBROOK D HOIST FAILURE – A STUDY OF SAFETY MANAGEMENT FAILURE

The construction and building industry (civil engineering, house building, building maintenance etc.) has long had the highest incidence of fatal and major injuries per employee of all industries. For example, according to the Health & Safety Executive, from 1981 to 1985 the incidence of such injuries in construction increased steadily from 164.0 to 231.8 per 100 000 employees, whereas the incidence for all industries barely altered (60.3 to 63.1). Since the early 1960s, four sets of Construction Regulations required systematic safety procedures on site.

Among these legal requirements are the need to appoint competent persons to oversee safety arrangements and to ensure regular inspection of lifting and other equipment. Many such inspections have to be done either daily or weekly whereas others, such as thorough examinations, have to be done either six-monthly or every two years. A series of statutory registers recording these inspections and the results have to be maintained on site. In addition to and overlaying these specific requirements, the Health & Safety at Work etc. Act 1974 places a duty on all employers to ensure so far as is reasonably practicable the health and safety of all their employees. They also have to draw up and revise as necessary a statement of their health and safety policy and the practical arrangements for carrying it out. More recently, the Management of Health and Safety at Work Regulations 1992 and the Construction (Design and Management) Regulations 1994 have required construction employers to manage health and safety in a competent and business-like fashion.

Littlebrook D was a large power station under construction at Dartford, Kent. The CEGB had contracted a major part of the civil engineering work, including construction of the cooling water system, to John Laing Construction Ltd. They in turn had subcontracted the construction of the shafts and tunnels to Edmund Nuttall Ltd. On 9 January 1978, a hoist operated by Nuttalls failed. The hoist cage fell more than 30 m to the bottom of a 60 m shaft. Four men died and five were seriously injured. The Health & Safety Executive conducted an investigation and published their report (*The Hoist Accident at Littlebrook D Power Station, 9 January 1978*).

Nuttalls were prosecuted and convicted under health and safety legislation. Subsequently, civil actions by those injured or by dependents were also successful. Considerable press publicity was given to what many regarded as a symptomatic failure of the construction industry in particular and employers in general to manage health and safety responsibilities effectively.

ANALYSIS

STAGE 1 SYSTEMS DESCRIPTION AND PARADIGM SELECTION

AWARENESS

The analyst was a consultant who wanted to gain greater understanding of the Littlebrook D hoist failure and to see if there were any lessons to be learned. In particular, he wanted to demonstrate to clients how such failures occur and how they can be prevented. His own world-view was very much influenced by the safety principle of 'self-regulation' proposed by Lord Robens (1972), i.e. those who create risks should manage them in a business-like fashion and those who work with such risks should co-operate to ensure the effective management of risks.

The official Health & Safety Executive (HSE) report concluded that the hoist's wire suspension rope broke at a part weakened by corrosion and devoid of lubricant. The deterioration occurred over a relatively short period and was not detected. Analysis of water in the shaft showed that it contained salt and the corrosion was consistent with the rope having been impregnated with salt water. Over the whole of the corroded length of rope at both sides of the fracture, the wire rope core was very corroded and many wires were broken. Tests revealed that at the fracture all the wires had lost over 50% of their tensile strength and the outer wires had lost 80%. In addition, both clamping units of the cage safety mechanism (fall arrester) were corroded and coated with a hard cement-like deposit weighing an estimated 80 kg +/- 25 kg. This deposit was visible evidence of the harsh service conditions and its presence should have alerted site staff to have high maintenance standards. At the time of the accident, the hoist cage was carrying nine passengers (one more than the specified maximum of eight).

The hoist manufacturers, ACE Machinery Ltd, specified in their handbook a monthly maintenance procedure including a rope examination. However, 'the exact pattern of routine maintenance could not be established since the contractors kept no record of such work. Site enquiries showed that maintenance work was carried out on a haphazard basis, mainly tending to coincide with the occasions on which repairs to the hoist were required. In the absence of even a simple site record, it was impossible to ascertain whether or not the hoist had been maintained in accordance with the manufacturer's handbook.'

Statutory six-monthly thorough examinations had been delegated to insurance company engineering surveyors (a common and acceptable practice). Such an examination had been due on or before 16 December 1977 but for various reasons the examination did not take place. Since the legal duties lay on Nuttalls, they should either have arranged for an examination by another competent person or taken the hoist out of commission until such examination had been done. Up to 9 January 1978 statutory weekly inspections had been carried out by Nuttall's own site staff, and at each inspection the entry for the hoist in the register read as 'in good order' or 'in good working order'.

Although Nuttall's safety policy set out general aims, it gave no clear indication about how these were to be achieved. 'Failure to specify detailed procedures was evident throughout the chain of management responsibility and put another burden on the site agent who, in addition to maintaining production rates and overall progress, was expected to ensure that "all machinery and plant... are maintained in good condition" and to maintain the site's registers, records and reports. Neither the site agent, his deputy (who had been appointed as site safety officer) nor the office manager had received clear guidance, training or allowance of time to undertake this responsibility.'

Although given overall responsibility for the site, the site agent 'clearly needed to be given adequate resources including advice, instruction and appropriately trained staff and suitable support by the organization.' Assistance on safety matters was intended to be available from a safety co-ordinator at Nuttalls headquarters who had visited Littlebrook D 13 times over the preceding 18 months. It is not clear whether assistance was requested or what assistance, if any, was rendered. The failure situation was summarized as a rich picture (Fig. 11.12) and as a spray diagram (Fig. 11.13).

COMMITMENT

The analyst, perceiving that his clients would be in positions comparable with Nuttall's managing director, induced the following commitment:

NUTTALL'S MANAGING DIRECTOR

'This accident has come as a terrible shock to the Board. Apart from the tragedy itself, our good name and reputation are at stake. We thought our safety policy, which is signed personally by me, was a very good one. As MD, I am ultimately responsible for both production and safety in all our operations. I need to find out what went wrong with our safety organization.'

Other potential clients could have been in positions comparable with the managing director of Ace Machinery, the site agent or other key figures but these possibilities were not pursued.

TESTING

- Is the potential client's task relevant to the failure situation? (Y)
- Is the commitment (of analyst and potential client) goal-orientated? (Y)
- Is analysis more appropriate than action? (Y)
- Is analysis need-driven rather than just to satisfy curiosity? (Y)

The test results indicate that the situation is worthy of systems analysis.

SEPARATION OF SYSTEMS

One important area in the situation that would be of interest to a potential client is safety versus production. Three systems deemed relevant to this area by the analyst are:

A: the Nuttall system for the safe excavation of tunnels at Littlebrook D;

B: the Nuttall system for purchasing, operating and maintaining lifting equipment;

C: the Nuttall system for formulating and executing safety policy.

For reasons of space, only system A is examined here. Typical components and an indication of a trial boundary for system A are as follows:

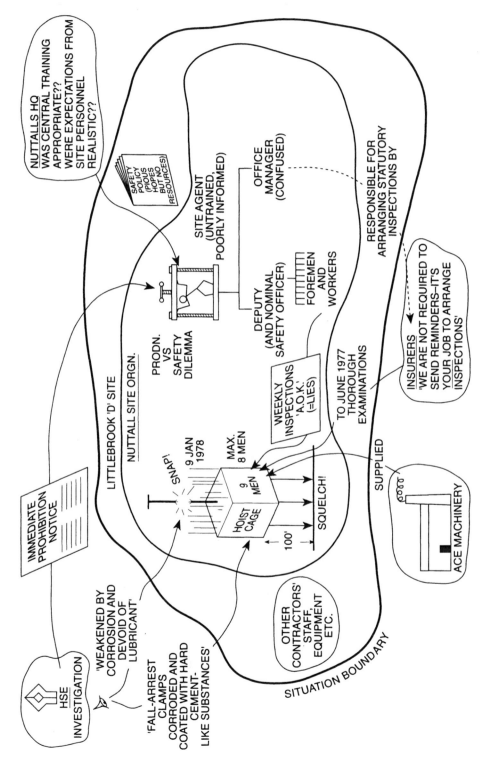

Fig. 11.12 A rich picture of the situation surrounding the hoist accident at Littlebrook D Power Station site (first iteration).

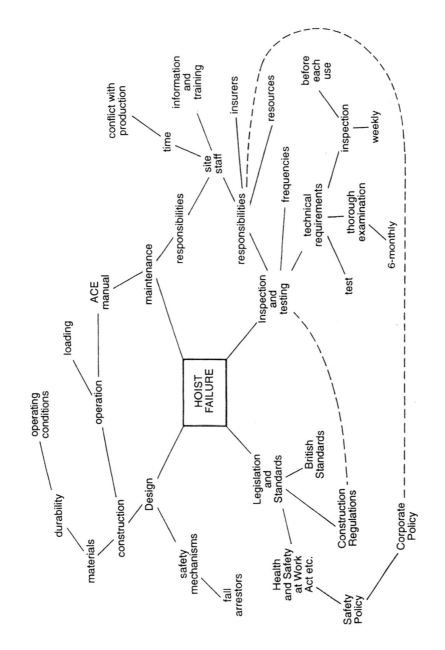

Fig. 11.13 Spray diagram of the situation surrounding the hoist accident at Littlebrook D.

Within the SYSTEM	*In the environment*
managing director	ACE Machinery
other directors	insurers
safety policy	HSE
resources	CEGB
site agent	John Laing Construction
office manager	HSW Act
deputy site agent	Factories Act
foremen	Construction Regulations
workers	wet, salty conditions
central training dept	
central safety dept	
safety committee	
trades union officials	
safety reps	
plant and equipment	
purchasing	
statutory registers	

System A is perceived as a key system because Nuttall's managing director was ultimately responsible for all safety matters in the company. He owned the failure problem. Since there appeared to be a discrepancy between the resources provided for production and those for execution of the safety policy, this system is highly relevant to understanding the failure. Systems B and C were also judged to be key systems.

SELECTING A KEY SYSTEM

System A was selected as the first of the three for detailed examination since it relates directly to the hoist accident at Littlebrook D, whereas systems B and C are of more general concern.

DETAILED ANALYSIS OF SYSTEM A

(A) COMPONENTS

The resolution of the trial components was adjusted and summarized as a system map (see Fig. 11.14).

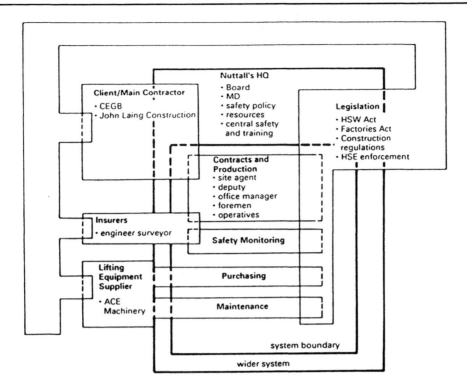

Fig. 11.14 System map of the Nuttall system relating to the Littlebrook D site (third iteration).

(B) INPUTS

- management skills, knowledge and training;
- engineering skills;
- workforce skills, knowledge and training;
- world-view of board;
- world-view of line managers;
- trade union influence;
- ACE hoist;
- client specification.

(C) OUTPUTS

- on-shore and off-shore shafts;
- cooling water tunnels (partly excavated);

- ineffective and under-resourced safety policy;

- poorly trained/informed workforce;

- poor maintenance;

- damaged hoist;

- five fatalities;

- four seriously injured.

(D) ENVIRONMENT (RESOLUTION ADJUSTED)

- legislation;

- client and main contractor;

- ACE Machinery Ltd;

- insurers;

- physical environment (wet, salty conditions, grout deposit etc).

(E) STRUCTURE (RESOLUTION ADJUSTED)

Apparent sub-systems were:

- board;

- contracts;

- purchasing;

- finance;

- central training;

- central safety dept.

(F) VARIABLES (RESOLUTION ADJUSTED)

- Nuttall's senior management;

- safety policy;

- safety resources;

- behaviour of site personnel;

- plant safety;

- safety monitoring;

- safety control.

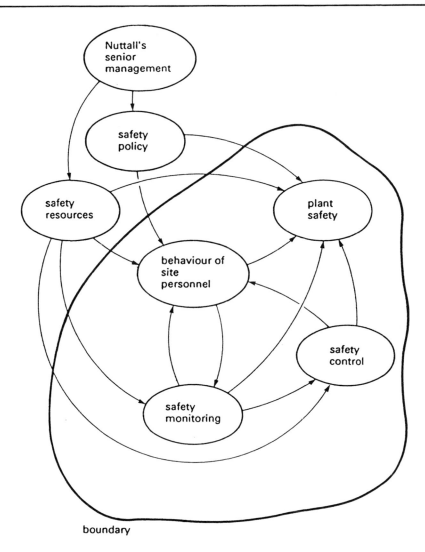

boundary

Fig. 11.15 Influences on the variables of the Nuttall system at Littlebrook D (second iteration).

(G) RELATIONSHIPS BETWEEN VARIABLES

Fig. 11.15 shows the relationship between variables.

(H) APPARENTLY SIGNIFICANT FAILURES

Four failure categories were identified:

A.   Failures in resource provision and distribution

- not enough time for site agent to exercise his responsibilities specified in the safety policy;
- no training resources provided for site personnel.

B   Failures in safety monitoring

- weekly statutory inspections were perfunctory;
- six-monthly statutory inspection omitted;
- failure of company safety co-ordinator adequately to monitor site safety arrangements.

C   Failure in safety control

- failure of company safety co-ordinator to co-ordinate and supervise safety arrangements;
- no regular preventive maintenance of hoists.

D   Failure in plant safety

- failure of single suspension rope;
- failure of fall-arrest safety clamps.

(I) SUITABLE PARADIGMS FOR COMPARISON

In addition to the formal system paradigm, the control, communication and fault tree paradigm are appropriate as indicated in Table 11.3.

STAGE 2 COMPARISON

Relevant aspects of the system description were superimposed on the formal system paradigm and the control, communication and fault tree paradigms as shown in Figs. 11.16 to 11.19.

Table 11.3 Paradigms apparently relevant to the Littlebrook D failure

Failure category	Suggested paradigm	Justification
A	control	lack of monitoring and control by site agent
	communication	safety policy not acted upon
B	control	safety inspections casual; arrangements not monitored
C	control	no preventive maintenance, arrangements not monitored and controlled
D	fault tree	mechanical failures

STAGE 3 MEANING OF COMPARISONS

Formal system paradigm versus the Nuttall system at Littlebrook D

paradigm

	desirable	undesirable
no/few discrepancies		
many discrepancies	X	

Discrepencies include:

(a)   from the wider system, an incomplete safety policy and limited resources;

(b)   control sub-system ineffective owing to overburdened site agent;

(c)   the maintenance sub-system seemed casual and ineffective (e.g. the cement-like grouting deposit that built up, the corrosion, lack of lubrication);

(d)   performance monitoring sub-system seemed casual and ineffective.

Control paradigm versus the Nuttall system at Littlebrook D

paradigm

	desirable	undesirable
no/few discrepancies		
many discrepancies	X	

Two major mismatches were:

(a)   no proper monitoring of safety;

(b)   no control action to restore proper safety monitoring or to ensure preventive maintenance.

This comparison confirms the interpretation from the FSP comparison.

Communication paradigm versus dissemination of Nuttall safety policy

paradigm

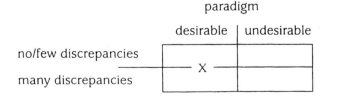

	desirable	undesirable
no/few discrepancies		
many discrepancies	X	

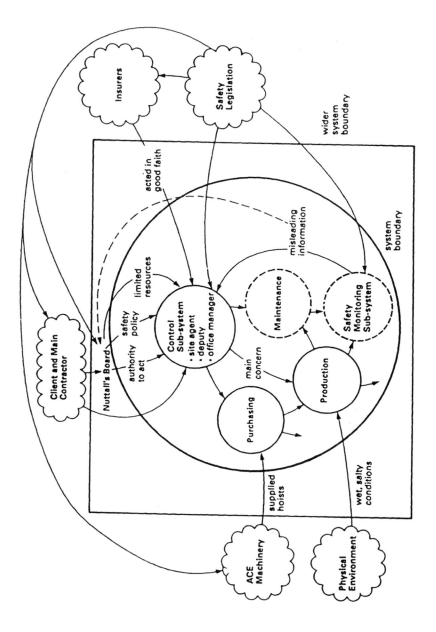

Fig. 11.16 The Nuttall system at Littlebrook D superimposed on the formal system paradigm (second iteration).

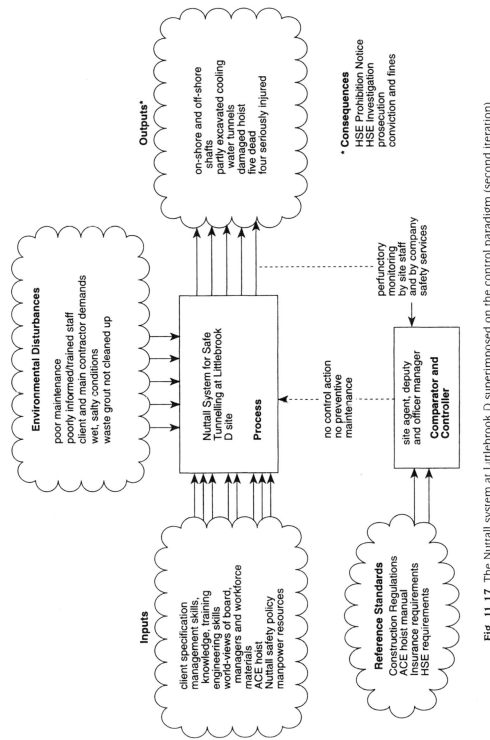

Inputs

client specification
management skills,
knowledge, training
engineering skills
world-views of board,
managers and workforce
materials
ACE hoist
Nuttall safety policy
manpower resources

Environmental Disturbances

poor maintenance
poorly informed/trained staff
client and main contractor demands
wet, salty conditions
waste grout not cleaned up

Nuttall System for Safe
Tunnelling at Littlebrook
D site

Process

Outputs*

on-shore and off-shore
shafts
partly excavated cooling
water tunnels
damaged hoist
five dead
four seriously injured

*** Consequences**

HSE Prohibition Notice
HSE Investigation
prosecution
conviction and fines

Reference Standards

Construction Regulations
ACE hoist manual
Insurance requirements
HSE requirements

site agent, deputy
and officer manager

**Comparator and
Controller**

no control action
no preventive
maintenance

perfunctory
monitoring
by site staff
and by company
safety services

Fig. 11.17 The Nuttall system at Littlebrook D superimposed on the control paradigm (second iteration).

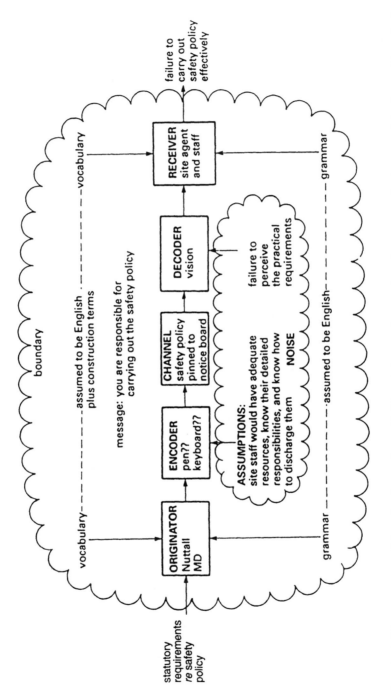

Fig. 11.18 Dissemination of Nuttall safety policy at Littlebrook D superimposed on the communication paradigm (second iteration).

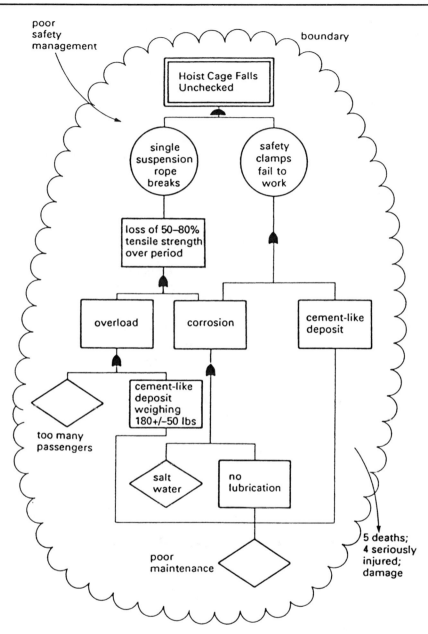

Fig. 11.19 The hoist failure at Littlebrook D superimposed on the fault tree paradigm (second iteration).

The information available (see Fig 11.8) is insufficient to confirm a mismatch. Ostensibly, there appears to be a match because the receivers read the policy documents and appeared to understand the message sent. However, the originator and receivers appeared to have different understandings of what the message meant. More data would have to be collected to examine this aspect further.

Fault tree model versus faults culminating in unchecked fall of hoist cage

	paradigm	
	desirable	undesirable
no/few discrepancies		X
many discrepancies		

There is a direct match: a hierarchy of faults culminating in the unchecked fall of the hoist cage.

STAGE 4 LESSONS

The failures examined offer the following lessons:

(a) Any large-scale excavation work ought to be under competent direction and control. There should be effective safety monitoring of every phase and aspect of the work.

(b) Communications of safety policy and directives from senior management (wider system) should take account of the resources of manpower, time, information, instruction, training and supervision needed to execute effectively those policies and directives on site.

(c) Plant and equipment whose failure would foreseeably result in death or injury should be inspected (i.e. monitored) and should undergo thorough preventive maintenance (i.e. control) at prescribed regular intervals by competent persons. Proper records should be kept and entries should be subject to regular independent cross-checking against the equipment concerned by senior personnel and/or independent auditors. These monitoring and control activities should be at least to the standard required by law.

POTENTIAL FOR CONTINUATION OF CASE STUDY

Systems B and C could be examined in a similar fashion. The focus of attention would then shift to corporate level rather than Littlebrook D. Since weaknesses in management at corporate level emerged in the lessons from system A, examination of systems B and C should provide interesting comparisons. Beyond the study of failures, attitudes towards the 'safety versus production' problem could form the basis of an SSM study.

SELECTED REFERENCES

The Hoist Accident at Littlebrook D Power Station, 9 January 1978, Health & Safety Executive, HSE Books

Robens (1972), *Safety and Health at Work*, Report of the Committee 1970–72, Chairman Lord Robens, Cmnd 5034, HMSO, London

Waring A.E. (1996), *Safety Management Systems*, ITBP

Managing Construction for Health and Safety, Approved Code of Practice for the Construction (Design and Management) Regulations 1994, Health & Safety Commission.

SUMMARY

The objectives of this chapter were to demonstrate the application of the SYSTEM FAILURES methodology through two case studies. Two points emerge from these studies. First, whereas both cases have been studied by others using non-systems approaches, the framework of SYSTEMS FAILURES methodology provides a disciplined way of gaining understanding from apparent failures and avoids mental 'leapfrogging' in the search for a cause. Second, whereas other methods may be good for certain tasks, they tend to focus on particular, narrow aspects of an apparent failure rather than on underlying causes which interact. The SYSTEMS FAILURES methodology integrates paradigm comparisons so that organizational behaviour and human factors are examined on a par with technical matters. With SFM, 'technical faults' are seen to be largely a *consequence* of organizational failures whereas other methods often relegate organizational failures to the category of 'contributory factors'.

12 SWITCHING AND COMBINING METHODOLOGIES

The objectives of this chapter are to:

- examine situations which might require application of more than one system methodologies;

- identify typical stages in a systems study when switching of methodologies might be appropriate;

- suggest techniques which assist in switching and combining system methodologies within a single study.

INTRODUCTION

So far, this book has described the use of systems methodologies as if 'problems' and situations present themselves in such a way that the choice of methodology is clear and obvious. For example, where conflict and unease are apparent SOFT SYSTEMS methodology would be appropriate. If the presenting problem is structured and there is a large measure of agreement about it, then HARD SYSTEMS methodology should be used, and so on. Unfortunately, the analyst is rarely faced with situations where the choice of methodology is clear cut.

Where the choice is unclear or ambiguous, how should the analyst proceed? Is it possible to apply more than one methodology during a single study? How would you know which methodology to use first? Can the analyst safely switch methodologies in the middle of a study? This chapter addresses such questions.

NB SYSTEM, HARD SYSTEM, SOFT SYSTEM and SYSTEM FAILURE in small capitals refer to metaphorical and perceptual constructs.

ASSESSING THE SYSTEMS TASK

As indicated throughout preceding chapters, the analyst will be concerned not only with world-views in the problem setting but also with his or her own world-view. The analyst's approach to perceived problems and to applying systems methodologies (or any other) will be influenced by that world-view. Look back, for example, at the introductory paragraphs to the Daleside case study in Chapter 11 to see how the analyst felt that his world-view had affected his whole stance to public housing. Another analyst would probably have approached the same task from a different angle and with different biases.

In deciding which methodology to use, there is no requirement to choose one rather than another. Individuals tend to favour one methodology rather than another. This is all right provided that natural bias is not taken to such an extreme that the analyst uses only one methodology for all cases. The analyst's own inclinations and initial assessment of the situation are likely to swing his or her decision towards one of the three methodologies. Intuitive hunches like this are often no worse than lengthy pondering, and have an advantage in that something of value will almost certainly be learned from a quick run through with any methodology. However, there are some guidelines which can help to improve efficiency.

SELECTING A METHODOLOGY

Many of the examples and case studies in both the 'hard' and 'soft' systems categories frequently have also a 'failures' character. Interventions in natural systems, such as the Dayak case, and in socio-technical systems such as the Bali case (see Chapter 6), often produce counter-intuitive outcomes (= failures). Problem situations amenable to SSM such as those at Lucrative, Air Traffic Control, and Northwood could very easily be justified as FAILURES cases. Therefore, if in any doubt when starting a systems study little will be lost by using the FAILURES methodology first. A lot can be learned even if there are apparently no significant failures. The analyst can then decide which, if any, of the HARD SYSTEMS and SOFT methodologies are going to be applied next.

If there is a large measure of agreement about the nature of the problem (or opportunity) and what is to be achieved, then HARD SYSTEMS methodology could be applied from the start. Where agreement is low or patchy, then SSM might be a better starting point.

To recap, any of the three approaches can be chosen to start the study but if in doubt use the SYSTEMS FAILURES methodology first. Having carried out an initial FAILURES study, you can then decide if either or both of the HARD and SOFT methodologies would be suitable as follow-up studies. However, a slavish approach to using systems methodologies is not recommended. Analysts are often up against time pressures which might preclude anything more than a superficial use of even one of the methodologies. In such cases, it is perfectly acceptable to use systems *ideas* along the way rather than trying a step-by-step 'cook-book' approach which will undoubtedly be more time-consuming.

SWITCHING METHODOLOGIES

There are occasions when switching methodolgies in mid-stream would be appropriate. Typically, a sensible switching point would be in the early stages of the HARD or SOFT approaches when sufficient description and analysis has been done to indicate that another methodology would be better. For example, if the analyst starts the HARD SYSTEMS methodology and discovers at systems description stage that FAILURES are manifest, then it may be prudent to find out more about them first so that counter-intuitive outcomes may be avoided. Thus, a switch to SYSTEM FAILURES methodology would be appropriate. Similarly, if it is impossible in the use of HARD SYSTEMS methodology clearly to identify objectives and constraints, it suggests that the analyst does not know enough about the systemic setting; switch to FAILURES methodology to gain understanding. However, it may be that uncertainties and differences of opinion arise about objectives, in which case switch to SSM.

If starting with SSM, the rich picture analysis may throw up apparently significant failures. It would probably be sensible at this stage to switch to SYSTEMS FAILURES methodology to gain greater understanding of the problem situation before returning to SSM. Nevertheless, having identified relevant systems there may be a large measure of agreement about them, in which case switch to HARD SYSTEMS methodology. After the debate stage of SSM, it is often useful to use a 'hard systems' approach in order to translate the 'whats' of the conceptual model(s) agreed upon into 'hows'. This may engender confidence at the implementation stage.

Of course, the problem situation may not remain stable throughout the period of study. If significant changes occur, this would be another indication for switching methodologies as the analyst sees fit.

Activity
Read the Northwood case study in Chapter 9. Identify a suitable point to switch to SYSTEMS FAILURES methodology and carry it out. Assess the understanding gained and consider how it might have affected the SSM study of Northwood presented in Chapter 9. You could also select any of the cases in earlier chapters and try switching methodologies.

SUMMARY

The objectives of this chapter were to (a) examine situations which might require application of more than one system methodology, (b) identify typical stages in a systems study when switching methodologies might be appropriate, and (c) suggest techniques which assist in switching and combining system methodologies within a single study.

Selecting, combining and switching systems methodologies is something of an art. There are no rights and wrongs about it but analysts who learn to do it skilfully tend to achieve more effective results than do those who simply resort out of habit to the one methodology they know best. If in doubt, use SYSTEM FAILURES methodology to start. Applying different methodologies in series can be very fruitful but sometimes you may have to switch methodologies in mid-stream. This can be done safely if the guidance above is followed. If time is short, use systems ideas and only as much of the formal methodologies as you think justifiable to assist the systems task.

13 DEVELOPING YOUR SYSTEMS SKILLS

The objectives of this chapter are to:

- provide guidance on how to apply systems-thinking in your work;

- summarize the range of sources of advice, guidance and learning which could assist in development of systems skills.

INTRODUCTION

As noted earlier in this book, applied systems requires a way of thinking rather than blind adherence to formulaic methods. It requires a reflexive and adaptive mind which is capable of trying new methods and techniques and 'bending the rules' when appropriate. This chapter seeks to widen the reader's approach to systems thinking beyond the three methodologies which form the core of this book, and to indicate sources which might assist in skill development.

SYSTEMS THINKING IN YOUR WORK

ASSUMPTIONS AND DEBATES

As discussed in Some Persepctives p. 5, systems work is inextricably bound up with long-standing debates and controversies about the nature of reality and the position of humans as observers, interpreters and interveners. Put another way, there are world-view clashes about world-views, for example:

- world-views about the nature of the social world;

- world-views about the neutrality of humans in what they perceive, interpret, consider important, and how they respond;

NB SYSTEM, HARD SYSTEM, SOFT SYSTEM and SYSTEM FAILURE in small capitals refer to metaphorical and perceptual constructs.

- world-views about the nature of organizations;

- world-views about individual and group behaviour such as attitudes, motivation, culture, power, learning etc.;

- world-views about systems ideas.

A competent systems thinker is aware of such complex factors and how they are likely to affect the approach to, conduct of, and outcomes from, the application of systems ideas.

OTHER SYSTEMS METHODOLOGIES AND TECHNIQUES

In addition to the three methodologies covered in this book, other system methodologies of note include:

- Viable Systems Methodology (VSM);

- Critical Systems Thinking (CST);

- Total Systems Intervention (TSI).

VSM is attributed to the systems thinker Stafford Beer and is based essentially on a cybernetic model of organization, i.e. it is based on ideas about intelligent machines. VSM addresses what are assumed to be the necessary and sufficient conditions for system viability. A VSM model of an organization typically includes recursions or 'nests' of lower-order systems, each of which repeats the viable functions of the next higher level of resolution or recursion.

Critical Systems Thinking (CST) seeks to combine aspects of functionalism and interpretism with radical humanism (seeking the emancipation of system actors or beneficiaries through system improvement). The analyst is required to make explicit his or her world-view in developing a constructive criticism of a particular SYSTEM. CST shares a number of characteristics with research methods such as organizational ethnography, participant observation and action research, and also explicitly allows for the complementary use of all other systems methodologies.

Total Systems Intervention (TSI) is a derivative of CST, which seeks to encourage creative thinking about organizations and their 'problems' TSI advocates the interactive combination of three components – system metaphors, 'a system of systems methodologies', and the individual methodologies themselves. TSI is an advanced methodology and Flood and Jackson (1991) who have pioneered it caution against a simple pragmatic 'pick-and-mix' approach to system methods within TSI. In other words, TSI is much more than applying the approach suggested in Chapter 12 of this book.

Methodologies such as Structured Systems Analysis and Design (SSADM) and Multiview are variants of, respectively, 'hard systems and 'soft systems' approaches which tend to be applied to the computing and IT field.

Cognitive mapping attributed to Colin Eden is a technique which seeks to elicit and characterize the typical knowledge/belief/expectation sets of one or more groups of people, usually in an organization. Cognitive mapping is a derivative of the well-known repertory grid technique for characterizing the personality of individuals. Its use in systems work centres on detailed identification of world-views, behaviour prediction, identification of desired changes and evaluating effects of system interventions.

SELF-CONFIDENCE

One sign of developed skills in practical systems thinking is the self-confidence to make the methodologies and techniques your own and to know when 'bending the rules' is justifiable. Systems work should not be about slavishly and blindly following orthodox rules thought up by someone else, nor should it be an excuse for breaking the faith just for the sake of it.

Systems work is like photography. The unskilled amateur photographer may be tempted to acquire a range of 'professional' accoutrements which he or she feels have to be used in order to demonstrate professionalism. The highly skilled professional photographer, however, knows exactly when and if such devices are needed and will recognize when rules need to be broken and how best to break them.

KEEPING UP-TO-DATE

The following are useful sources of up-to-date information on developments in practical systems thinking:

Systems Practice bimonthly academic journal, Plenum Publishing Corporation, 233 Spring Street, New York, NY 10013, USA.

The Systemist quarterly learned journal, United Kingdom Systems Society, published by Byword Publications, 29 West Downs Close, Fareham, Hants PO16 7HW, England

Systems students and practitioners should also consider joining:

The United Kingdom Systems Society, Department of Computing and Information Systems, University of Paisley, Renfrewshire PA1 2BE

COURSES

In the UK, the following institutions offer courses which are either wholly or significantly concerned with systems:

City University, Department of Systems Science, St John Street, London EC1V 0HB, England.

University of Hull, Department of Management Systems and Sciences, Hull HU6 7RX, England, and its affiliated Centre for Systems Studies, Newlands House, Hull HU6 7TQ.

Lancaster University, Lancaster Management School, Lancaster LA1 4YX, England.

The Open University, Systems Department, Faculty of Technology, Walton Hall, Milton Keynes, Bucks MK7 6AA, England.

University of Paisley, Department of Computing and Information Systems, Paisley, Renfrewshire PA1 2BE, Scotland.

University of Salford, Information Systems Research Group, Department of Mathematics and Computer Science, Salford M5 4WT, England.

Glossary

Here, and throughout the book, the author has adopted the convention of using SMALL CAPITALS to indicate that the terms SYSTEM, HARD SYSTEM, SOFT SYSTEM and SYSTEM FAILURE should be regarded as 'perceived' rather than actual. This is to avoid the wearisome repetition of the prefix 'perceived' throughout the text.

A

abstract system: One that is essentially theoretical or symbolic, e.g. a computer programming language.

actor: A person perceived to play a role in a human activity system; a social 'actor'.

adaptive control: Moderating action taken by a SYSTEM to maintain its output(s) at a desired level by monitoring output(s), comparing with required level, and counteracting any discrepancy; closed loop control involving feedback signals.

algorithm: Any well-defined set of operations for solving a particular problem; may be expressed in words or diagrammatically.

B

black box model: Input – process – output in which process is represented by a notional 'black box'; the assumption is that the contents of the black box may be ignored.

boundary: A conceptual boundary between the components of a SYSTEM and the system's environment.

BS 7850. British Standard guidance on Total Quality Management.

C

cascade paradigm: Concept and model of a chain reaction; the simplest cascade is a 'domino' chain but real-world cascades are usually multi-component and involve multiple causal loops.

CATWOE: Mnemonic for the test of adequacy of a Root Definition in soft systems methodology; stands for Customers, Actors, Transformation, Weltanschauung, Owner, Environment.

Checkland method: See soft systems methodology.

client: The person who commissions a system study and to whom the analyst formally reports.

client-set: All those with whom a systems study seeks to gain credibility.

closed system: A system which is not perceived to have any interaction with an environment; real-world systems are rarely closed systems.

cognitive mapping: A technique based on repertory grid technique which seeks to identify the characteristic knowledge, beliefs and expectation sets of a group of people.

communication paradigm: Concept and models which describe the encoding, transmission and decoding of information; can be human-human, human-machine or machine-machine.

component: An identifiable part of a system's structure.

conceptual model: A notional model of a concept.

control: Action taken by a system to maintain its activity or output at a pre-determined level; see adaptive and non-adaptive control.

control paradigm: Model which represents the control concept including the components of control and their relationships.

Critical Systems Thinking: A constructively critical approach to human activity 'systems' which seeks system improvement and empowerment of system actors and owners.

culture: Unwritten and usually unadmitted attitudes, beliefs, values, rules of behaviour, ideologies, habitual responses, language, rituals, 'quirks' and other characteristics of a particular group of people; cultures can be identified at different levels, e.g. nations, societies, organizations, departments, interest groups.

D

designed technical system: A notional system of technical components designed and constructed by humans; not necessarily a mechanical system.

E

emergence: A collection of properties which characterize a particular notional system but which could not be attributed to any of the system's components in isolation, e.g. customer satisfaction; the result of synergy between components; see synergy, holism and systemic.

engineering reliability: A measure of how successful an engineered system is likely to be in completing its mission; usually measured as a probability in the range 0 to 1.0.

engineering reliability models: Models which represent various ways in which the reliability of engineered systems may be affected, e.g. fault trees, cascades.

environment: (1) A conceptual area surrounding a SYSTEM outside its boundary; components in a SYSTEM's environment affect the system but whereas components in the system may affect those in the environment they have no control over them. (2) The physical and social environments of people.

ETHICS: Effective Technical and Human Implementation of Computer Systems, a socio-technical systems approach developed by Professor Enid Mumford.

F

fault tree paradigm: An engineering reliability concept and model which enables the possible causes of a fault or apparent failure to be charted as a sequence or hierarchy of preceding events.

feedback: Signals from monitoring of outputs from a process are fed back to a comparator which checks for discrepancy between output level and desired level; characteristic of closed loop or adaptive control.

feedforward: Signals representing a desired level of output are fed to an actuator which adjusts the process so as to produce that level of output; characteristic of open loop or non-adaptive control.

formal problem-solving: A formal procedure for solving well-structured and understood problems having limited range of known possible solutions; having defined the problem and considered the resources available, the task is essentially a cost-benefit appraisal of the possible solutions; not a 'systems' approach.

formal system paradigm: A model which provides the essential framework of components and processes needed for a SYSTEM to function, e.g. decision, control, monitoring, communication; applies especially to human activity systems.

functionalist world-view: A world-view which suggests that everything has a pre-ordained role and function; the structures of business and industry and how they operate are taken for granted; 'problems' exist to be 'solved'; consistent with HARD SYSTEMS methodology.

H

HARD SYSTEM: One perceived to have well-structured components and definable, quantifiable attributes which lend themselves to prediction and control.

HARD SYSTEMS methodology: A systems methodology which assumes that a perceived problem exists to be solved, or an unmet need or opportunity fulfilled; analysis involves detailed description of SYSTEMS and a rigorous evaluation of potential strategies; client-set world-view is relevant throughout.

HAZOPS: Hazard and Operability Studies designed to check and challenge assumptions about the operational safety of process plant and equipment.

hierarchy: The concept of relationships in which sets of items are subordinate to others in some way e.g. a family tree, a set of objectives.

holism: A concept often expressed as 'the whole is greater than the sum of its parts'; encompasses the concepts of emergence, synergy and systemic properties.

holon: An alternative term for 'system' proposed by Professor Peter Checkland in order to avoid 'problems' associated with the wide misuse of the term 'system'; crucially, 'what a holon (system) shall contain is determined by the observer'.

homeostasis: Self-maintaining activity consistent with adaptive, closed-loop control; characteristic of biological systems but may be applied to human activity SYSTEMS with caution.

human activity system: One perceived to involve people apparently carrying out some purposeful activity; the system content is conceptual rather than real-world, i.e. it is determined by the observer.

human factors paradigms: Concepts and models which represent particular aspects of human behaviour e.g. learning, stress, group dynamics.

I

information system: A system conceived and designed to provide users with information on prescribed topics.

interpretive world-view: A world-view which does not regard everything as having a pre-ordained role and function although it does value social order; the structures of business and industry and human activity in general are seen as being socially constructed; many real-world 'problems' perceived to require coping and learning strategies rather than 'solutions'; consistent with SSM.

ISO: International Standards Organization.

ISO 9000: International standard specification for quality management systems.

issue: A topic about which there is (overt or covert) disagreement among social actors; a bone of contention.

iteration: The process of repeating actions; a standard activity in systems analysis in order to develop clarity and understanding or improve design.

J

JSM: Jackson Structured Method; a HARD SYSTEMS approach to information systems analysis and design.

K

key figure: A social actor in a human activity SYSTEM whom the observer considers to exercise a special or important role.

L

LSDM: Learmonth and Burchett Structured Development Method; see SSADM.

M

management system: (1) A notional system relating to management of an organization or operation. (2) A structured systematic means for ensuring that an organization, or a defined part of it, is capable of achieving and maintaining high standards of specified performance.

measure of assessment: A means of determining the anticipated results of a number of different proposed options in hard systems methodology and formal problem solving, both quantitative and qualitative measures are usually needed.

mess: A 'system of problems' which defies resolution simply by trying to solve individual problems (Ackoff); typical of apparently intractable 'wicked' problems of human activity SYSTEMS; a starting point for SSM.

MRP-II: Manufacturing Resource Planning; a HARD SYSTEMS approach to production management.

N

natural system: A system which is not man-made and perceived to exist in the natural world e.g. the weather.

non-adaptive control: Control which does not rely on monitoring process output, and adapting to any discrepancy between output and desired state; feedforward or open-loop control.

O

open system: A SYSTEM which interacts with an environment; and adaptive system.

organization: (1) The processes of forming, maintaining and dissolving human relationships; (2) A structure of such relationships as in 'the' organization; (3) A human activity SYSTEM perceived to relate to 'the' organization; (4) The process of organizing or co-ordinating resources in a systematic way for best efficiency in their application; (5) A company, corporation, firm, enterprise, society or other body.

owner: (1) A 'system owner' is the person who has ultimate authority over its existence; (2) A problem owner is the person who has the task of resolving it.

P

paradigm: A model of components and their inter-relationships which describes a concept.

political processes: Processes in human activity SYSTEMS by which various power factors (e.g. authority, influence, knowledge, information, world-views) affect the course and outcomes of thinking and action.

power: An emergent property of social interaction within a particular context; a complex phenomenon (see political processes and Some Perspectives p. 5).

primary task: The essential task of a human activity SYSTEM, e.g. the primary task of a motor manufacturer is to make motor vehicles.

problem: A source of puzzle, annoyance, frustration or harm to someone; problems are assumed not to exist outside people's heads.

process: A system component which changes continuously; 'doing' of some kind.

purposeful: Consciously willed behaviour involving creative choice.

purposive: Pre-ordained or pre-conscious behaviour resulting from a complex mixture of heredity and previous cultural and other experience.

R

real world: The world outside the artificial world of the laboratory.

reductionism: A process of reducing complexity to simpler and more manageable components; an inherent part of modelling in HARD SYSTEMS methodology; reductionist models assume that all the fine structure that is lost is insignificant to the task.

reification: Regarding something as an object even if it is intangible, e.g. the money supply.

relevant system: In SSM, a hypothetical or notional system initially deemed by the analyst to be relevant to the 'mess' and ultimately tested for relevance on the actors.

resolution: The degree of detail covered in a system diagram; the number of components that needs to be adjusted to be informative and to avoid swamping a reader.

rich picture: An evocative visual summary of a situation or 'mess', drawn at the start of SSM but may also be used in SYSTEMS FAILURES methodology.

root definition: The precise definition of a relevant SYSTEM in SSM.

S

SASDM: Structured Analysis and Systems Design; a HARD SYSTEMS approach to information systems developed by DeMarco and Yourdon.

socio-technical system: A SYSTEM conceived as having both engineered or designed components and human activity components e.g. an information system of which computers form a part.

SOFT SYSTEM: One relating to human activity.

SOFT SYSTEMS methodology: A methodology intended for use where a human activity SYSTEM exhibits crisis, conflict, uncertainty or unease among the social actors; also called the Checkland methodology; two main forms – basic seven-stage form (Checkland 1981) and developed form (Checkland and Scholes 1990).

SSADM: Structured Systems Analysis and Design Methodology; a 'HARD SYSTEMS' approach to information systems developed for the Central Computer and Telecommunications Agency by Learmonth and Burchett Management Systems.

SSM: see SOFT SYSTEMS methodology.

strategy: An overall plan of action to achieve a desired objective.

stress paradigm: A human factors paradigm which represents how a human being adapts to a variety of stressors.

structure: Relatively stable and unchanging components of a SYSTEM; the 'doers' and the 'done to'.

sub-system: An identifiable component of a SYSTEM which itself has the characteristics of a system.

synergy: Interaction between system components to produce an output greater than the sum of component outputs; see emergence and holism.

system: A concept of a recognizable whole consisting of a number of parts which interact in an organized way; characterized by inputs, outputs, processes, a boundary, an environment, an owner, emergent properties, control and survival; addition or removal of a component affects both the SYSTEM and the component.

system description: A structured way of describing a SYSTEM.

SYSTEM FAILURE: An apparent shortcoming in a SYSTEM which causes someone concern or is otherwise detrimental to someone.

systematic: An ordered and organized way of doing something.

systemic: To do with a SYSTEM and implying holism and emergence.

systems engineering: A HARD SYSTEMS approach to the design and construction of technical or engineered systems.

T

Total Quality Management (TQM): The management philosophy and practices which aim to harness the human and material resources of an organization in the most effective way to achieve the objectives of the organization.

Total Systems Intervention: A derivative of Critical Systems Thinking developed by Flood and Jackson which advocates the interactive combination of system metaphors, 'a system of system methodologies' and the individual methodologies themselves.

transformation: The essential process of a notional relevant system in SSM.

V

value: A belief or set of beliefs which is not testable in a fully objective way, e.g. religious beliefs, political views, moral standpoints.

value system: A number of values which interact.

Viable Systems Methodology: A systems methodology originated by Stafford Beer which adopts a cybernetic model of the necessary and sufficient conditions for organizational effectiveness.

W

Weltanschauung: see world-view.

wider system: A system outside the SYSTEM which authorizes the latter's existence, sets policy, provides resources etc., e.g. a parent company represents the wider system of a subsidiary.

world-view: A complex set of perceptions, attitudes, beliefs, values and motivations which characterize how an individual or group of people interpret the world and their existence; characteristic biases; closely allied to ideational culture.

Y

YSM: Yourdon Structured Method; a HARD SYSTEMS approach to information systems.

REFERENCES AND FURTHER READING

Ackoff R.L. (1971), Towards a system of system concepts, *Journal of Management Science*, **17** (11).

Allen V.L. (1982), *Social Analysis: a Marxist Critique and Alternative*, The Moor Press, Shipley.

Arinze B. (1992), Decision Support Systems (DSS) development using a model of user inquiry types: methodological proposals and a case study, *Systems Practice*, **5** (6), pp 629–650.

Astley W.G. and Van de Ven A.H. (1983), Central perspectives and debates in organization theory, *Administrative Science Quarterly*, **28**, pp 245–273.

Avison D. and Wood-Harper T. (1990), *Multiview: An Exploration in Information Systems Development*, Alfred Waller, Henley-on-Thames.

Bacharach S.B. and Lawler E.J. (1980), *Power and Politics in Organizations: the Social Psychology of Conflict, Coalitions and Bargaining*, Jossey-Bass Inc, San Francisco.

Beer M., Eisenstat R.A. and Spector B. (1990), Why change programs don't produce change, *Harvard Business Review*, **68** (6), pp 158–166.

Bignell V. and Fortune J. (1984), *Understanding Systems Failures*, Manchester University Press, Manchester.

Board of Banking Supervision (1995) Report of the Inquiry into the Circumstances of the Collapse of Barings, Chairman E.A.J. George, HMSO, London.

Booth R.T., Raafat H. and Waring A.E. (1988), *Machinery and Plant Integrity, Module ST2*, Occupational Health & Safety Open Learning, Portsmouth University.

Bryman A. (1988), *Doing Research in Organizations*, Routledge, London.

Buchanan D.A., Boddy D. and McCalman J. (1988), Getting in, getting on, getting out, and getting back, in *Doing Research in Organizations*, ed. A. Bryman, Routledge, London pp 64–67.

Burrell G. and Morgan G. (1979), *Sociological Paradigms and Organizational Analysis*, Heinemann, London.

Bynner J. and Stribley K.M. (1979), *Social Research: Principles and Procedures*, Longman/Open University Press, Harlow.

Carter P. and Jackson N. (1991), In defence of paradigm incommensurability, *Organization Studies*, **12** (1), pp 109–127.

Carter R., Martin J., Mayblin B. *et al.* (1984), *Systems, Management and Change – a Graphic Guide*, Harper & Row, London.

Checkland P. (1981), *Systems Thinking, Systems Practice*, John Wiley & Sons, Chichester.

Checkland P. and Davies L. (1986), The use of the term Weltanschauung in soft systems methodology, *Journal of Applied Systems Analysis*, **13**, pp 109–116.

Checkland P. and Scholes J. (1990), *Soft Systems Methodology in Action*, John Wiley & Sons, Chichester.

Churchman C.W. (1985), Perspectives of the systems approach, in W.G. Bennis *et al.* (eds), *The Planning of Change in Organizations*, 4th edition, Holt, Rinehart and Winston, New York. pp 253–259.

Clare C. and Loucopoulos P. (1987), *Business Information Systems*, Paradigm.

Clegg S. (1980), Power, organization theory, Marx and critique, in S. Clegg and D. Dunkerley (eds), *Critical Issues in Organizations*, Routledge, London. pp 21–40.

Clegg C., Kemp N. and Legge K. (1985), *Case Studies in Organization Behaviour*, Harper & Row, London.

Cummings T.G. (1980), *Systems Theory for Organization Development*, John Wiley & Sons, Chichester.

Cutts G. (1987), *Structured Systems and Design Methodology*, Blackwell Scientific Publications, Oxford.

Davies L.J. (1988), Understanding organizational culture: a soft systems perspective, *Systems Practice*, **1** (1), pp 11–30

Deal T.E. and Kennedy A.A (1986), *Corporate Cultures: Rites and Rituals of Corporate Life*, Addison-Wesley.

Denzin N.K. (1978), *The Research Act*, McGraw Hill.

Diamond M.A. (1986), Resistance to change: a psychoanalytic critique of Argyris and Schon's contributions to organization theory and intervention, *Journal of Management Studies*, **23** (5), pp 543–561.

Dixon N.F. (1981), *Preconscious Processing*, John Wiley & Sons, Chichester.

Donaldson L. (1985), *In Defence of Organization Theory*, Cambridge University Press.

Douglas M. (1992), *Risk and Blame: Essays in Cultural Theory*, Routledge, London.

Eden C., Jones S. and Sims D. (1983), *Messing About in Problems*, Pergamon Press, Oxford.

Espejo R. and Harnden R. (1989), *The Viable Systems Model*, John Wiley & Sons, Chichester.

ESRC (1993), *Report of the Commission on Management Research*, Economic and Social Science Research Council.

Finlay P.N. and Wilson J.M. (1991), Validation for decision support systems: recent developments and findings, *Systems Practice*, **4** (6), pp 599–610

Flood R.L. and Jackson M.C. (1991), *Creative Problem Solving: Total Systems Intervention*, John Wiley & Sons, Chichester.

Fortune J. and Peters G. (1995), *Learning from Failure: the Systems Approach*, John Wiley & Sons, Chichester.

Glendon A.I. and McKenna E. (1995), *Human Safety and Risk Management*, Chapman & Hall, London.

Hardy C. (1985), The nature of unobtrusive power, *Journal of Management Studies*, **22** (4), pp 384–399.

Ho J.K.K and Sculli D. (1994), A multi-perspective systems-based framework for Decision Support Systems design, *Systems Practice*, **7** (5), pp 551–563.

Holling C.S. and Goldberg M.A. (1973), *Managing the Environment*, US Government Printing Office.

Jackson M.C. (1991), *Systems Methodology for the Management Sciences*, Plenum, New York.

Jeffcutt P. (1991), *From interpretation to representation in organisational analysis: post-modernism, ethnography and organisational culture*, paper presented at The New Theory of Organisations Conference, Keele University, April 1991.

Johnson G. (1987), *Strategic Change and the Management Process*, Basil Blackwell, Oxford.

Johnson G. (1992), Managing strategic change – strategy, culture and action. *Long Range Planning*, **25** (1), pp 28–36.

Klein D. (1985), Some notes on the dynamics of resistance to change: the defender's role, in W.G. Bennis *et al* (eds), *The Planning of Change in Organizations*, 4th edition, Holt, Rinehart and Winston, New York.

Kluback W. and Weinbaum M. (1957), *Dilthey's Philosophy of Existence: introduction to Weltanschauungslehre*, translation of an essay, Vision Press (out of print).

Knights D. and Morgan G. (1991), Strategic discourse and subjectivity, *Organization Studies*, **12** (2), pp 251–273.

Korman A.K. and Vredenburgh D.J. (1984), The conceptual, methodological and ethical foundations of organizational behaviour, in M. Gruneberg and T. Wall (eds), *Social Psychology and Organizational Behaviour*, John Wiley & Sons, Chichester. pp 227–254.

Kuhn T.S. (1970), *The Structure of Scientific Revolutions*, University of Chicago Press.

Layzell P.J. and Loucopoulos P. (1987), *Systems Analysis and Development*, Chartwell-Bratt.

Lewis B.N., Horabin I.S. and Gane C.P. (1967), *Flow Charts, Logical Trees, and Algorithms for Rules and Regulations*, Civil Service College Occasional Paper No 2, HMSO.

Littler C. (1985), Taylorism, Fordism and job redesign, in D. Knights *et al.* (eds), *Job Redesign: Critical Perspectives on the Labour Process*, Gower Publishing. pp 10–29.

Locke E.A. (1984), Job satisfaction, in Gruneberg M. and Wall T. (eds), *Social Psychology and Organizational Behaviour*, John Wiley & Sons, Chichester. pp 93–117.

Lundberg C.C. (1990), Surfacing organizational culture, *Journal of Managerial Psychology*, **5** (4), pp 19–26.

Mangham I. (1979), *The Politics of Organizational Change*, Associated Business Press, London.

Mar'ashi J. (1995) *Conceptual Challenges in the Islamic System*, Industrial Management Institute, Tehran, Iran.

Miller G.A. (1956), The magical number seven, plus or minus two: some limits on our capacity for processing information, *Psychological Review*, **63**, pp 81–97.

Morgan G. (1986), *Images of Organization*, Sage, London.

Oborne D. and Gruneberg M.M. (1983), *The Physical Environment at Work*, John Wiley & Sons. Chichester.

Oliga J. (1990), Power-ideology matrix in social system control, *Systems Practice*, **3** (1), pp 31–49.

Open University (1984), T301 *Complexity, Management and Change – a Systems Approach*, course texts, revised 1993.

Pettigrew A. (1973), *The Politics of Organizational Decision Making*, Tavistock.

Pettigrew A. (1985), *The Awakening Giant – Change and Continuity in ICI*, Blackwell.

Pettigrew A. (1987), Context and action in the transformation of the firm, *Journal of Management Studies*, **24** (6), pp 649–670.

Pettigrew A., Ferlie E. and McKee L. (1992), *Shaping Strategic Change*, Sage, London.

Pfeffer J. (1981), *Power in Organizations*, Pitman.

Pfeffer J. (1982), *Organizations and Organization Theory*, Pitman

Reason P. and Rowan J. (1985), *Human Inquiry: a Sourcebook of New Paradigm Research*,

Reed M. (1991a), *Organizations and modernity: continuity and discontinuity in organization theory*, paper presented at The New Theory of Organizations Conference, Keele University, April 1991.

Reed M. (1991b), From paradigms to images: the paradigm warrior turns post-modernist guru, *Personnel Review*, **19** (3), pp 35–40.

Roberts N., Andersen D., Deal R. *et al.* (1983), *Introduction to Computer Simulation – a System Dynamics Modelling Approach*, Addison-Wesley, Reading, Mass.

Rosen M. (1991), Coming to terms with the field: understanding and doing organizational ethnography, *Journal of Management Studies*, **28** (1), pp 1–24.

Rowe C.J. (1985), Identifying causes of failure: a case study in computerised stock control, *Behaviour and Information Technology*, **4**(1), pp 63–72.

Sarma V.V.S. (1994), Decision-making in complex systems, *Systems Practice* **7**(4), pp 399–407

Schein E.H. (1985), *Organization Culture and Leadership*, Jossey-Bass Inc., San Francisco.

Schwenk C.R. (1989), Linking cognitive, organizational and political factors in explaining strategic change, *Journal of Management Studies*, **26** (2), pp 177–187.

Smircich L. (1983), Concepts of culture and organizational analysis, *Administrative Science Quarterly*, **28**(3), pp 339–358

Smith H.W. (1970), *Strategies of Social Research*, Prentice Hall/Open University Press, Bletchley, Bucks.

Toft B. (1994), *Behavioural aspects of risk management*, paper presented at the Association of Insurance and Risk Managers in Industry and Commerce Annual Conference, University of Warwick, 1–4 April 1994, AIRMIC Conference Proceedings, London.

Turner B.A. (1988), Connoisseurship in the study of organizational cultures, in *Doing Research in Organizations*, ed. A. Bryman, Routledge, London pp 108–122.

Turner B.A. (1992), *Organizational learning and the management of risk*, paper presented at British Academy of Management 6th Annual Conference, Bradford University, 14-16 September 1992.

Vickers G. (1983), *Human Systems are Different*, Harper & Row, London

Waring A.E. (1989), *Systems Methods for Managers: a Practical Guide*, Blackwell Scientific Publications, Oxford (out of print).

Waring A.E. (1992), *Organizational culture, management and safety*, paper presented at British Academy of Management 6th Annual Conference, Bradford University, 14–16 September 1992.

Waring A.E. (1993), *Management of Change and Information Technology: Three Case Studies*, PhD Thesis, London Management Centre, University of Westminster.

Waring A.E. (1994), *Power and culture in organisations and their implications for management of risk*, paper presented at Changing Perceptions of Risk conference, Risk and Hazard Management Research Group, Bolton Business School, 27 February – 1 March 1994.

Waring A.E. (1996), *Safety Management Systems*, Chapman & Hall, London.

Waring A.E. and Glendon A.I. (1997 forthcoming), *Management, Risk and Change*, International Thomson Business Press, London.

Westley F.R. (1990), The eye of the needle: cultural and personal transformation in a traditional organization, *Human Relations*, **43** (3), pp 273–293.

INDEX

ABOUT THE AUTHOR

Dr Alan Waring is a consultant specializing in management, risk and organizational change issues in which he regularly uses systems thinking. His wide experience covers industries such as offshore and onshore oil and gas, financial institutions, railways, ports, manufacturing, explosives, airlines, shipyards, local government and many others. Assignments have included work in Europe, the USA, Singapore and Iran. His associate team numbers approximately twenty. Address for contact:

Alan Waring & Associates, 67 Crows Road, Epping, Essex CM16 5DH,
tel. 01992 574844, fax. 01992 572844